Emily Dickinson

Emily Dickinson

A POET'S GRAMMAR

Cristanne Miller

Harvard University Press

Cambridge, Massachusetts, and London, England   1987

The texts of Emily Dickinson's poems and letters are reprinted by
permission of the publishers and the Trustees of Amherst College from
The Poems of Emily Dickinson, edited by Thomas H. Johnson,
Cambridge, Mass.: The Belknap Press of Harvard University Press,
Copyright 1951, © 1955, 1979, 1983 by the President and Fellows
of Harvard College; from *The Complete Poems of Emily Dickinson*, edited
by Thomas H. Johnson, Copyright 1914, 1929, 1935, 1942 by
Martha Dickinson Bianchi, Copyright © renewed 1957, 1963 by
Mary L. Hampson, by permission of Little, Brown and Company; and
from *The Letters of Emily Dickinson*, edited by Thomas H. Johnson,
Cambridge, Mass.: The Belknap Press of Harvard University Press,
Copyright © 1958, 1986 by the President and Fellows of Harvard
College.

Publication of this book has been aided by a grant from the Andrew
W. Mellon Foundation.

This book is printed on acid-free paper, and its binding materials have
been chosen for strength and durability.

Library of Congress Cataloging-in-Publication Data

Miller, Cristanne.
    Emily Dickinson, a poet's grammar.

    Bibliography: p.
    Includes index.
    1. Dickinson, Emily, 1830–1886—Language.
2. Dickinson, Emily, 1830–1886—Sources. I. Title.
PS1541.Z5M48   1987   811'.4   86-22836
ISBN 0-674-25035-4 (alk. paper)

I read in *Goedel, Escher, Bach* a reformulation of Goedel's Theorem, in which Hofstadter proposed that for every record player there were records it could not play because they would lead to its indirect self-destruction. And it struck me that if you squared this you would get a hypothesis that for every language there were perceptions it could not express because they would lead to its indirect self-destruction. Furthermore, if you cubed it, you would get a hypothesis that for every culture there are *languages* it could not use because they would lead to its indirect self-destruction. This made me wonder: what would happen to American culture if women did have and did use a language that expressed their perceptions?

Suzette Haden Elgin, *A First Dictionary and Grammar of Laadan*

Acknowledgments

Tᴴᴵꜱ ʙᴏᴏᴋ has come slowly into being; I trust that the many friends and colleagues who have contributed to its final form know from my private thanks how much I have valued their support and advice. A few, however, also deserve public recognition: Janel Mueller, for first inspiring and guiding me in the practice of stylistic criticism; Suzanne Juhasz, for reading more than one version of the manuscript and always being willing to "talk Dickinson" with me; and Robert Ferguson, for his unfailing readiness to brainstorm or give advice and encouragement—first to keep on writing, then to stop when the book was done. I have enjoyed financial and institutional support from Pomona College, the National Endowment for the Humanities, the Women's Studies Research Center of the University of Wisconsin in Madison, and the Newberry Library, as an Exxon Education Foundation Fellow. During my year at the Women's Studies Research Center and the Newberry Library, Yvonne Costello, Eric Cheyfitz, and Diane Robins gave valuable suggestions for improving the manuscript. Lynn Keller contributed the invaluable close sharing of ideas that comes from collaborative work—ours on Dickinson and Elizabeth Bishop. Thanks beyond words go to Dale and Betty Miller— to my father for teaching me to hear the words I read, and to my mother for caring that I read them.

Contents

Emily Dickinson

The poems and letters in this text will be referred to by number (the letter numbers preceded by L) and quoted from Thomas H. Johnson's *The Poems of Emily Dickinson* (Cambridge, Mass.: Harvard University Press, 1955) and *The Letters of Emily Dickinson* (Cambridge, Mass.: Harvard University Press, 1958). Information taken from Richard B. Sewall's *The Life of Emily Dickinson* (New York: Farrar, Straus and Giroux, 1974) will be cited in the text as *Life* (with volume and page number).

ONE

Letters to the World

Could mortal lip divine
The undeveloped Freight
Of a delivered syllable
'Twould crumble with the weight.   (1409)

L ANGUAGE is poetry, Emily Dickinson said, when it "makes my whole body so cold no fire ever can warm me," when "I feel physically as if the top of my head were taken off" (L 342a). According to this definition, poetry reveals itself in the immediate, unambiguous response of a reader to a text. Defining poetry from the perspective of an impressionistic reader is a curious move for any poet, but it is particularly curious for a poet whose own cryptically elusive poems baffle even sophisticated readers. The language of Dickinson's poetry is elliptically compressed, disjunctive, at times ungrammatical; its reference is unclear; its metaphors are so densely compacted that literal components of meaning fade. Yet Dickinson believes that a "syllable" has meaning when it is "delivered"; a word "just / Begins to live" "When it is said" (1212), when it is "made Flesh" (1651) in an act of communication. For the syllables and words of her poems to live, they must speak. One of the primary difficulties for the modern reader of Dickinson's poetry is to understand this tension between the poet's partially articulated desire to speak to an audience, to move her reader, and her largely unarticulated decision to write the riddling, elliptical poetry she does. This tension, however, is at the root of the peculiar urgency in Dickinson's poems. Dickinson writes as she does because of a combination of factors: her belief in the extraordinary power of language, her responses to the language she reads in mid-nineteenth-century America, and her sense of herself as woman and poet.[1] These are the contexts in which I discuss the language of Dickinson's poetry.

1

To balance the varying types of information recovered in examining the details of Dickinson's language use, her ideas, and her life in nineteenth-century Amherst, one must employ various methodological strategies. Looking for meaning in a poem's language alone, the reader finds extraordinary multiplicity. The poet's metaphors and extended analogies, her peculiar brevity, lack of normal punctuation, irregular manipulation of grammar, syntax, and word combination all invite multiple, nonreferential interpretations of what she means. Tempering this multiplicity with a historical understanding of the poet's life and the language theories and practice available to her focuses the possibilities of meaning. Taking the further step of reading Dickinson's individual poems as parts of the larger puzzle of her whole creative work more clearly establishes a poem's bounds. This book follows the act of interpretation from unrestricted play with language to play within the overlapping and clarifying spheres of interpretive linguistic, structural, historical, and biographical analysis. I attempt to create a range for the understanding of Dickinson's language strategies and poems that is both focused and multidimensional.

As an example of what I mean by focused and multidimensional, let me read through a poem I shall return to frequently in the course of the book:

> Essential Oils – are wrung –
> The Attar from the Rose
> Be not expressed by Suns – alone –
> It is the gift of Screws –
>
> The General Rose – decay –
> But this – in Lady's Drawer
> Make Summer – When the Lady lie
> In Ceaseless Rosemary –   (675)

This poem is, first, about making perfume. A simple reading would be the following: Attar (essence of roses) is expressed by "Screws," that is, a process involving screws, not by natural growth in the sun. The natural or general rose decays, while the rose of perfume outlasts even its maker (or wearer). The connotations of "Essential" and "expressed," however, suggest other readings: the articulate expression of "Essential Oil" (essence of any kind—poetry? love?) requires the transformation of experience into consciousness, or language. The pun in *express* makes it difficult to separate pain ("Screws" of experience) from articulate realization (verbal expression); pain and consciousness may be one. The rose or life that lives only in the sun, unexpressed, does not put forth essence.

In my reading, as in most critical readings of the poem, Dickinson here develops the idea that essence, or poetry, comes only with "Screws."[2] The pain endured in this refining expression compensates its maker by conferring a kind of immortality on her. In the last stanza, essence—whether perfume, a purer soul, or poetry—will outlast its maker, even if it is hidden away from the world. It is like a sachet that scents the underclothes of a "Lady's Drawer" and provides the lingering, underlying scent of her life. The Lady may die, but her expressed essence continues to create, be fertile, "Make Summer." That essence, in turn, can give Attar or underlying scent, meaning, to other lives.

Here Dickinson plays off her century's widespread conception of woman as the ministering angel in the house and of poet as sensitive, suffering soul. The woman's conscious offering of herself to the needs of others, to the "Screws" of omnipresent demand, reduces her selfish or earthly concerns to the point where she becomes pure, essential spirit, the Romantic soul. As the poem also implies, and as one sees in most nineteenth-century fiction, attaining such purity coincides with the woman's death. Just as petals must be crushed to produce essence, the woman's (or poet's) life is crushed through self-sacrifice or suffering to produce her pure soul; and, like a sachet, even in death that soul beautifies or scents all it touches. This poem further implies, however, that the poet (or woman) chooses the conscious suffering of "Screws" over the easy life of "Suns" for the sake of the product (be it poem or healthy family) and of her indirect immortality, even if that immortality is never known beyond the confines of her "Drawer." Because of this choice, the Attar of her life—both as pure soul and as expressed essence—acts ceaselessly in the private sphere of her home, or wherever her self and products are cherished.

By presenting poetic creation metaphorically as the expressing of essence and suggesting a connection between this process and a woman's life or death, Dickinson strikingly anticipates twentieth-century feminist metaphors for female creativity. Using current feminist constructions, Dickinson's "Lady" can be seen as both spiritual and biological producer of essence, and (re)production as an essentially female art and act (although identifying sexuality with "Screws" more closely

resembles Freudian notions of women's masochistic enjoyment of pain
than it does current feminism). On the literal level, expressed essence
or perfume is the property of women; they wear it. The poem then
places this essence "in Lady's Drawer"—where, as sachet, it scents her
clothing, and by metonymy her body. Reading "Drawer" as a pun on
"drawers" further makes "essence" the Lady's own, perhaps even the
scent or power of her sexuality. In Dickinson's dictionary, "Drawer[s]"
may be "undergarment" or "that which draws or attracts, or has the
power of attraction" as well as "a sliding box in a case or table, which
is drawn at pleasure."[3] Itself the product of "Screws," "Essential Oil"
in "Lady's Drawer / Make Summer," or brings the time of fertility,
"When the Lady lie . . ." As manipulator of "Screws," as object
crushed by the process of expression, and as wearer of drawers, the
Lady creates her Attar as well as using it. Although one need not
conclude that Dickinson claims poetry as belonging to women's sexual
and reproductive power, the poem allows this direction of interpretation. Dickinson's practice of keeping her own poems hidden in a
chest in her bedroom underlines the conjunction of poetic creation
and woman's experience in this poem.

The dominant metaphor of "Essential Oils" suggests that language,
too, must undergo transformation in the creation of poetry. Expression
is not natural—in fact, Joanne Feit Diehl calls it an "anti-natural
activity" for Dickinson;[4] it entails the application of screws to the
"Rose" of language as much as to experience or life. Such application
reveals itself in the language of this poem. For example, four of the
poem's verbs are without inflection, that is, unmarked for person,
function, or tense: *Be, decay, Make,* and *lie.* Although Dickinson uses
uninflected verbs in various ways, in "Essential Oils" this ungrammatical form helps create a sense of timeless essence. Leaving a verb
uninflected returns it to its basic stem or root form, giving it the
flavor of primary or essential activity. In their substitution of an
essential or root for a historical form, these verbs embody the process
of transformation from General Rose to Attar that is the subject of
the poem. Further, and more typical, evidence of the "Screws" of
expression in this poem are its lack of standardized punctuation,
frequent dashes, lack of clear antecedent for the pronouns "it" and
"this," and the uncertain identity and role of the Lady. All of these
transformations or disruptions of what is normally expected in language work toward creating multiplicity of meaning and an indeter-

minate reference, two characteristics that open questions of meaning but frustrate the referential or informative communication most language provides. Like the rose, language is crushed into essence in this poem.

"Essential Oils" revolves around paradoxical contrasts. Elevated "Essential Oils" require homely "Screws"; immortal "Attar" mingles with the scent symbolizing mortality (rosemary was used to scent corpses as well as being a common herb of the kitchen); "Screws" distort but the act and the product may give an intense, if excruciating, pleasure. Only the combination of natural beauty and distorting transformation "Make Summer," as in the Christian tradition only death brings "Ceaseless" life. The Lady's private or hidden self, like the oil of the Rose, is released or born through suffering and only then may become the most precious of perfumes. Although in no way directly autobiographical, the poem provides a self-portrait of Dickinson as private and female poet, creating the "gift" of poetry through the transforming distortions of her linguistic and metaphorical "Screws." The product of "Screws" is not the scent of a single rose but the essence of the type (the General Rose); analogously, reading a poem returns us not to the poet's particular experiences (the rose) but to the essence of her life.

As in "Essential Oils – are wrung," Dickinson typically makes the poet's labor analogous to ordinary life. The poet's letters to neighbors and friends suggest that the analogy may stem from her daily, practical conflation of ordinary and poetic expression: the language of Dickinson's poems is not fundamentally different from the language of her everyday life. In letters as well as in poems, Dickinson's language is densely compressed, metaphorical, disjunctive; syntax is inverted; words are coined and used ungrammatically. Dickinson even drafts some of her letters, making—as in drafts of her poems—lists of optional words or phrases where she is not satisfied. Both letters and poems balance informality and formality, colloquialism and complexity, intimacy and distance. The set line length and regular meter and rhyme of her verse no doubt encourage syntactic inversion or ellipsis or an occasional archaism, like the truncated participial adjective "create" for "created" in "Of all the Souls that stand create –" (664). Equally inverted or elliptical prose passages from letters, however, indicate that poetry's formal restriction is merely an encouragement to such distortion, not its cause. Her letters may be as elliptical syntactically and metaphorically as her poems—for example, as in an 1868 note (L 324) to her sister-in-law, Susan Gilbert Dickinson:

> Going is less, Sister, long gone from you, yet We who take all with us, leave not much behind – Busy missing you – I have not tasted Spring – Should there be other Aprils, We will perhaps dine –
>
> > Emily –

or in an 1879 note to a neighbor, Mrs. Henry Hills, written on the death of her infant son: "'Come unto me.' Beloved Commandment. The Darling obeyed" (L 595). The extent of Dickinson's unconventional manipulation of language reveals itself more clearly in the broader context of her ordinary communications with family and friends than in her poems alone.

Not surprisingly for one who was preoccupied with language, Emily was the letter writer of the Dickinson family, taking over her mother's function of keeping her brother Austin informed about the doings at home and passing on her parents' and sister's messages.[5] To Austin, in an early letter, she writes, "At my old stand again Dear Austin, and happy as a queen to know that while I speak those whom I love are listening" (L 45). In this role she commands the attention of her family on both sides: she gives the messages of one and receives at least briefly and at a distance the undivided attention of the other. The power of the letter lies partly in making her central to people she loves, at least "while" she is speaking. Letter writing presumes communication with an audience, and Dickinson is "happy as a queen" while her audience is secure.

The attraction of letters for the poet also lies in the particular kind of communication that writing entails. From her early youth, Dickinson thought of language's power in connection primarily with its written form. Joseph Lyman remembers her early as saying, "We used to think, J . . . when I was an unsifted girl and you so scholarly that words were cheap and weak. Now I dont know of anything so mighty. There are [those] to which I lift my hat when I see them sitting princelike among their peers on the page. Sometimes I write one, and look at his outlines till he glows as no sapphire."[6] One Dickinson speaker dealt "words like Blades . . . / And every One unbared a Nerve / Or wantoned with a Bone" (479), but the written word outlives its dealer:

A Word dropped careless on a Page
May stimulate an eye
When folded in perpetual seam
The Wrinkled Maker lie

Infection in the sentence breeds
We may inhale Despair
At distances of Centuries
From the Malaria —   (1261)

In letters, she comments "a Pen has so many inflections and a Voice but one" (L 470); "We bruise each other less in talking than in writing, for then a quiet accent helps words themselves too hard" (L 332). On reading that George Eliot had died, she writes: "The look of the words as they lay in the print I never shall forget. Not their face in the casket could have had the eternity to me" (L 710). The distance between pen and voice makes the language seem more powerful because it becomes more absolute:

> A Letter always feels to me like immortality because it is the mind alone without corporeal friend. Indebted in our talk to attitude and accent, there seems a spectral power in thought that walks alone —   (L 330)

> What is it that instructs a hand lightly created, to impel shapes to eyes at a distance, which for them have the whole area of life or of death? Yet not a pencil in the street but has this awful power, though nobody arrests it. An earnest letter is or should be life-warrant or death-warrant, for what is each instant but a gun, harmless because "unloaded," but that touched "goes off"?   (L 656)

Dickinson's "Letter" here is obviously epistolary, but she may also be punning on the alphabetical letter, suggesting there is a "spectral power," a "life-warrant" in any written word. "What a Hazard a Letter is!" she writes late in her life (L 1007).

In her poems, too, Dickinson writes of the letter as a powerful form. Prayers to or thoughts of an absent "Lord" (God or "Master") are letters to him, she writes in "You love the Lord — you cannot see —" (487). In a late fragment, the bliss of exchanging letters raises the human state above the divine: "A Letter is a joy of Earth — / It is denied the Gods — " (1639). In "The Way I read a Letter's — this —" (636), she makes reading a letter the most intimate form of communication possible: it requires locked doors, absolute solitude, and as great a distance as possible from others to "Peruse how infinite I am / To no one that You — know —." The speaker of this poem apparently longs to hear from a secret lover (she sighs for "lack of Heaven — but not / The Heaven God bestow —"), but the poem's opening indefinite article—"a Letter"—indicates that all letters require this attention and produce a similar ecstasy, or perhaps even that love letters are the prototype for all letters.[7] In her earliest poem about a letter, the sentimental "In Ebon Box, when years have flown" (169), the speaker's unfinished sentence and closing exclamation imply it is ridiculous to suppose that even old letters are "none of our" continuing, daily "affair!" Because their message is secret (it cannot be overheard); because they partake in the power of all written language; and because they demand the undivided attention of their reader, letters provide a kind of communication somewhere between that of holy prayer and secular seduction.

Dickinson wrote copious letters throughout her life. The conjunction between this written correspondence and her life of *belles lettres* or "letters" is as deep as the homonym itself. In a poem written probably in 1862, one of her most productive years, Dickinson even characterizes her poet/speaker as a letter writer.

> This is my letter to the World
> That never wrote to Me —
> The simple News that Nature told
> With tender Majesty
>
> Her Message is committed
> To Hands I cannot see —
> For love of Her — Sweet — countrymen —
> Judge tenderly — of Me   (441)

This poem modestly represents the poet as a neighborly correspondent. She passes on Nature's "Message" or "simple News" in a friendly letter, and we are to judge her "tenderly" for the sake of the original speaker, Nature, not for her gifted translation of nature's truths. The writer disappears behind the supposed transparency of her message. In the fiction of the poem she does not create, she gossips.

The poet's artlessness is patently a pose here. Few of Dickinson's poems bear any resemblance to "simple News," and she is always, albeit indirectly, a part of the subject of her poems. Nonetheless, the metaphor of poet as letter writer aptly characterizes Dickinson's art, first because of the stylistic similarities of her poems and letters, and second because several of her poems were literally "letter[s] to the World," either mailed alone without other comment or included in more conventional letters. The element of controlled intimacy, and through it controlled power, that written communication provides is a key to Dickinson's method in her poems as it is to her reliance on letters for exchange with her friends.

All epistolary correspondence assumes some kind of separation or distance, whether unavoidable or willed. In the great age of letter writing, Samuel Richardson writes that "the converse of the pen . . . makes distance, presence" and then goes "presence" one further; a letter "brings back to sweet remembrance all the delights of presence; which makes even presence but body, while absence becomes the soul."[8] For Dickinson this is exactly what happens. Distance creates the possibility of real or full presence; absence "becomes" the soul both in flattering it, allowing it to appear at its best, and in giving it the safety and control to appear, to speak without inhibition. Even when her correspondents were within easy visiting range, Dickinson's primary "converse" remained that of the pen.

Despite the claim of her poem on letter writing, "the World" wrote to Dickinson with great regularity and with continued invitations to be more a part of it than she desired to be. For much of her life, Dickinson did not want to see people. Mabel Loomis Todd, who spent hours at the Dickinson house with Austin and Lavinia, and whose affair with Austin had Emily's tacit approval, saw the poet for the first time after her death; yet the two women had spent hours in the same house and exchanged friendly messages for four years.[9] Visitors report coming to see their friend and then speaking to her only from another room or the opposite end of a staircase. Yet the poet carried on a prolific correspondence. According to Sewall, "it is clear that we have only a fraction, and probably a small one" of Dickinson's letters. That small fraction includes ninety-three known correspondents, several of whom she wrote to often and for years (*Life* II, 750–751). Apart from her letters to friends at a distance, Dickinson sent frequent notes to neighbors and almost daily notes across the lawn to Sue or her children, especially after she stopped visiting "The Evergreens," as Austin and Sue's house was called. These letters and notes provide a perfect analogue for the confiding but noninformative voice of Dickinson's poems. In the poems as in life, she is oracularly chatty, a neighbor who invites you in and then speaks to you elliptically from behind her closed door.

Generally, both letters and language help the poet overcome the barriers of separation between herself and her loved ones while yet serving to protect her from immediate or direct intimacy with them. Dickinson wants too much from people and can imagine that she gets what she wants from relationships with them only if she keeps real contact at a minimum. Through letters the poet can control relationships, meeting her correspondents only in an "imaginative" or "aesthetic union," that is, a union that can only with difficulty (or by death) be taken from her because she has constructed it herself through and in language.[10] Even more than letters, poetry allows Dickinson both to express the urgent intimacy she feels and to establish the distance that allows her to maintain control of her actions, if not of her feelings. Dickinson seems intuitively to understand the psychological paradox that encourages least inhibited awareness and expression of feeling when there is least risk her feeling will be acted upon. If she maintains distance between herself and those she loves, she can allow herself to desire them and to express those desires openly. By combining the separation of written communication with the ambiguity of address and metaphor inevitable in verse, Dickinson frees herself for her most profound self-expression.

In practical terms, letters and poems appear to be complementary forms of the same kind of communication for the poet. In some letters Dickinson changes from prose to verse in mid-sentence, as if both were the same medium. For example, she writes to Thomas Wentworth Higginson (L 280):

I found you were gone, by accident, as I find Systems are, or Seasons . . . Carlo [the poet's dog] – still remained – and I told him –

Best Gains – must have the Losses' Test –
To constitute them – Gains –

My Shaggy Ally assented –

These lines were never developed into a longer poem, but in other letters Dickinson lifts lines from finished poems and incorporates them into her prose, as in this letter to Helen Hunt Jackson: ". . . The Summer has been wide and deep, and a deeper Autumn is *but the Gleam concomitant of that waylaying Light —*" (L 937). The phrase I have italicized appears as the last two lines of a poem written approximately a year earlier—"The farthest Thunder that I heard" (1581, ca. 1883). Around the time she wrote the poem, Dickinson also sent its first stanza to Sue.

The hymn or "common" meter and the rhyme of most of Dickinson's poems seem so natural to her that she occasionally falls into their rhythm in the middle of a paragraph, without marking it as verse. For example, she includes the following lines in a letter to Sue (L 288, 1864; I have italicized the metered phrases):

Sweet Sue —

. . .

   Take back that "Bee" and "Buttercup" — I have no Field for them, though for the Woman whom I prefer, Here is Festival — Where my Hands are cut, Her fingers will be found inside —

. . .

   Take the Key to the Lily, now, *and I will lock the Rose —*

In the same light vein, the poet writes in meter and rhymes to a neighbor, probably as a Fourth of July greeting (whole text of L 509, ca. 1877):

"My Country, 'tis of thee," has always meant the Woods — to me — "Sweet Land of Liberty," I trust is your own —

More often, however, the poet lapses into verse to express what she cannot say in prose. For example, probably to Samuel Bowles, Dickinson writes "Because I could not say it — I fixed it in the Verse — for you to read — when your thought wavers, for such a foot as mine" (L 251); to Higginson, she writes "I have no Saxon, now" (L 265);[11] to her cousins, "Let Emily sing for you because she cannot pray" (L 278). As these apologies suggest, Dickinson is most apt to write in meter when she is responding to a crisis or is particularly upset. A letter written shortly after her favorite nephew's death provides an extreme example. Here the poet writes prose in almost continuous alternating iambic tetrameter and trimeter, in one "stanza" even using rhyme. This long and extraordinary letter (L 868) concludes:

> He knew no niggard moment – His Life was full of Boon –
> The Playthings of the Dervish were not so wild as his –
> No crescent was this Creature – He traveled from the Full –
> Such soar, but never set –
> I see him in the Star, and meet his sweet velocity in every-
> thing that flies – His Life was like the Bugle, which winds
> itself away, his Elegy an echo – his Requiem ecstasy –
> Dawn and Meridian in one.
> . . .
> Without a speculation, our little Ajax spans the whole –
>
> Pass to thy Rendezvous of Light,
> Pangless except for us –
> Who slowly ford the Mystery
> Which thou hast leaped across!
>   Emily.

The regular recurrence of stresses and sounds in poetry seems to have a calming effect on the poet. In an early letter to Higginson, she apologetically but assertively links poetic formality with her capacity to speak, apparently in response to his suggestion that she loosen the strictness of her short lines' meter and rhyme: "[I] could not drop the Bells whose jingling cooled my Tramp" (L 265). Poetic form allows Dickinson greater revelation and more precise expression of feeling than the more common or "Saxon" demands of prose. The poet's distortions of grammar and syntax as well as her use of "jingling" meter, stanzas, and rhyme may provide a purely formal discipline she needs to be able to articulate chaotic or rebellious feeling and thought.

The physical distance created by letter writing and the metaphorical distance created by opaque and elliptical language function as metaphorical equivalents, and the poet draws on both repeatedly in various forms. She increases the given distance of epistolary correspondence through a near-total lack of reference to the events of her everyday life and by striking various poses. In letters and poems sent to her close friends, these poses would be easily identified and were intended primarily to console or amuse. When the aunt signs herself "His

Niece." or "Dick – Jim –" to her nephew Ned (L 291 and L 604), everyone knows she is spoofing. At the other end of the spectrum, when a 31-year-old woman who has already written at least 400 poems speaks with a child's overwhelmingly modest hesitation and signs herself "Your Scholar" (L 268, July 1862) in writing to Higginson, who knows her only through her telegraphic letters and through poems she says are not about herself, he is likely to take the pose seriously— which he and generations of readers in fact did. Just as one cannot assume the detail of Dickinson's poetry is autobiographical, one cannot trust that she will represent herself fully or accurately in a letter. Austin remarks about her letters to Higginson, "Emily definitely posed in those letters" (*Life* II, 538), and a family friend comments about the published letters, "she did attitudinize for her own pleasure."[12] Dickinson tells even her closest epistolary friends remarkably little about the events of her life. Death and illness are the only personal events she alludes to with any regularity, and even these are most often elliptically cast.

Dickinson's practice of mailing the same poem in more than one letter is related to her practice of posing. This serves as a warning to her twentieth-century readers that poems mailed in letters may be deceptively personal; they were not conceived solely in the light of a single friendship. In the context of any one mailing, a poem seems to be occasional, referring to particular events and the private relationship between writer and reader. Certainly, some couplets sent with gifts from her garden or kitchen to neighbors were occasional in origin and were used only once (for example, the lines quoted earlier in the letter to Higginson). The poems themselves, however, are a different matter. For example, in a letter probably sent to Samuel Bowles, Dickinson begins with the highly personal: "Dear friend If you doubted my Snow – for a moment – you never will – again – I know . . ." and includes the anguishing poem "Through the strait pass of suffering – / The Martyrs – even – trod" (792). The poet made a fair copy of this poem for herself before she mailed it to Bowles, however, and she mailed another copy of the same poem to Sue.[13] The multiple copies suggest that the poet's primary intent in writing the poem was not to present herself as a martyr to Bowles or to point toward any single occasion, whatever the impetus for sending him the poem might have been. In the letter to Sue, the poem would seem to have a different reference and perhaps significance. The poem expresses a truth that Dickinson values and finds useful. Like any poem, it allows her to share her emotional present without revealing its event and detail.

My favorite example of Dickinson's double mailing occurs with a poem (494) found in two clean copies after her death. Both were written on embossed stationery, signed "Emily –," and folded as if they had been put in envelopes. One of the copies begins:

> Going to Him! Happy letter!
> Tell Him –
> Tell Him the page I did'nt write –
> Tell Him – I only said the Syntax –
> And left the Verb and the pronoun out –
> Tell Him just how the fingers hurried –
> Then – how they waded – slow – slow –
> And then you wished you had eyes in your pages –
> So you could see what moved them so –

And ends coyly:

> Tell Him – just how she sealed you – Cautious!
> But – if He ask where you are hid
> Until tomorrow – Happy letter!
> Gesture Coquette – and shake your Head!

The other copy begins "Going – to – Her! / Happy – Letter!" and substitutes "Her" for "Him" throughout.[14] For the poet, the poem exists beyond any personal use she may put it to. It is more general in address and broader in theme than a single mailing or context would signify.

That Dickinson knows the "you" of letters (and mailed poems) may be deceptively personal we see in her caustic response to a letter that Mrs. Holland mailed jointly to her and her sister Lavinia: "A mutual plum is not a plum. I was too respectful to take the pulp and do not like a stone. Send no union letters" (L 321). As reader, Dickinson is unwilling to accept any but the explicitly singular, personal address. A letter's "you" should not be expandable: "A mutual plum is not a plum"; its message, like the plum's fruit, should be only for oneself. As poet, however, Dickinson knows that a poem's audience will always expand and contract; its "you" can be simultaneously as personal as

Sue next door and as unspecified as the unknown future audience, or as abstract as that same pronoun used in a sentence like "You take three eggs . . ." In her poems, Dickinson would have it both ways: she addresses multiple audiences with the intimacy of speaking privately to a close friend. For the recipient of a poem, it would be difficult if not impossible to detect the fraud.

Dickinson's use of her poems in letters suggests one way in which she may have intended them to be read: they are private messages universalized by a double release from private circumstance. As noted in "This is my letter," their audience is unlimited; the addressee is "the World," although she would speak to its members one by one under the ambiguity of the pronoun "you." Second, the speaker in the poems is more a dramatic than a personal "I." To Higginson, the poet writes of her poems: "When I state myself, as the Representative of the Verse – it does not mean – me – but a supposed person" (L 268). Although we must read this disclaimer skeptically, it carries some truth. Dickinson uses the experience of her life and world to create what Weisbuch has aptly called a "sceneless" poetry. The poems stem from her life, but they do not point to it; there is no direct reference to a particular act of the poet or even necessarily to her real voice in the statement or voice of a poem. Dickinson's "I" is always a character stemming from her experience, and in that way it reveals her character, but no "I" is simply the poet. Nonetheless, patterns of posing reflect the disguised self: Dickinson's varied poses and strategies of indirection are as illuminating of her psychology as a more straightforward account of her life would be. Although the poet's language is not transparent, we do see her in it.

Dickinson is ingeniously redundant in providing explanations for her manipulation of distance and intimacy through her manipulation of language. As seen earlier, she desires the analogous features of controlled distance and ambiguously revealing language both because all communication threatens "life-warrant or death-warrant" and because such concentrated distillation is necessary for "Essential" expression. Protection of the reader from the poet's truth and of herself from her reader's response, however, also figures largely as an explanation for her choices of language. In letters and poems, Dickinson implies that she must speak as she does out of regard for her audience (including herself). Language is so powerful that it cannot be used in undiluted form. Moreover, its shot cannot be precisely controlled. In her most famous poem on the subject, Dickinson substitutes "Truth" for "language" as the substance of power, but the effect is identical and the remedy for the danger implies that truth and language are the same.

> Tell all the Truth but tell it slant –
> Success in Circuit lies
> Too bright for our infirm Delight
> The Truth's superb surprise
> As Lightning to the Children eased
> With explanation kind
> The Truth must dazzle gradually
> Or every man be blind –   (1129)

By the logic of this poem, indirection or "slant" in language protects the hearer, and the speaker's or poet's role becomes implicitly maternal. The thoughtful user of language protects her readers/children from frightening truth by talking around it, "easing" the "Lightning" she will "tell." This maternal image of the poet, like the poet as letter writer, presents a strong contrast to the more common nineteenth-century portrait of the poet as a wielder of lightning, like Zeus, Jove, or Thor, whose bolts announce his omnipotence and divinity. Dickinson tells everything slant. Her method of telling does not diminish the impact of her truth, just as "kind" explanations do not diminish lightning's power, but it—like the mother—can prevent readers from seeing the full danger her "Truth" puts them in.

Dickinson also maintained physical and psychological distance from friends and family partly because she required it for her own emotional equilibrium. Even given her tendency to pose and to write in hyperbole, Dickinson's responses to relatively ordinary events show her to be unusually sensitive. For example, about 1878, after nearly twenty years of living next door to her sister-in-law, she writes the following note, perhaps after Sue has returned from a trip: "I must wait a few Days before seeing you – You are too momentous. But remember it is idolatry, not indifference" (L 581). Twenty-five years earlier, when apparently in love with Sue, Dickinson writes:[15] ". . . in thinking of those I love, my reason is all gone from me, and I do fear sometimes that I must make a hospital for the hopelessly insane, and chain me up there such times, so I wont injure you" (L 77). Dickinson avoids seeing friends because they mean too much to her rather than because they mean so little. In an affectionate letter to Mrs. Holland, she writes: "Pardon my sanity, Mrs. Holland, in a world *in*sane, and love me if you will, for I had rather *be* loved than to be called a king in earth, or a lord in Heaven" (L 185). If Dickinson cared less about these relationships or needed her friends less, she might be able to allow them closer access to her.

Slanted truth and disjunctive language, like the pretense that she is conveyor of nature's "News," protect the writer from having to bear full responsibility for her messages. Complex and elliptical language is not immediately understood. Readers of Dickinson's poems and letters may doubt all they read in her cryptic ambiguity, and thus not blame the poet for saying what they do not want to hear from her. She is protected from sounding as radical or rebellious as she often is because understanding those aspects of her writing requires some complicity from her reader; since readers must work at understanding her texts, they must therefore to some extent be capable of recognizing a possibility of meaning before they can find it. The differences between late nineteenth century and modern readings of several poems show how extremely reader receptivity may affect the interpretation of a poem. Only after a reader becomes sensitive to, for example, gendered possibilities of meaning are those elements of Dickinson's poems recognized.[16] The opacity and multiplicity of the language likewise prevent—or allow—readers who do not recognize gender as an element of perception to overlook entirely that aspect of her poems while feeling confident about their reading. The poems' linguistic and metaphorical complexity allows Dickinson's readers to see her truths only as they are capable of admitting them.

Because, somewhat paradoxically, distorted language or communication at a distance increases Dickinson's willingness to speak, writing provides an avenue for more intimate and passionate expression than she feels comfortable with face to face. This is a truth all letter writers know. Even more than talking in the dark, writing letters allows private feelings to be articulated in a language half art, half hyperbole, with the assurance that these feelings will be heard and the safety of not being watched while they are spoken. In person, the poet could scarcely have said: "Thank you for having been" (to Mrs. Holland, 1873; L 399); or "I should be wild with joy to see my little lovers. The writing them is not so sweet as their two faces that seem so small way off, and yet have been two weeks from me – two wishful, wandering weeks" (to Louise and Frances Norcross, ca. 1863; L 286); or in the much-corrected draft of a letter to Otis Lord (L 562):

> Dont you know you are happiest while I withhold and not confer – dont you know that "No" is the wildest word we consign to Language?
>
> . . . It is Anguish I long conceal from you to let you leave me, hungry, but you ask the divine Crust and that would doom the Bread.
>
> That unfrequented Flower

In writing from a distance, Dickinson may give all in language that she withholds in fact. This returns us full circle to the poet's own excuse for including poems in prose: "Because I could not say it – I fixed it in the verse – for you to read." From the greater distance of poetic "letters" or language more formally patterned and constrained than her prose, she may play out thoughts and feelings that have no easily expressed place in her life.

Almost all of Dickinson's unusual uses of language contribute to the same limited number of basic effects: multiplicity of meaning, indeterminacy of reference and degree of personal involvement in the poem, and the establishment of a diction that swings between stylized aphorism and the informality of speech. Multiplicity, indeterminacy, and a fluctuating tone provide the poet with the linguistic and psychological freedom she needs to express, or inscribe, herself. Dickinson sees her place in the world primarily in terms of contrasting and shifting polarities. She—as daughter, woman, person uninvolved in the public sphere, female poet—has relatively little power, strength, or independence. In this capacity she speaks either defiantly and defensively or with longing. She resents her position, and she desires the enabling approval of the withheld love and power (in the drama of her poems, at least metaphorically male). Yet at the same time— again as daughter, woman, poet—she knows the responsibility of her daily tasks and the power of her voice. She speaks with authority, in pure essence, or else carefully, with the "infirm Delight" or outright suspicion of her audience in mind. In her poems Dickinson uses both the strategy of the weak, in her attempt to win over the world as lover, and the strategy of the strong, in her attempt to win against it as rival. The narratives of most poems adopt some version of the former strategy; the language of all her poetry reveals the latter.

The fascination of reading Dickinson's poetry is one and the same with the frustration of reading it. As Keller says, the poet does tease. The power of her words lies at least partly in their (and her) ability to give more than a reader can entirely understand but not enough to satisfy the desire to know. Regardless of how many times you read her best poems, and how many times you persuade others that you know what they "mean," you feel the tickle of unsolved mystery in the poem; you do not convince yourself that you have gotten to the bottom of it; the poem, like the poet herself, is never quite your own. She is an intimate correspondent you cannot see—a literal truth during her lifetime in Amherst as it is a metaphorical truism now. Perhaps in attempting to communicate intimately without giving herself away—again both literally and metaphorically—Dickinson has created a language as meaningful and as free of determined meaning as any English can be. In the grammar that follows, I attempt to indicate the most fruitful directions of response to particular features of Dickinson's language in the hope of revealing more of the poet than has previously been seen.

TWO

A Grammar

Reading a poem . . . is often like learning a language.
When we learn a language we develop the capacity to have
intuitions about its structure. A grammar is a special kind
of statement about these intuitions.

James Peter Thorne, "Stylistics and Generative Grammars"

I N CREATING this grammar, I have assumed that the language
of poetry differs from other language primarily in its greater
use of structural and formal elements to convey meaning. In
most ordinary uses, language transmits a message. In poetry, meaning
may lie as much in the interaction of semantic content and form as
in a message that can be isolated from the poem. The more a poem
calls attention to its formal elements by various foregrounding techniques, the more the reader is likely to learn about its meaning from
them. If we assume as a norm language that calls no attention to its
formal properties by deviating from the conventions of standard communication (that is, an utterance intended solely to communicate a
message), then Dickinson's poetry is richly deviant. That there may
in fact be no such norm makes Dickinson's poetry no less rich. Because
Dickinson's poems contain several constructions that are unusual even
in comparison with traditional poetic uses of language, reading them
is largely a process of deciphering the connections between what their
language says and what it may mean.

In this grammar I describe the striking continuous and occasional
features of Dickinson's language use in order to explore how structure
and syntax affect meaning in her poems. Because its intent is ultimately interpretive, the grammar does not confine itself to linguistic
and structural analysis of the poems; however, the interpretive elements of my analysis are not meant to suggest that mine are the only
possible interpretations. The grammar is not a stylistic dictionary;
one cannot reductively plug in the suggestive effect of a type of

language use every time an instance of that use occurs. All units of meaning are subject to the semantic and structural environment of their (con)text. Neither does it resemble grammars of ordinary language: it generates no rules for poetic usage and provides no comprehensive system of linguistic classification for the poet's actual language use. The grammar does analyze tendencies of meaning, following readings of particular poems. In its broadest element, the grammar seeks to reveal the values and assumptions that underlie Dickinson's manipulations of language. Whether these same language features would have similar or identical effects and reflect similar values in another poet's work would have to be the subject of a separate inquiry. My sense is that the features of language use that characterize Dickinson's poetry characterize various poets' language in differing degrees, and thus that my grammar may be useful in explaining the effects of other poets' uses of similar language patterns.

At times the grammar will simply point to extensive work that has been done elsewhere.[1] At other times the grammar departs from strict analysis of poetry and language to provide notes on historical or contemporary uses of language that may have influenced Dickinson's use. I do not discuss Dickinson's vocabulary, even such wonderfully Dickinsonian words as "Circumference" and—her name for herself— "Daisy." Nor do I analyze patterns of metaphorical usage; this subject has provided the basis for volumes of criticism already.[2]

The organizational principle of the grammar is twofold: it introduces categories of language use first on the basis of their importance to Dickinson's poetry generally, and second following the order dictated by a prolonged analysis of the language in the five sample poems, particularly "Essential Oils – are wrung." On a first reading of this poem, or any poem by Dickinson, two qualities of language stand out: it is highly compressed and highly disjunctive. Since compression is the single most characteristic element of Dickinson's poetry, I begin the grammar with a discussion of its patterns and effects.

TEXTS OF THE POEMS

> Essential Oils – are wrung –
> The Attar from the Rose
> Be not expressed by Suns – alone –
> It is the gift of Screws –

The General Rose — decay —
But this — in Lady's Drawer
Make Summer — When the Lady lie
In Ceaseless Rosemary —   (675)

8. Ceaseless Rosemary —] Spiceless Sepulchre.

He fumbles at your Soul
As Players at the Keys
Before they drop full Music on —
He stuns you by degrees —
Prepares your brittle Nature
For the Ethereal Blow
By fainter Hammers — further heard —
Then nearer — Then so slow
Your Breath has time to straighten —
Your Brain — to bubble Cool —
Deals — One — imperial — Thunderbolt —
That scalps your naked Soul —

When Winds take Forests in their Paws —
The Universe — is still —   (315)

5. Nature] substance   12. scalps] peels
9. time] chance   13. take] hold
14. Universe — is] Firmaments — are

This was a Poet — It is That
Distills amazing sense
From ordinary Meanings —
And Attar so immense

From the familiar species
That perished by the Door —
We wonder it was not Ourselves
Arrested it — before —

Of Pictures, the Discloser —
The Poet — it is He —
Entitles Us — by Contrast —
To ceaseless Poverty —

Of Portion – so unconscious –
The Robbing – could not harm –
Himself – to Him – a Fortune –
Exterior – to Time –   (448)

My Life had stood – a Loaded Gun –
In Corners – till a Day
The Owner passed – identified –
And carried Me away –

And now We roam in Sovreign Woods –
And now We hunt the Doe –
And every time I speak for Him –
The Mountains straight reply –

And do I smile, such cordial light
Upon the Valley glow –
It is as a Vesuvian face
Had let it's pleasure through –

And when at Night – Our good Day done –
I guard My Master's Head –
'Tis better than the Eider-Duck's
Deep Pillow – to have shared –

To foe of His – I'm deadly foe –
None stir the second time –
On whom I lay a Yellow Eye –
Or an emphatic Thumb –

Though I than He – may longer live
He longer must – than I –
For I have but the power to kill,
Without – the power to die –   (754)

5. in] the –   18. stir] harm
16. Deep] low   23. power] art

> To pile like Thunder to it's close
> Then crumble grand away
> While Everything created hid
> This – would be Poetry –
>
> Or Love – the two coeval come –
> We both and neither prove –
> Experience either and consume –
> For None see God and live –   (1247)

COMPRESSION

More a quality of language than a particular use of it, compression denominates whatever creates density or compactness of meaning in language. It may stem from ellipsis of function words, dense use of metaphor, highly associative vocabulary, abstract vocabulary in complex syntax, or any other language use that reduces the ratio of what is stated to what is implied. Samuel Levin claims that a greater use of compression is one of the three major features differentiating poetic from ordinary language (the other two being poetry's greater uses of unity and novelty).[3] Using Dickinson's verse as his test model, Levin argues that the deletion of part (or parts) of a sentence is frequently nonrecoverable in poetry; the omitted part cannot be recalled from the deep structure of the sentence. In contrast, ordinary speech permits only recoverable deletions. Compression stemming from nonrecoverable deletion—or compression that creates gaps in meaning—particularly distinguishes the language of poetry from that of prose.

To gain the full effect of Dickinson's compression, one must place her poetry in the context of the poetry she was most familiar with and that was most popular in America in her time. Among her American contemporaries, Emerson was relatively concise. In "The Snowstorm," a poem Dickinson borrowed from, he writes:

> Announced by all the trumpets of the sky,
> Arrives the snow, and, driving o'er the fields,
> Seems nowhere to alight: the whited air
> Hides hills and woods, the river, and the heaven,
> And veils the farm-house at the garden's end.

Longfellow, whom Dickinson quoted almost as often as she quoted Shakespeare,[4] writes in "The Evening Star":

> Lo! in the painted oriel of the West,
> Whose panes the sunken sun incarnadines,
> Like a fair lady at her casement, shines
> The evening star, the star of love and rest!

Dickinson evidently cared less for James Russell Lowell, but had certainly read several of his poems.[5] "The Present Crisis," a popular poem in Dickinson's time, begins:

> When a deed is done for Freedom, through the broad earth's
>   aching breast
> Runs a thrill of joy prophetic, trembling on from east to
>   west,
> And the slave, where'er he cowers, feels the soul within him
>   climb
> To the awful verge of manhood, as the energy sublime
> Of a century bursts full-blossomed on the thorny stem of
>   Time.

Now turn back to:

> Essential Oils – are wrung –
> The Attar from the Rose
> Be not expressed by Suns – alone –
> It is the gift of Screws –   (675)

or to:

> 'Twas Love – not me –
> Oh punish – pray –
> The Real one died for Thee –
> Just Him – not me –   (394)

Compression characterizes Dickinson's syntax but also the structure of her poems. As these examples show, her poetic line, often her stanzas, and the poems themselves are shorter than those of her contemporaries.[6] The brevity Dickinson achieves could only result from fully conscious deviation from the poetic language of the time.

Although Dickinson's compression in language takes any number of forms, it tends to function in three complementary ways. First, compression increases the ambiguity and multiplicity of meaning in a poem; it allows the poet to express more than one thought at a time or to disguise one thought behind another. As seen in her letters, veiled statement allows Dickinson to express what may be unpopular or dangerous thoughts and to articulate complex feelings. Second, compression may convey the impression of withheld power: the poet may conceal her strength. Eric Auerbach, for example, attributes the Bible's grandeur to its use of compression. Referring to Genesis 1, he writes that its "impressive brevity . . . is in such contrast to the immense content and . . . for that very reason has a note of obscurity which fills the listener with a shuddering awe."[7] The poet herself writes:

> I fear a Man of frugal Speech —
> I fear a Silent Man —
> Haranguer — I can overtake —
> Or Babbler — entertain —
>
> But He who weigheth — While the Rest —
> Expend their furthest pound —
> Of this Man — I am wary —
> I fear that He is Grand —   (543)

Because it may conceal strength, silence threatens. Not to show one's power may make it seem greater. As Dickinson says in another poem:

> When Etna basks and purrs
> Naples is more afraid
> Than when she shows her Garnet Tooth —
> Security is loud —   (1146)

Third, and partly as a continuation of its implicit grandeur, compression may suggest untold profundity. As in the sibyls' oracles, cryptic revelation seems to hold great meaning.

Compression takes relatively simple form in the primary sample poem, "Essential Oils – are wrung." Here, in the space of six lines, short sentences move the reader from the general "Essential Oils" to the particular, immortal "this" without clarifying reference but also without apparently breaking the continuity of the poem's subject. Note the change in subject that occurs at the beginning of almost every line:

> Essential Oils – are wrung –
> The Attar from the Rose
> Be not expressed by Suns – alone –
> It is the gift of Screws –
>
> The General Rose – decay –
> But this – in Lady's Drawer . . .

First, "Oils" become "The Attar." Such increasing specificity promises that the following lines will explicate the initial aphorism. Instead, however, the poem moves back to abstraction with the aphorism and "It" of line 4. By the convention in English that a pronoun points back to its nearest possible antecedent, "It" refers to "The Attar"; but here the pronoun's prominent place in the line and the preceding dash make it appear broader in reference than "The Attar" suffices to explain. Similarly, "this" in line 6 stands by conventional procedure for "this [Rose]." Yet that reading, too, is insufficient to account for the effect of the open pronoun—as indicated by readings of the poem that find poems and hopes of immortality as well as perfume (the synecdochic Rose) in the "Lady's Drawer." The poem makes its reader perform the interpretive work of connecting individual statements to create a coherent, complex understanding of the poet's theory of the creation of poetry; it provides the bones of minimal thought which we must flesh into personal statement and idea by creating the connective, explanatory links for ourselves.

To summarize, compression allows for protective ambiguity, conveys a sense of the speaker's withheld power, and implies a profundity beyond the obvious import of its message. In "Embarrassment of one another / And God" (662), the poet states: "Aloud / Is nothing that is chief." The "chief" elements of Dickinson's thought often lie in the spaces of unspoken meaning between the words she does say. Whether she intends to disguise her own power, to speak subversively, to express structurally her personal ethic of renunciation, to follow a tradition of poetry that speaks with archetypal, not personal, intimacy,[8] or any combination of these, Dickinson's extreme compression largely accounts for the multiplicity of meaning in her poems, and for their provocative, riddling quality.

Recoverable Deletion

Although its pervasiveness and, therefore, its effect are unusual, much of the compression of Dickinson's poetry is grammatical, or recoverable, under the rules of ordinary language use. Such deletion resembles ellipsis in meter: the poet may elide syllables because doing so enables the use of certain metrical effects (most often, maintaining the appropriate pattern and number of syllables in a line) without sacrificing clarity or meaning. Dickinson often deletes an auxiliary verb, a repeated subject or verb, or an implied pronoun to maintain the rhythm of a line, intensify its meaning, or avoid redundancy, without confusing the poem's statement. For example, in the cryptic last stanza of "My Life had stood" (754), much of the omitted language is easily recoverable with a little rearranging of the syntax:

> Though I may live longer than He [may live]
> He must [live] longer than I [live]
> For I have but the power to kill,
> Without [having] the power to die

The difficulty of this stanza stems from its paradox and its inverted syntax, not from compression. Ellipsis of words contributes to the poetic effect of compression by the frequency of its occurrence, not by its novelty.

Nonrecoverable Deletion

Like recoverable deletion, nonrecoverable deletion may serve primarily to increase the density of a poem. It may also affect a poem's meaning more directly, by creating a syntactic or logical ambiguity. In "This was a Poet" (448), for example, there are several ways to recover the complete (or deep) syntax of the first line's cryptic "It is That." One might fill in the deletions of the first stanza as follows:

This was a Poet – It is [the fact] That [this was a poet which]
Distills amazing sense
From ordinary Meanings –
And [distills an] Attar [that is] so immense . . .

Or the second sentence might begin: " . . . It is That [(the poet), which] Distills . . ."; or "It [the poet] is that [which] . . ."; or "This [poem] was a Poet – It [the text] is That [which] . . ." Recovery of the deleted syntax here is inseparable from interpretation of the poem. In nonrecoverable deletion, this is always the case.

Dickinson often creates the gap of nonrecoverable deletion through asymmetry. "He fumbles at your Soul" (315) provides an example. In this poem, Dickinson provides no initial point of comparison for the speaker's comparatives. The speaker hears Hammers "fainter," "further," "Then nearer"—than anything she has ever experienced or imagined? Or than they were previously (wherever they were then)? The scene has no external point of reference or context; consequently, "nearer" could be any distance, and the threat could be of any magnitude. The deletion causes no confusion about the speaker's expectant anxiety, and thus no confusion in basically understanding the poem, but it does prevent us from locating the speaker in any way outside the poem's terms. It sets the poem off balance. This kind of minor nonrecoverable deletion obscures the difference between recoverable and nonrecoverable holes of meaning in a poem. Because there is so much deletion in Dickinson's poems, and because some of it is both nonrecoverable and essential to understanding the poem, the reader approaches all deletion cautiously, expecting indeterminacy or multiple meaning at every instance. Were Dickinson's poems less compressed, less economical as a whole, important nonrecoverable deletions would be easier to isolate and the poems would invite less actively expectant reading.

Dickinson's most characteristic type of nonrecoverable deletion is to omit phrases providing the logical links between consecutive statements or between stanzas. Turning again to "He fumbles at your Soul," she provides, for example, no explanation of how the couplet "When Winds take Forests in their Paws – / The Universe – is still – " concludes or summarizes the preceding lines. Does she omit "Similarly"? Or, "[The effect of having one's soul scalped is like that which occurs] When Winds take Forests in their Paws – [:] The Universe is still"? Or does she omit some longer phrase that would explain her move from the first metaphor to the second? The effect of deleting connecting phrases is often to juxtapose narrative and abstract statements, or differing metaphorical contexts. Because there is no connecting phrase, we are not sure if consecutive statements are meant to be additive, analogous, or contrasting. In "He fumbles at your Soul," is the human realm of vulnerability and terror like that of winds and forests or different from it?

In an essay on what effects various optional transformations of the simple subject-verb (object) statement at the grammatical root of any sentence may have on a writer's style, Richard Ohmann notes that D. H. Lawrence uses deletion as a "stylistic alternative to conjunction."[9] Dickinson does the same. Her nonrecoverable deletions allow a freedom of association and narrative movement that may only be possible for a mind freed from the felt necessity of marking—or even acknowledging—every step of its way, as transitional conjunctions do. Extreme use of compression may accompany an unwillingness to adhere to the explanatory conjunctions or phrases of logical, full-bodied argument. The blank *and* replaces temporal or adverbial connectives, thereby marking that some connection exists but omitting to clarify it. This kind of compression is classically called *parataxis,* although in classical parataxis the deletion may be recoverable while in Dickinson's work what is omitted between sentences or phrases is most often nonrecoverable or multiply recoverable, depending on the reader's interpretation of the poem.

Parataxis

Dickinson tends to write either in short, simple, subject-verb-object sentences or in highly clausal, complex sentences. The former syntax characterizes the majority of her sentences and is paratactic. Successive short sentences or sentence units allow a particularly quick movement from metaphor to metaphor, or from abstract pronouncement to particular example back to pronouncement, or from scene to apparent conclusion as in "He fumbles at your Soul." Consequently, the opportunities for understated connection are multiple. Dickinson juxtaposes the stages of an idea or story rather than explaining their progression.

For example, short, simple sentences allow the quick movement from event to event in "My Life had stood – a Loaded Gun" (754). Here, the abrupt sentence and stanza movement calls attention to the shifts in tense and in subject almost from line to line and gives the reader no syntactic breathing space in which to ponder the implications of the shifts. The poem proceeds for the most part through simple conjunction using *and,* a type of parataxis that Dickinson uses frequently: "My Life had stood . . . And now We roam . . . And now We hunt . . . And every time . . . And do I smile . . . And when at Night I guard . . . To foes of His . . . Though I than He." Dickinson presents the skeleton of an archetypal story here, lingering briefly only in the last stanza to speculate on what the future of such a violent self-realization and unequal relationship of power (Owner to gun, or gun to doe) must bring. The poem is so dazzling and baffling partly because each stanza provokes its own line of interpretation as well as the need to connect its direction with that of the preceding line or lines. A poem that provided even part of the explanatory connection required to make sense of this string of events would have to be much longer and would be correspondingly less rich in suggestion for the reader.

Parataxis could be called a disjunctive or coordinate linking of ideas rather than a thematic or subordinate linking. Information is presented sequentially, without hierarchical restriction or conjunction. According to William Card's statistical conclusions about the relative frequency with which coordinate conjunctions appear in English prose, Dickinson's verse is highly paratactic. In his study of essays by 22 twentieth-century writers, the coordinate conjunctions *and, or, but, yet, for, nor,* and *so* are used to connect 8.5 to 8.75 percent of typical English sentences.[10] In contrast, 43.4 percent of the 2,174 sentence connectors in his sample are pronouns, and another almost 18 percent consist of *this, that, these,* and *those.* Conjunctive adverbs (*however, indeed, thus, therefore, rather, instead,* and so on) account for about 7.3 percent of all connectors in his study, and nominal or adjectival connectors account for about another 5.7 percent. Dickinson uses almost no conjunctive adverbs and few nominal or adjectival connectors (the only frequently used one is "more"). In a random sampling of 16 of her poems, out of 71 sentence connectors (not including pronoun connectors),[11] 39, or almost 55 percent, are accounted for by *and, but, or,* and *so.*[12] If one omits pronoun connectors from Card's study, coordinate conjunctions account for about 23.5 percent of connectors—less than half the number found in Dickinson's poems. Furthermore, Dickinson is as apt to juxtapose sentences without any connector as she is to use a coordinate conjunction; thus her poetry is more paratactic than this primitive count of coordinating conjunctions reveals.

Janel Mueller claims for parataxis generally an "inexhaustible potential in the production of new sentences—the very core of linguistic creativity."[13] This creativity is twofold. The syntax of parataxis is itself inexhaustible: an infinite number of sentences may be joined by the use of *and* or without any intervening conjunction. At the same time, the effect of joining sentences without explanation beyond the contextually ambiguous *and* often resembles that of metaphor. The hole of meaning which, filled, would explain the relation of one event or proposition to the next is left unfilled. Here the potential for meanings is perhaps not "inexhaustible," but it does not yield to single or right conjunction. All explanation is interpretive, not syntactic.

This form of nonrecoverable deletion is also emotionally powerful. Auerbach implies that paratactic syntax is suited to a focus on "matters concerned with the inner life" rather than with the description of outward events. Using Augustine's prose as an example, he argues that conjunction with *and* in particular creates effects we associate with subjective expression, namely spontaneity and informality. Through parataxis, Dickinson too gives the impression of artlessness. Her juxtaposition or simple linking of independent claims helps create the dramatic and impulsive effect of a speaking voice, often that of childishness or naiveté.[14] As seen earlier in "My Life had stood," however, and as Mueller suggests, the lack of hypotactic connection may also create rich semantic or contextual ambiguity. Borrowing from Auerbach's description of Genesis, the contrast between extreme brevity and powerful content contributes to the large "note of obscurity" in Dickinson's poems and makes her, like the frugal man of her poem, sound "Grand."[15] The simplicity of paratactic syntax both makes the speaker's voice sound impulsive or natural and increases the elevating ellipticism or obscurity of her message. Thus the same syntactic device leads to comparisons with a child's voice and with that of the author of the Bible—what was long thought to be the voice of God. As I will discuss in Chapter 3, Dickinson's lifelong familiarity with the Bible, with church hymns, and with the paratactic or conjunctive styles of earlier writers (especially George Herbert and Sir Thomas Browne) most likely influenced her style.

Parataxis in the form of juxtaposed lines and sentences may have various functions and present various difficulties to the reader. When the juxtaposed sentences are parallel syntactically, they are often so reduced in syntax that the poem reads like a riddling analogy or a single long sentence, with the relationships of an object to its subject or of the poem's parallel elaborations to its first claim becoming increasingly ambiguous. A simple example occurs in a poem that enumerates its stages and thus keeps at least an ordered sequence of actions clear:

> Finding is the first Act
> The second, loss,
> Third, Expedition for
> the "Golden Fleece"
>
> Fourth, no Discovery —
> Fifth, no Crew —
> Finally, no Golden Fleece —
> Jason — sham — too.   (870)

At first one supposes that "is" links each Act to its action, in an inversion of the first line's form. After the fifth line, however, each Act marks the progressive discovery of what does not exist, revealing that there was no "Finding" at all. The "too" of the last line reveals that the first Act is as much a "sham" as the rest. Because the first lines have no context, Jason's expedition and "sham" seem to represent all "finding" and quest. Every hopeful venture may end thus. "'Morning' — means 'Milking' — to the Farmer" (300) works similarly, using compressed parallel syntax and moving from the apparent to the metaphorical, although this time becoming less specific instead of more in its reference to others' lives. The poem ends:

> Epicures — date a Breakfast — by it —
> Brides — an Apocalypse —
> Worlds — a Flood —
> Faint-going Lives — Their lapse from Sighing —
> Faith — The Experiment of Our Lord —

Parataxis may work democratically to equalize the steps in an argument or attempts at description. No order is assigned the successive assertions, and there may in fact be no logical or necessary order. For example, "Essential Oils – are wrung" begins with a simple aphorism. The next two lines, presented without conjunctive transition, provide more specific content: not just any "Essential Oils" but "The Attar from the Rose / Be not expressed by Suns – alone." The following line either restates the aphorism equally succinctly or provides new terms for understanding "Attar," presumably the same as "Essential Oils": "It is the gift of Screws." The argument develops through the juxtaposition of new terms for what appears to be the same event or claim. Changing the order of the statements might initially confuse the reader (and would certainly destroy the stanza's form), but it would have little effect on the cumulative statements of the poem.

Several poems, like "Essential Oils," begin with a brief aphorism that serves as the thematic key or as the primary analogy for the rest of the poem: "Absence disembodies – so does Death" (860), the speaker of another poem states; "Remembrance has a Rear and Front – / 'Tis something like a House" (1182); or "Paradise is of the option." (1069)—one of Dickinson's few first lines that ends with a period. Equally often Dickinson begins a drama with very short juxtaposed sentences, only gradually expanding into hypotactic explanation and connection, as for example in "My Cocoon tightens – Colors teaze – / I'm feeling for the Air – " (1099), where the following sentences are two, then three, then four lines long. Other poems begin: "The Sun went down – no Man looked on – / The Earth and I, alone, / Were present at the Majesty – " (1079); or "I cannot want it more – / I cannot want it less – / My Human Nature's fullest force / Expends itself on this." (1301); or "He put the Belt around my life – / I heard the Buckle snap – / And turned away, imperial" (273); or "Praise it – 'tis dead – / It cannot glow – / Warm this inclement Ear / With the encomium it earned . . ." (1384). The sharp economy of the sentences and their abrupt succession give Dickinson's poetry an elevated and emotionally charged or tense quality, even when the subject is playful.

Conjunction with *and* offers more specific complexities than juxtaposition, as an analysis of "My Life had stood – a Loaded Gun," shows. In this poem, six of the first sixteen lines begin with "And":

My Life had stood – a Loaded Gun –
In Corners – till a Day
The Owner passed – identified –
And carried Me away –

And now We roam in Sovreign Woods –
And now We hunt the Doe –
And every time I speak for Him –
The Mountains straight reply –

And do I smile, such cordial light
Upon the Valley glow –
It is as a Vesuvian face
Had let it's pleasure through –

And when at Night – Our good Day done –
I guard My Master's Head –
'Tis better than the Eider-Duck's
Deep Pillow – to have shared –

The first "And" is asymmetric and altogether grammatical. In a common instance of conjunction reduction, it links three verbs to their common direct object ("Me"). The order of the verbs is irreversible, and their connection to one another and to their context is clear. The phrase "And now We" of lines 6 and 7 also appears to be asymmetric; it introduces the contrast of successive present actions to the past of the first stanza.[16] The speaker is liberated from the stasis of her past and recounts moment by moment the successive activities of her new life: "And now . . . And now . . ." The continuous reference of "And (every time I speak . . .) / The Mountains . . . reply" (my parentheses), however, forestalls this temporal, asymmetric interpretation. "And now" may refer to simultaneously ongoing rather than successive actions of the speaker's present.

Roaming and speaking may logically be seen either as parts (subsets) of hunting or as three separate actions. In the latter case, there would be no temporal reason for this ordering of the verbs; the *and*s would be symmetrical. Yet as we continue reading, a situational development appears that may explain the ordering of these phrases and point to a thematic climax: We roam, We hunt, I speak for Him, I smile, "And when . . . / I guard . . . / 'Tis better." With the line-initial "I guard" Dickinson gives us our clue to the pattern by her first—and in this poem single—foregrounding of the speaker as actor. The speaker has moved from the plural, temporally dislocated and relatively nonspecific "And now We roam" to increasingly singular and personal action. She moves from a veiled differentiation of feminine speaker/Gun from Master within concerted action (we hunt the Doe), to distinction within the unity (I speak for Him), to solitary action (I smile), to the choice of solitary over unified and intimate action (I guard, not share his pillow).

The poem's increasing use of restrictive clauses (every time I speak . . . do I smile . . . When I guard), where the speaker's action provides the restricting factor, strengthens the sense of her increasing control, although these (hypotactic) restrictive clauses keep her influence indirect, out of the subject position or grammatical spotlight. The *And*s of this poem's procession are ambiguously symmetrical or asymmetrical. Their progress is sequential, not causal, but it can be seen to have some logical basis in the speaker's development from passive object to ambiguously independent and indirect actor. Through their noncommital and unobtrusive mediating the speaker proceeds to minor claims of independence and then to claims of enormous destructive power, although she concludes by musing over its—and a Gun/Life's—futility.

As Lakoff explains, to understand the use of a conjoining *and*, the reader must often make presuppositions about the overt elements in both halves of the sentence (or in both sentences) and then make deductions from those presuppositions. Reading *and* asymmetrically, we presuppose, for example, that *speak, smile,* and *guard* are more intimate actions than roaming and hunting, and we deduce therefore that this difference as well as the change from plural to singular subject may explain the order of the narration. Reading *and* symmetrically, we would presuppose some identity in all the linked actions (roaming, hunting, speaking, smiling, guarding) and perhaps find their common denominator in the presupposition that hunting involves all the other activities; consequently, smiling like Vesuvius and guarding her Master's head would be equivalent actions to hunting the Doe. Explanation may then require the further leap to metaphorical interpretation: each of these actions involves destroying, subverting, or denying some aspect of the feminine, whether as object (doe), cultural expectation (of cheering and comforting smiles), or social role (sharing a man's bed instead of guarding it). Syntax allows for both, and perhaps other, readings of this sequence of coordinate conjunctions. As this poem shows, parataxis may be a tool of suspense, one more form of rich ambiguity.

Typically, repeated *and*s create a sequence of blanks in a Dickinson poem. They mark the place where some unspecified and perhaps unknown movement in logic or narrative has occurred, a place that may be filled only in retrospect and tentatively with a conjoining phrase more specific than *and.* Thus *and*s may function as a veil to prevent the reader from seeing where the speaker is going. They may also allow the speaker latitude behind that veil to move from one feeling or idea to the next without having to acknowledge either the progression or her motives. Like more obvious (syntactic) forms of nonrecoverable deletion, paratactic *and*s obligate the reader to establish a sentence's missing links.

Dickinson's other frequently used coordinate conjunctions—*but* and *or*—function differently from *and.* Although they, too, often cover a point of nonrecoverable deletion in a poem's narrative or logic, their more obvious function is to mark points of choice or contrast. Where the use of *and* requires the reader to imagine all explanatory conditions or situations of relation, the use of *but* and *or* typically provides at least the context of the contrast.

Syntactic Doubling

Dickinson creates syntactic and semantic ambiguity in several poems by using a single phrase to cover two nonparallel syntactic contexts or to describe two different subjects, usually without marking the division of these contexts by punctuation. The poet deletes what would be the repeated phrase, even though its repetition is considered necessary by all normal grammatical rules. The undeleted phrase, consequently, must function twice, and it makes equal sense in both of its possible contexts. An example from ordinary speech would be "John eats the apple was large": "the apple" functions as direct object of "John eats" and subject of "was large." For want of a technical label, I call this repeated feature of Dickinson's language "syntactic doubling." This doubling is the most striking form of Dickinson's compression, and it is the one she uses with the greatest thematic consistency. An example of doubling occurs in the lines of "He fumbles at your Soul" examined earlier for asymmetry. Syntactically, the phrase "Then so slow" is ambiguous; it is parallel to and continues both the

description of how the soul hears the tormentor's hammers ("Further
. . . Then nearer – *Then so slow*"), and the description of how He
approaches ("He stuns . . . prepares . . . *Then so slow* . . . Deals").
Contiguity demands the former reading, but the latter sentence seems
incomplete without the conjunction "Then" to introduce its final verb.
The phrase "so slow" works twice in the poem; it describes both the
fearful perception of the soul and the awful approach of the tormentor.
Consequently, it collapses the two separate actions into one. Dickinson
makes the soul's observation of its tormentor inseparable from the
tormentor's blow—an appropriate way to introduce the climax of this
moment of mental agony, and to anticipate the concluding couplet's
leap from antagonistic soul and tormentor to the natural partners,
forests and winds.

Syntactic doubling frequently occurs at points where the speaker of
the poem becomes indistinguishable from her subject as the agent of
some action.[17] Another example occurs in the well-known "A Bird
came down the Walk" (328), where either the bird or the observer
may be fearful. According to punctuation, context in the poem, and
syntax, the middle line of the following three could apply to either
the preceding or the following line:

> He stirred his Velvet Head
>
> Like one in danger, Cautious,
> I offered him a Crumb

As in "He fumbles," here the weakening of distinctions between self
and other, or subject and object, immediately precedes the climax of
the poem, again an event that transforms the terms of the parties'
previous acquaintance. In "A Bird came down the Walk," the bird
flies away and the speaker observes the miraculousness of the flight
while simultaneously creating its miraculousness through her extraordinary description. The transport seems to belong to both bird and
speaker and identifies them as mutual subject of the poem. These
lines follow:

> And he unrolled his feathers
> And rowed him softer home –
>
> Than Oars divide the Ocean,
> Too silver for a seam –

> Or Butterflies, off Banks of Noon
> Leap, plashless as they swim.

Like other nonrecoverable deletion, syntactic doubling acts to multiply the possibilities for interpretation in a poem, to increase indeterminacy. More particularly, by using this form of compression to identify the speaker of a poem with its subject, Dickinson suggests that the speaker's articulation—even in pointing to a definite event—half-creates all she sees. Such identification also allows for the speaker's (and poet's) indirect presentation of self, sometimes leading to revelations it would be risky or embarrassing to make in more explicit form.[18]

Compression, then, creates density of narrative and of epistemological argument. It allows rapid movement between the stages of both—occasionally even allowing the omission of a stage in that movement. Extreme density, in turn, is largely responsible for the polysemous quality of Dickinson's language. The poems suggest so much in such short space that, like the wary speaker of "I fear a Man of frugal Speech," the reader must "weigh" each word in attempting to locate the source of a poem's tone or line of play.

Patterned Contrast with Polysyllables

In the first line of "Essential Oils – are wrung," a dash separates the line into noun phrase and verb phrase, or primary latinate or foreign and Anglo-Saxon or native elements; it separates "Essential Oils" from "wrung" or the process of wringing essence from the common.[19] The polysyllabic glide of "Essential," the capital letters, long vowels, alliterative *l* and *s* sounds, and the general elevation of "Essential Oils" (unlike the more common and less evocative synonym "perfume") all stand in contrast to the monosyllables, uncapitalized letters, short vowels, and homeliness of "are wrung." The first line gives us in small, or in compressed form, the contrast of the rest of the poem: attar does not fall naturally from the rose; not "Suns" but "Screws" express it. Beauty and bountiful growth do not suffice for the creation of essence.

The tension of this poem between latinate or generally foreign-derived elements ("Attar") and Anglo-Saxon or common elements ("Screws") recurs throughout Dickinson's poetry, particularly when the latinate words are polysyllabic and of a special, elevated vocabulary (for example, that of religion, philosophy, or royalty). Allen Tate associates these two features of her diction—"words of Latin or Greek origin and, sharply opposed to these, the concrete Saxon element"—with "immortality, or the idea of permanence" on the one hand, and "the physical process of death or decay" on the other. Dickinson uses "the Latin for ideas and the Saxon for perceptions—the peculiar virtue of English as a poetic language."[20] Juhasz sees the primary categories of contrast as words of space and time and words of ideas: "Dickinson's poems reveal a structure based on the encounter, dramatic and reciprocal, between the dimensional and conceptual vocabularies."[21] As her notion of a reciprocal encounter suggests, contrast does not always imply opposition. In fact, it is the close yoking of these vocabularies that creates the rich tension of the contrast. To take a brief example without syllabic contrast, the "Sheets of Place" that lightning "exhibits" on a landscape in the poem "The Soul's distinct connection / With immortality" (974) gives a powerful immediacy to the idea of lightning by assigning an abstract spatial concept (place) to a common object (sheets), itself a metaphor for the sudden brightening and great expanse of the sky. As in this example, when the contrasting vocabularies are joined by the genitive *of* or by a copular verb, they constitute a metaphor, as any predication of an abstract onto a concrete or a concrete onto an abstract quality necessarily does. Although not every contrast involves metaphorical predication, different levels or types of vocabulary, etymological difference, or difference in length and sound, and few contrasts establish a tension as simple as the semantic distinction Tate claims, contrast does generally involve a combination of semantic difference and difference in levels of diction and sound.

Whether the primary categories are polysyllabic and monosyllabic, latinate and native, or abstract and concrete, patterns of contrast structure much of Dickinson's poetry. As in "Essential Oils – are wrung," or the "Ethereal Blow" of "He fumbles," the contrast may establish a thematic paradox (precious Attar is the result of painful labor, of Screws; a knockout blow is ethereal); or it may emphasize the breadth of a single state (the daisy's "Dark Sod" forgotten in "Extasy – and Dell –"). As Lindberg-Seyersted observes, Dickinson often uses concrete words and imagery to define abstractions: "Revolution is the Pod / Systems rattle from" (1082); "Experiment to me / Is every one I meet" (1073); "All Circumstances are the Frame / In which His Face is set − " (820); "Exultation is the going / Of an inland soul to sea" (76); "Crisis is a Hair" (889). In these examples, polysyllabic and/or latinate abstraction is defined by monosyllabic, native words representing concrete objects or actions. The same contrast of abstract and concrete reference occurs in definitions that do not contain a corresponding etymological or a syllabic contrast: for example, "'Hope' is the thing with feathers" (254), "To be alive − is Power" (677), or "Power is only Pain − / Stranded, thro' Discipline" (252).

Much of Dickinson's most startling imagery plays on the contrasts of the native, known object or fact with the exotic or abstract: "Quartz contentment" (341); "Queen of Calvary − " (348); "I dwell in Possibility − / A fairer House than Prose − " (657); "Moats of Mystery" (1609); or—again without the syllabic contrast—"A Mob of solid Bliss −" (1532), and the more homely "I can wade Grief − / Whole Pools of it −" in contrast to the always unsettling "push of Joy" (252). Despite the occurrence of paired contrasting monosyllables or native words, like "push of Joy," latinate and native, abstract and concrete, polysyllabic and monosyllabic elements of contrast interact with such regularity in Dickinson's poetry that the complete absence of one type of contrast when the others are present is more surprising than its presence would be.

Dickinson apparently likes polysyllabic words of foreign and elevated vocabularies as much for their potential humor and for their alliterative solidity as for their value in structural contrasts. A slant of light may be an "imperial affliction" (258); a hummingbird appears as "Resonance of Emerald −" (1463); a spider that "on my reticence / Assiduously crawled" lives in "Perpetual presumption" (1167); a beetle can "From Eminence remote / Driv[e] ponderous perpendicular / His figure intimate" (1128). As these examples suggest, Dickinson often uses elevated and polysyllabic phrases in such strictly compressed contexts or to describe such homely subjects that they appear ludicrous, out of balance. She may mock their extravagance and her subject even while she enjoys using them.

Polysyllabic and latinate words, when densely combined, may also bury the argument of a poem so deep in abstractions that the speaker is effectively protected from revealing any emotional response. For example, in the following convoluted and unusually polysyllabic lines, the poem has no clear emotional tone or message:

A nearness to Tremendousness –
An Agony procures –
Affliction ranges Boundlessness –
Vicinity to Laws

Contentment's quiet Suburb –
Affliction cannot stay
In Acres – It's Location
Is Illocality –   (963)

The poem claims, in simple paraphrase, that agony brings us close to or procures boundlessness. The redundantly polysyllabic abstraction of the claim, however, makes this paraphrase difficult and leaves the speaker's relation to the claim uncertain. It is unclear, for example, just what agony or affliction does procure. The three first explanatory words provided are all more common as adjectives than nouns: we know what *near, tremendous,* and *boundless* mean. Made substantive, however, the meanings are less clear, and the imprecise spatial marking of "nearness" and of the verb "ranges" makes the sufferer's position even less certain. These awkward noun forms, like the later "Illocality," suggest that agony removes us from a known or definable place. Polysyllabic circumlocution appropriately describes a place that is neither here nor there and has substance only as insubstantial qualities might be imagined to have: "nearness to Tremendousness" is neither local nor circumscribed. The poem is not as simple as my opening paraphrase.

Somewhat paradoxically, and whether used humorously or not, the poet's polysyllables have the effect of emphasizing aurally the poems' general compression. Dickinson's poetry consists largely of one-syllable or two-syllable Anglo-Saxon-derived words. As Richard Howard determines statistically, of the 110 words that Dickinson uses more than 50 times in her poetry, more than 85 percent are of Anglo-Saxon origin. Moreover, although these 110 words represent less than 1.5 percent of the poet's vocabulary (not counting what he calls "structural" words), they make up slightly more than 25 percent of her total uses of words.[22] The skeleton of plain language established by these frequently repeated Anglo-Saxon words—perhaps a legacy of her Puritan forebears—gives Dickinson's foreign-derived language special prominence in the poems.[23]

A polysyllabic word may comprise all or most of a line. The following quotations present a few of the countless instances where this occurs: in "I cannot be ashamed" (914), "Magnitude / Reverses Modesty" and ". . . a Hight so high / Involves Alpine / Requirements"; in "Bloom – is Result – to meet a Flower" (1058), "To be a Flower, is profound / Responsibility –"; in the more familiar "Because I could not stop for Death" (712), "The Carriage held but just Ourselves – / And Immortality." The metrical regularity of Dickinson's lines combines with the word's isolation in such cases to make each of its syllables distinct; the weak penultimate syllable of "Immortality" holds its place in the line as firmly as any monosyllabic noun might. Readers may not glide over unstressed sounds in the word as they might if it were to appear in a longer line and a richer syntactic context.

The poet plays semantically on the metrical lengthening of her polysyllabic words. For example, in "She rose to His Requirement – dropt / The Playthings of Her Life" (732), it is virtually impossible to read the first line metrically, that is, giving "Requirement" three syllable positions. Partly because of the dash following it and partly because so many of Dickinson's lines end in polysyllables, "Requirement" seems to fill the line (to take four syllables), and "dropt" is as much a metrical surprise as it is a thematic one. By the end of the first line, the poet has already undercut her initial claim that the wife's new "honorable" position involves any real elevation. An earlier poem (305) weights all three syllables of "difference" to highlight the idea of distinction in its first line: "The difference between Despair / And Fear – is like the One" between the "instant" before "a Wreck" and the instant after, or between the pronunciation of "difference" with and without the often elided, mid-word syllable. In Dickinson's world, these are distinctions that count. Despite the enormous compression of her poetry generally, there is little elision in Dickinson's polysyllables. The clarity of each syllable, with its individual stress level and sound, gives a weight and delicate edge of wonder to these words that is unlike any other poetic effect I can think of.

Perhaps partly because of this effect, Dickinson is fond of ending poems with heavily polysyllabic lines: "Gaze perplexedly!" (66); "For our mutual honor, / Immortality!" (68); "Night's possibility!" (106); "In Ceaseless Rosemary – " (675); "Unto Her Sacrament – " (751); "Through their Comparative." (800); "Be wholly beautiful – " (801); "Of His Diameters – " (802); "To notoriety." (987);

"No Emolument." (1357). Because in English few polysyllabic or latinate words of more than two syllables have a final stressed syllable, Dickinson's poems often end on a secondary or tertiary stress. Especially when she combines the weak final stress with an imperfect or slant rhyme (for example, "decay" with "Rosemary"), her poems end on a mediate, holding note, with a chord quietly or only partially resolved rather than with the clean "masculine" rhyme of most nineteenth-century poetry.

Foreign-derived and polysyllabic words make readers recognize what splendors of vocabulary the poet knowingly forgoes in her compression. Her frugality, they remind us, emerges from hoarded "Syllables of Velvet – / Sentences of Plush, / Depths of Ruby, undrained," (334) rather than from an impoverished lexicon. By their contrasting length and elevated status—their general richness of contribution to the tone—latinate and polysyllabic words increase the effect of frugality and of understated substance in the poems.

DISJUNCTION

In his theory of foregrounding, Jan Mukařovský defines the function of poetic language as maximizing the deautomatization of language through variation from an established norm. Poetic neologism especially, he states, is formed "with considerable violence to the language, as regards both form and meaning."[24] The more stabilized the norm of standard language and of traditional poetic form, the greater the variation from that norm a poet can take and still write what is heard as poetry. Dickinson uses most of the traditional unifying features of poetry—rhyme, meter, stanzas, and verbal, syntactic, thematic, and figurative repetitions. As quoted earlier, she writes in an early letter to Higginson, "[I] could not drop the Bells whose jingling cooled my Tramp" (L 265). This underlying regularity of meter, rhyme, and stanza forms and the correspondence of her line to syntactic phrase boundaries "cool" the surprise of her disruptive punctuation, inverted and elliptical syntax, occasional metrical irregularity, off-rhyme, and general ungrammaticality. These traditional features, however, also make her disruptions startling by setting them off so quietly.[25] In spite of the simplicity and ordering unity of its major structural features, Dickinson's poetry rivals twentieth-century poetry in its disruption of expected patterns of style and meaning.

As any exploration of the history of English poetry quickly reveals, disjunction is nothing new to poetry. It appears to be a fundamental organizing principle of Old English poetry and is an accepted if not a desired result of the paratactic conventions of the seventeenth- and eighteenth-century "plain" style.[26] There, as in Dickinson's poems, abrupt shifts of tone and immediate subject frequently occur between stanzas or sections of a poem. In Dickinson's poems, however, disjunction also occurs repeatedly and prominently in all levels of style. The fragmentation of "Essential Oils" results as much from disjunction as from compression, as even a glance at the first line reveals. Here, a dash separates the noun phrase from its predicate: "Essential Oils – are wrung –". Dickinson heightens the effect of fragmentation by substituting a dash for the expected period at the end of the line. Disjunction occurs most often in Dickinson's poetry through breaks in the middle of a phrase that we do not expect to be broken. These breaks are often caused by deletion or punctuation, or a combination of the two. A similar effect occurs in semantic or grammatical breaks, where striking word contrast or unexpected grammatical experimentation disrupts the movement of a sentence or line.

To take another example, in "This was a Poet" disjunction occurs again in punctuation and syntax, but also in plot and tone. The poem begins with a two-stanza sentence, then abruptly changes to highly fragmented, repetitive sentences in the two concluding stanzas. The first stanzas (without line breaks or mid-sentence capitals) run: This was a poet – It is that distills amazing sense from ordinary meanings – and attar so immense from the familiar species that perished by the door – we wonder it was not ourselves arrested it – before –. Up until "– before –" the first two stanzas contain only three dashes, each marking a major clause boundary. In contrast (and again without line breaks or mid-sentence capitals), the third and fourth stanzas run: Of pictures, the discloser – the poet – it is he – entitles us – by contrast – to ceaseless poverty – Of portion – so unconscious – the robbing – could not harm – himself – to him – a fortune – exterior – to time –. In these stanzas, a dash or comma interrupts every second or third word. The change in tone corresponds to that in syntax: the marveling tone of the first stanzas becomes a clipped, less certain, skeptical or outright ironic tone in the third and fourth stanzas. Dickinson expresses her ambivalence toward this "Poet" through juxtaposed but unconnected statements, that is, through nonrecoverable deletion. She omits explanation and conjunction in combining the halves of this poem, just as she omits them in linking the final couplet of "He fumbles at your Soul" to the body of that poem. Nonrecoverable deletion is closely related to all the disjunctive strategies of Dickinson's poems.

In its broadest effect, disjunction undercuts the reader's expectation of finding ordered meaning. Language that knowingly disrupts culturally shared ordering patterns (such as those of sentence structure, grammar, punctuation) seems to give structural body to a larger comment on that society's order as well. Especially when the formal disruptions reflect thematic variance from cultural ordering patterns, they seem to voice a belief that the world is not harmonious, that life is neither reasonable nor easy, that there is no natural or divine plan of things keeping meaning safe from the threat of incipient chaos. Disjunction, however, also provides the foundation for profoundly creative experimentation with language. The new combination or ordering of meaning by definition demands some breaking up of previous combinations; disjunctive units of meaning allow for creative reordering of what formerly appeared to be conclusively known. Dickinson does not write in a new language—that would be absurd, primarily because then no one would understand her. Rather, she reorders meaning along associative, analogical lines in order to express what was before inexpressible or unseen and out of a love of play with language. Dickinson's language is essentially, not superficially, disjunctive.

Variants

Like many writers, Dickinson edited her poems. Unlike most others, she did not always decide between variant possibilities for a thought or phrase even in fair copies of a poem. Most of Dickinson's poems exist in finished, single form. Of the remaining several, however, some in fair copy contain one or more variants for a word or line without indicating which choice the poet preferred. Other poems exist in differing fair copies, suggesting that the poet altered her text for various readers or that she changed her mind about which version she liked best.[27] In both these groups of poems, an examination of a poem's variants provides a more complete sense of Dickinson's conception of the poem, unfinished or ambiguous as it may be. Because most of the poems were never prepared for publication, there is not always an authoritative text; the poem includes all its textual variants.

Even when Dickinson does apparently make a final choice between variants, comparing that choice with earlier versions of the poem can sharpen our sense of the final text. In different poems, then, variants either remain an undeleted and thus still important part of what are, by conventional standards, unfinished poems, or they provide evidence of Dickinson's creative processes and thus contribute to a reader's understanding of how a poem reached completion. All variants may bring us closer to the poet's own thoughts about her poems.

Dickinson's variants are at times approximate synonyms, broadening the possibilities for what any single choice might mean. In "He fumbles at your Soul," for example, she writes "The Firmaments — are still" before settling on "The Universe — is still" in a copy she sends to Sue. Both choices suggest all-encompassing effect, the first by its unusual plural (all skies or heavens) and the second by its inclusiveness (all that exists anywhere, heaven or earth). Whatever has happened to the speaker, or to the metaphorical "Forests," brings all worlds, all heavens to motionless silence. The variant of the preceding line ("When Winds take [hold] Forests in their Paws"), however, does not work this simply: winds *taking* forests and winds *holding* forests create different paradigms of action. When "Winds *take* Forests," the act is aggressive and exceptional: the moment of contact, of taking hold, the moment of changing relationship between the two elements moves all worlds to stillness. This fits with the aggressiveness of the unknown "He" toward the speaker in the poem. The earlier variant, "When Winds *hold* Forests," makes the closing couplet an epitaph rather than an analogously devastating event. The period after the speaker has been scalped is like that when winds hold forests: all is completely still, in hushed stasis, perhaps even in harmonic rest. Holding suggests care, protectiveness, prolonged inaction (or gentle action). The moment is one of breathlessness following a storm; it leaves one in an eerie but soothing state of balance, instead of in the tension of waiting to see what follows scalping, or the winds' taking of forests. Dickinson's choice of "take" over "hold" tells us something about her final—or latest known—intentions in the poem.

Variants stand in almost dialectical opposition to each other at the end of "Essential Oils — are wrung." In Chapter 1, I discuss the poem's conclusion using the final line of the text in fascicle 34: "When the Lady lie / In Ceaseless Rosemary." Dickinson sent a copy of this poem to Sue, however, which leaves the lady "In Spiceless Sepulchre." With this conclusion the lady's burial seems literal and permanent. In

Facsimile of Dickinson's poem "He fumbles at your Soul" (315), from *The Manuscript Books of Emily Dickinson*, ed. Ralph Franklin (Cambridge, Mass.: Harvard University Press, 1981), reproduced by permission of the Houghton Library, Harvard University.

contrast to the "Lady's Drawer," which holds eternal "Summer" because of the attar hidden there, the "Sepulchre" of the lady is "Spiceless." "Ceaseless Rosemary" suggests both the contrast of the woman's death to her poems' immortality and a kinship in ceaselessness of maker and product; "Spiceless Sepulchre" suggests only contrast. This latter concluding line implies that the poet transforms only roses, not herself, into essence; consequently, like the natural "General Rose," she decays.

Dickinson's tentative substitution of "art" for "power" in the penultimate line of the fascicle copy of "My Life had stood – a Loaded Gun" ("For I have but the art to kill, / Without – the power to die –") alters this poem by contributing additional and in some ways contradictory information. Killing, this variation suggests, is analogous to creating. Killing may involve the attention to aesthetic detail, the meticulous care, of art, or art may result from explosive, destructive force similar to that of killing. A complete reading of the poem would have to consider the relation of art to power, especially to relationships of power, and of both to aggressive hostility. By providing both choices, Dickinson requires that we consider both.

Particularly in a text like "My Life had stood," where no clean copy of the poem exists, Dickinson's textual variants provide evidence that her poems originated as processes of thought based on the play of cumulative possibilities of meaning. More strongly even than the ambiguities of compression and syntax, variants contribute to the multiplicity of a text by requiring the reader's participation in establishing the text of a poem. Any act of interpretation requires a stable text, although interpreting a poem may involve several acts of interpretation and therefore make use of several textual variations. In poems with multiple word choice the reader must continuously stabilize the text by choosing what belongs in it and at the same time repeatedly return to account for the other, unchosen, possibilities of the poem's meaning.

Punctuation

The most cursory glance at Dickinson's poems shows that she regarded punctuation as a matter of style and personal expression to the same extent that she regarded language in this way. The early editors of her poems, with their penchant for tidying, varied in their decisions about the need to even out the poet's meters, improve her rhymes, or correct her spelling and word choice, but they uniformly standardized her punctuation. They did not take their cue from the poet in doing so.

As Lindberg-Seyersted notes, Dickinson gives no sign of being flexible about her style of punctuation. She lists alternative words in poems; she apologizes for her misspellings and modernizes archaisms in later copies of early poems; but she never apologizes for her unorthodox punctuation or provides variants for it, and where she does alter it from copy to copy it is not done consistently to standardize her marks.[28] Dickinson documents her concern with punctuation in the well-known querulous letter to Higginson complaining about an editorial decision of the *Springfield Republican* to alter the punctuation in one line of her "A narrow Fellow in the Grass." She writes: "Lest you meet my Snake and suppose I deceive it was robbed of me – defeated too of the third line by the punctuation. The third and fourth were one – I had told you I did not print –" (L 316). Even given the hyperbole of the writer's complaint, if a single alteration "defeats" the poem of a line, what does greater alteration of punctuation do?

Although modern editors and critics largely agree that "correcting" Dickinson's punctuation alters the flavor if not the sense of the poems, the editorial problems of deciding which punctuation to correct silently and of how to interpret Dickinson's several ambiguous slanting marks remain. For example, most editors correct Dickinson's misplaced apostrophes (the poet consistently adds an apostrophe to the possessive *its*—it's—and uses a premature apostrophe in contractions ending in *nt*—ca'nt, did'nt, twas'nt, and so forth).[29] They decide that this idiosyncrasy is meaningless, as I do, solely on the basis of a judgment that neither the tone nor the content of the poems is altered by adhering to her apostrophes. Whether, or how, to reproduce the poet's various slanting marks in standard type remains the largest editorial question. Several critics have attempted to categorize her "pointing marks," dividing her slanting lines into (among others) angular slants, vertical slants, elongated periods, stress marks, and half-moon marks, and differentiating them according to their position above, at, or below the writing line. No one has argued convincingly, however, that such categorizations in any appreciable way affect our reading of the poems. To my mind, representing her slanting marks typographically as dashes—as Johnson and almost every editor and critic following him does—reproduces well the effects Dickinson apparently intended, in spite of the standardization this imposes upon what are, in her own hand, idiosyncratic and ambiguous forms.[30] In the discussion that follows I refer to any slanting mark in the manuscript of her poems that is not evidently a comma or period as a dash.

Even the amateur reader of Dickinson's poems instantly recognizes this poet's verse by her repeated use of the dash. Sometimes the poet's dashes merely replace conventional punctuation, but often they occur where a comma (or any other mark in standard usage) would be unnecessary or wrong. These dashes correspond to pauses for breath or deliberation, or to signs of an impatient eagerness that cannot be bothered with the formalities of standard punctuation. Dickinson's dashes operate rhetorically more than syntactically. Overall, they create a suggestion that the mind at work in the text is unfettered by normal rules of logical procedure. As the reader of Dickinson further knows, they are also infectious. To spend much time with a mind that allows itself such fascinating stops and shifts is to fall into the habit of allowing oneself to move more freely between topics and thoughts. Dickinson's punctuation, like her poetry, teaches the reader to trust the play of the mind.

Dickinson's dashes often function in predictable ways: to isolate words whose meanings suggest isolation or otherwise to reflect the semantic content of the words they surround, and to create suspense in a text. A simple example of punctuation reflecting semantic content occurs in the line "Urging the feet – that would – not – fly –" ("Better – than Music! For I – who heard it –", 503). Commas, which Dickinson often uses interchangeably with the dash, and an unexpected line break combine with dashes to create a similar imitative effect in the second stanza of "After great pain, a formal feeling comes –" (341):

> The Feet, mechanical, go round –
> Of Ground, or Air, or Ought –
> A Wooden way
> Regardless grown,
> A Quartz contentment, like a stone – [31]

The pauses between almost every word in the first lines quoted and then between every phrase echo the ponderousness and reluctance of the speaker's movement. Dashes perform a different dramatic function in lines 12 and 13 of "He fumbles at your Soul" (following "Your Breath has time to straighten –"):

Your Brain – to bubble Cool –
[He] Deals – One – imperial – Thunderbolt –

This poem's suspense began with the initial comparison of the tormentor's fumbling to "Players at the Keys / Before they drop full
Music on –". The unusual simile indirectly poses the question of what
"He" will do to your soul that is equivalent to "full Music." The
disjointedness of the lines quoted above makes the poem move most
slowly as it reaches its climactic action, which increases the reader's
curiosity. Like the speaker, the reader waits in suspense. The arrested
movement of the poem may also reveal the speaker's dazed astonish-
ment: she can barely bring herself to utter what has happened to her.

The effect of these dashes can be more precisely analyzed. In line
13 of "He fumbles," dashes isolate and thereby emphasize each word.
After preparatory, almost sensual fumbling, He requires a single blow
to devastate your innermost being—"imperial" being so obvious in
the blow's force that it does not even require the stress of capitalization. The casual "Deals" implies that His effort and attention are
minimal, thereby making His power seem more awful. This is mere
play for Him; it is like "dealing" a game of cards or any common
blow. We are touched minimally, by "One" thunderbolt, by what is
analogous to his "Paws" (not the brutal claws, or teeth). In contrast
to line 13, the following line—"That scalps your naked Soul"—
remains unfragmented, marked only by a single capitalization, as
though after an "imperial – Thunderbolt" nothing could be a surprise;
things more horrible might have happened. The effect is less dreadful
than the paralyzing suspense.

Dashes foreground key words of difference; they make important
thematic words more distinct. Often Dickinson uses dashes to emphasize points of analogy in the poem, spatially marking the focal
words to give each additional weight. For example, in the lines from
"To pile like Thunder,"

This – would be Poetry –

Or Love –

"Love" is separated from its analogical partner by line and stanza break
as well as by dashes. Rather than isolating the two terms, however,
the white space foregrounds the parallel between "Poetry" and "Love"

by making the appearance of "Love" a greater surprise. The movement of the poem is toward connection of states usually regarded as separate, and the syntactically ambiguous dash concluding the first stanza both allows the sentence to continue (if we read the dash as dash) and makes the continuation a surprise (if we read the dash as end punctuation, which it often is in Dickinson's poetry). Generally, as here, the isolation of a word is more likely to call attention to the surprise of its relationship with others of the poem's terms than to isolate it in a naming function, even when—as in "To pile like Thunder"—the poem's intent is to define ("To pile like Thunder . . . would be Poetry – / Or Love –"). A further point in this context is that the dash following "Love" and completing the first sentence of the poem is no more apparently conclusive than that following Poetry; the definition may still be open for other phenomena equivalent to these.

As these examples indicate, in Dickinson's poetry the dash's primary function is rarely syntactic, to mark a tangential phrase for the reader or enclose a narrative aside.[32] Rather, dashes typically isolate words for emphasis, provide a rhythmical syncopation to the meter and phrase of a line, and act as hooks on attention, slowing the reader's progress through the poem.

Dickinson uses the period infrequently, and most often in her very early and late poetry. The five representative poems I have chosen are entirely characteristic in their prolific use of the dash and lack of periods. Although some poems do end with a period conventionally used, Dickinson is apt to use the period ironically, to mock the expectation of final certainty. Her periods superficially fulfill the reader's expectation that the poems will conclude instead of just ending, while the poems in fact rarely do conclude. At least as often as with periods, Dickinson ends sentences and poems with a question or exclamation mark, and several poems have no closing punctuation.

More than the dash, the question mark signifies Dickinson's desire to unsettle rather than to conclude in her poems. Sirkka Heiskanen-Mäkelä claims generally that Dickinson's open syntax makes each poem a "'statement' of questions that must remain unanswered," but this questioning is also often explicit.[33] Poems that begin with exclamations or assertions, for example, may end in doubt. The emphatic and ironic "Title divine – is mine!" closes "Is *this* – the way?" (1072); "I found the words to every thought / I ever had – but One –" ends "How would your own – begin? / Can Blaze be shown in Cochineal – / Or Noon – in Mazarin?" (581). The tribute to Elizabeth Barrett

Browning which begins haltingly, in almost deifying admiration ("Her
– 'last Poems' – / Poets – ended – / Silver – perished – with her
Tongue –"), ends with a peculiar twist. The speaker reasons that,
since it is "dull – conferring" praise or prizes on the already immortal
(dead) poet, her grave must be "sufficient sign" of her greatness. The
speaker then, however, indirectly and jealously asserts how better she
than Robert Browning might have buried his wife:

> Nought – that We – No Poet's Kinsman –
> Suffocate – with easy wo –
> What, and if, Ourself a Bridegroom –
> Put Her down – in Italy?   (312)

Using an unanswered question instead of a definite statement spares
the speaker from the hubris of outright comparison, but it also leaves
the degree of difference unspecified and thus leaves the greatest potential for difference in what she, as Bridegroom, might have done.
Because it remains unanswered and because it is incomplete to begin
with, the question is also multiple here. "What, and if" may be
meant competitively, as I hypothesize: Dickinson thinks that she, as
poet, could better memorialize Barrett Browning than Browning can.
Or she may long to share the Kinsman's privilege of participating in
the funeral service, out of her grateful love to the dead poet. Or
perhaps she wonders how much more affected she would have been
by the poet's death had she also been the one to bury her. The reader
creates the question in attempting to answer it.

This poem's concluding question also reveals the ways in which
questions may function as assertions in Dickinson's poems. However
open-ended in form they may be, they structure the experience they
refer to simply by directing the focused attention of doubt where they
do.[34] The speaker's questions are aggressive in the poem "Why – do
they shut Me out of Heaven?" (248). This poem begins with two
questions, the second immediately coloring the apparent innocence of
the first: "Did I sing – too loud?" The poem ends with an indirect
comparison that directly accuses God of being less generous than the
speaker would be in His position:

> Oh, if I – were the Gentleman
> In the "White Robe" –

> And they – were the little Hand – that knocked –
> Could – I – forbid?

A threatening question creates a similar indirect assertion at the conclusion of "God made a little Gentian" (442); here the speaker asks, "Creator – Shall I – bloom?"[35]

In several poems the question appears as something resembling a teaching device, the kind of rhetorical question asked of children in order to instruct them without having to play the authority directly. In poem 447, Dickinson asks briefly:

> Could – I do more – for Thee –
> Wert Thou a Bumble Bee –
> Since for the Queen, have I –
> Nought but Bouquet?

Here, the answer is clearly no. The poem's question calls attention to the comparison (Queen, Bumble Bee) and to the speaker's role, leaving the analogy itself flexible in its implications. When Dickinson defines gratitude ("Gratitude – is not the mention / Of a Tenderness"), the poem concludes with an illustration proving that silence should not be taken as absence of feeling:

> When the Sea return no Answer
> By the Line and Lead
> Proves it there's no Sea, or rather
> A remoter Bed?   (989)

Be sensible, these questions admonish; figure these things out for yourself from your own knowledge of the world. The teaching tone takes an accusatory edge in poem 490, which is structured around two extended questions asked, one surmises by the subject, of no lesser authority than God:

> To One denied to drink
> To tell what Water is
> Would be acuter, would it not
> Than letting Him surmise?

> To lead Him to the Well
> And let Him hear it drip
> Remind Him, would it not, somewhat
> Of His condemned lip?

The repeated (and already redundant, because of the larger question form) "would it not" underscores the questioner's ironic stance. She is convinced that the practice of telling a sufferer what "He" cannot have is cruel. Why, she pointedly wonders, beyond sadistic enjoyment of another's misery, give her knowledge of a heaven, or perfection, or joy she could otherwise merely abstractly "surmise"? In all these questions, the primary power of the speaker lies in the freedom to ask them. She may demand answers of any authority; the fact that she will not receive answers beyond those she creates for herself by framing them is unimportant in comparison with the self-assertion implied in the asking.

Dickinson's poems characteristically either begin in apparent certainty and move to apparent doubt (as in the examples above), or begin with a question and end by undercutting the adequacy of the expected answer. An example of the latter occurs in "Who were 'the Father and the Son' / We pondered when a child, / And what had they to do with us" (1258), which concludes:

> We blush, that Heaven if we achieve —
> Event ineffable —
> We shall have shunned until ashamed
> To own the Miracle —

Or a poem resembling "Essential Oils — are wrung" in its insistence that precious expression results from painful experience begins with the challenge "Dare you see a Soul *at the White Heat?*" (365) and ends with ambiguous and uncertain victory: "Least Village" or person has "it's Blacksmith" who hammers and heats "these impatient Ores . . . Until the Designated Light / Repudiate the Forge —". The final verb is either an archaic subjunctive, casting doubt on the possibility of achieving this state, or an uninflected verb, suggesting a timelessness corresponding to the moments of pure ore or "Essential Oil" that "Make Summer." In either case, this moment of transcendence and transformation cannot be conveyed in standardized English and does not seem to take place in real time.

The exclamation mark occurs most frequently early in Dickinson's writing years and, like italics and the dash, gives the poetry an air of breathless or urgent speech. An exclamation mark italicizes its entire statement, often indicating that the statement is a surprise or a departure from what has gone before. In this sense, although the exclamation expresses certainty rather than the uncertainty of the question, the two marks of punctuation function similarly. As conclusions to poems, both indicate that what appears to be true is not always to be trusted, that surprising events may disrupt impressions or assumptions held to be true. For example, the meditative poem "I shall know why – when Time is over – / And I have ceased to wonder why –" ends "I shall forget the drop of Anguish / That scalds me now – that scalds me now!" (193). The combined exclamation mark and repetition emphatically move the reader's attention from the poem's metaphysical question about divine justice to "wonder" at the speaker's present suffering. In one version of another poem the exclamation mark works ironically: "I should have been too glad, I see – / Too lifted – for the scant degree / Of Life's penurious Round –" (313) begins with three stanzas of left-branching syntax, and even in the fourth stanza the poet never finishes the initial sentence by saying what it is that would have made her "too glad." The poem concludes with a series of paradoxes and two exclamations:

> Defeat – whets Victory – they say –
> The Reefs – in old Gethsemane –
> Endear the Coast – beyond!
> 'Tis Beggars – Banquets – can define –
> 'Tis Parching – vitalizes Wine –
> "Faith" bleats – to understand!

Like the extended and incomplete statement of revelation—"I should have been too glad, I see"—these simple paradoxes undercut the speaker's claim that she now understands by the very redundancy of their certainty. The truism that beggars define banquets does not explain why *she* is a beggar, or why she should have had to relinquish her feast. The exclamation provides tonal quality—whether of irony, as in this poem, or of urgency, or of surprise. Its repeated use contributes to the impression that the voice of the poem is spontaneous and intimate; there is no pretense of decorum or artificial formality here.

Capitalization

Like her punctuation, Dickinson's capitalization is not easy to deter-
mine. Although most of the letters in her manuscripts are either
clearly capital or not, some are of an in-between size. How they are
reproduced in type may have as much to do with an editor's expectations as with the poet's intent. For example, in "He fumbles at your
Soul," the *s* beginning "stuns" of line 4 and that beginning "Soul" in
line 12 are of about the same medium size in the manuscript, but
Johnson considers only the latter a capital in his standardization of
Dickinson's handwriting for type. The decision is logical: Dickinson
has already clearly capitalized "Soul" in line 1, and she more often
capitalizes nouns than verbs in the poems. Nonetheless, following
this pattern of her capitalization (and the earlier British and American
habit of capitalizing nouns) encourages inconsistency; an editor will
tend to overlook questionable capitals when they occur at the beginning of verbs, adverbs, or function words but to consider letters of
the same shape and size capital when they occur at the beginning of
a noun.[36]

Dickinson's capitalized words simultaneously suggest concrete, immediate presence and belie it. They give her words a symbolic referentiality. Perhaps partly for the practical reason that so many of
Dickinson's capitals begin nouns, multiple capitalized words may lend
particular substantiality to ideas or things. Even when the capitalized
nouns are themselves insubstantial ("Essential Oils"), the stress of
capitalization gives the words added weight in the line. The poet
draws our attention to the objects and ideas, the named things of her
poetry, by capitalizing their names.

To demonstrate: taking a random ten poems (302, 402, 502, 602,
702, 802, 902, 1002, 1102, 1202) as a sample and not counting the
first word of each line or the word "I," Dickinson capitalizes 108
nouns, 10 adjectives, 2 verbs and no words of any other grammatical
category.[37] As another example, in "I started Early – Took my Dog"
(520—again, not counting the first word in each line or "I"), Dickinson capitalizes 24 out of the poem's 25 nouns, 9 out of 10 subject
and object pronouns, 5 out of 6 adjectives, but only 1 out of 19 verbs
and 1 of 4 adverbs ("Took" and "Early"). The poems I have chosen as
representative for this grammar demonstrate the same pattern. In
these five poems the poet capitalizes a total of 85 words, again not
counting "I" or the first word of a line; 62 are nouns, 9 are adjectives,

13 are pronouns (and all of these occur in the two poems "This was a Poet" and "My Life had stood"), and 2 are conjunctions. There are no mid-line capitalized verbs, adverbs, or function words besides the conjunctions. This stress on the substantives (nouns and adjectives) of a poem functions both to emphasize the naming word as an entity important in itself and, correspondingly, to increase the effect of substantiality, and thus an implicit referentiality when the noun is concrete, supporting those words. Of course, a capitalized noun in fact refers no more directly or immediately than an uncapitalized one; the more emphatic form, however, suggests a difference in quality.

On the other hand, a capitalized noun also seems to represent its class, and to that extent it functions symbolically. For example, in "My Life had stood – a Loaded Gun," the word "Gun" is metaphorical: we understand it to represent repression or containment and potential explosively destructive power, particularized in the concrete form of the tool of a powerful "Owner." The capitalization here has much the effect of capitalized personifications or allegorizations of things and qualities in Spenser's *Faerie Queene* or Bunyan's *Pilgrim's Progress*—or in much popular nineteenth-century American literature. Similarly, the capitalization of "Essential," "Oils," "Attar," "Rose," "Suns," and "Screws"—that is, every noun but "gift" in the first stanza of poem 675—encourages us to read the poem allegorically, as the poet's theory of poetic creation. By flagging so many of her substantives, Dickinson seems to invite the reader to make as much of them as he or she will.

Experimental Grammar

Nouns

Because much of her language sounds extraordinary, Dickinson is assumed to coin a large number of words and to use words from exotic sources. For the most part, however, the unusual sound of her language stems from the transposition of classes of words by simple appropriation (a verb is used as a noun, for example, without a change in its form), from the transformation of words from one class to another by adding or omitting suffixes, and from unusual juxtapositions of words (the violation of selectional restrictions). In his vocabulary study, Howard reports that coined words amount to only slightly more than 2 percent of Dickinson's total vocabulary (a percentage comparable to that in poetry by Keats, Lanier, and Emerson), and that her vocabulary does not contain an uncommon proportion of words from special sources. The poet's vocabulary is uncommon, he finds, because of its small number of "high-frequency" words (words that occur eight times or more per thousand lines of poetry), because of its high ratio of verbs to nouns and adjectives, and because of the poet's "singular" experimentation with the form and class of words.[38]

Most of Dickinson's form/class grammatical experiments involve adjectives and nouns: adjectives, verbs, and adverbs function as nouns, and nouns function, most often, as adjectives. Dickinson will transform anything into a noun or adjective. Action becomes object in "The Daily Own – of Love" (580), "The overtakelessness" (1691), or with "Piles of solid Moan –" (639). Adjectives may act as nouns: "Brow to Barefoot!" (275), "I sometimes drop it, for a Quick –" (708) and "The fairer – for the farness – / And for the foreignhood" (719). Adverbs become nouns: "an Until –" (779), "a Sportsman's Peradventure –" (925). Nouns and verbs become adjectives with the addition of the suffix -less: competeless, recordless, postponeless, repealless, stopless, graspless, pauseless, perturbless, reportless, floorless—to name just a few of Dickinson's uses of this suffix.[39] Noun becomes adjective in the famous snake poem "A narrow Fellow in the Grass" (986): "His notice instant is"; and with "more angel" in "The World – stands – solemner – to me –" (493). An abstract noun becomes capable of action, or quantified, in "The Plenty hurt me – 'twas so new" (579); "But Epoch had no basis here / For Period exhaled." (1159); "across the June / A Wind with fingers – goes –" (409); and with "a blame" (299). Transforming an insubstantial property into a noun—as in "The Adequate" of hell (744)—implies that the object, quality, or event in question can only be named indirectly, through a grammatical subversion of the distinction between quality and object.

Using a word of one grammatical class to function as another disguises a complex predication. Juxtaposing words that do not function together in normal usage creates a kind of parataxis, for which the reader must work out the appropriate relationship. To give a simple example: "The Daily Own – of Love" gives distinct body to possessiveness, perhaps in reflection of the physical quality of the feeling, and certainly in analogy with the ownership of more mundane and quantifiable possessions. "The Daily Own – of Love / Depreciate the Vision –" suggests that once love becomes a daily affair (and is in that sense "owned") it decreases in worth. Or the unusual "Own" and uninflected "Depreciate" may imply that allowing love to be possessive, especially in a constant or "Daily" way, decreases one's appreciation of love generally; or more simply that any love gained is less desired than a love that remains unrequited. Making a noun function as an adjective, a verb function as a noun, and so on requires a semantic explanation provided only by lengthy and speculative paraphrase. The discourse of the poem indicates the direction these reconstructions of meaning and syntax should take, but it does not clarify the ambiguity altogether. Form/class experimentation, in other words, is a particularly effective and metaphorical form of compression. Through these unusual combinations, Dickinson may create resonant and complex predications using just a few words.

The "gift of Screws" provides a semantic instance of Dickinson's play with form and meaning. Here each word is used grammatically, but because Dickinson uses the copular (or abbreviated auxiliary) "is" for the previous notional "Be . . . expressed," the action of creating in the line "It is the gift of Screws" is carried implicitly by the noun "Screws." "Screws" is a metonymy for a process that involves screwing; Attar is expressed through, or as a gift of, that process. In the same poem, "Ceaseless Rosemary" gives Rosemary an unexpected temporal and active edge. "Ceaseless" ordinarily describes only activities or time-bound events (as in ceaseless motion). "Ceaseless Rosemary," then, is not just immortal (the logical synonym for "Ceaseless") but ceaselessly active with whatever rosemary may do—produce its own scent? keep the corpse smelling like a living part of the earth? grow in kitchen gardens? represent the common work of a housewife? As a combination of adjective and noun, "Ceaseless Rosemary" is entirely grammatical. The combination of these words, however, violates semantic rules of selectional restriction, thereby implicitly predicating qualities of the noun (in this case predicating motion of Rosemary) that are inappropriate to it. The same jar in expectation of how one word will modify or join with another occurs in the phrase "Vesuvian smile" or in the predications "Your Breath has time to straighten – / Your Brain – to bubble Cool"; normally, a smile does not explode destructively, nor does breath have form capable of controlled flexibility nor the brain share properties of motion and temperature with water. Like her grammatical form/class substitution, Dickinson's semantic violation of selectional restrictions increases the complexity and metaphorical density of a poem.

Dickinson's liberties with the standard singular and plural number of nouns, like her form/class experimentation, affect the possibilities for direct unambiguous reference and hence generally move the poem in the direction of the metaphorical. By altering the expected use of number, the poet at times makes her subject more diffuse and at others creates a more particular sense of her subject, giving the illusion of increased referentiality. Both effects alter one's conventional perception of things in the world.

To begin with the greater particularity of the singular number: when a speaker wishes she were "a Hay —" (333), for example, or has the bird on her "Walk" drink "a Dew / From a convenient Grass —" (328), the indefinite article "a" sharpens the image otherwise created by these mass nouns. Making a plural or mass noun singular does not identify any dew or grass, but it suggests that one could. "Hay," for example, does not grammatically distinguish its parts except in the separate categories of "stalks," "bundles," and so on. A *hay* is not possible in English.⁴⁰ By making her speaker "a" hay, however, Dickinson implies that she would stand out from the rest of the grasses— even if the point of difference existed only in her own imagined singularity. In "a Glee among the Garret" (934), the singular glee seems specifiable, perhaps traceable to a particular cause, and the plural Garret seems more a repeated event than a place repeatedly returned to. Through her casual use of the singular where one expects a plural number, Dickinson suggests that even under the apparently most anonymous circumstances single reference, and singularity, is possible.

Marking a plural noun as singular or making a singular noun plural (as with "among the Garret" or "thronging Mind —", 751, or "Whole Chaoses," 806) disrupts the possibility of reference. The poet's favorite combination of singular and plural reference occurs in the pronouns "ourself" and "themself." The singular "self" attached to a reflexive plural pronoun seems to undermine individuality by identifying numbers of people in a symbolic one. For example, in a poem later containing the unambiguously singular "And so I bear it big about / My Burial —" Dickinson writes:

> If we demur, it's gaping sides
> Disclose as 'twere a Tomb
> Ourself am lying straight wherein
> The Favorite of Doom.   (858)

Here the speaker includes her lover, and perhaps also the reader, in her experience ("Ourself") without departing from the narration of her own singular position ("am lying"). Reversing this multiplication of herself in "Those fair − fictitious People" (499), Dickinson begins with the plural "we" and "ourselves" and ends with the stanza:

> Esteeming us − as Exile −
> Themself − admitted Home −
> Through gentle Miracle of Death −
> The Way ourself, must come −

In this poem, "Themself" and "ourself" emphasize that although we all die, each instance of death involves only one solitary "self." Similarly, we "deem ourself a fool −" (320) and "We" question, "What, and if, Ourself a Bridegroom −" (312). The disruption of conventional number (is it I or we who act and speak?) places these poems in the universal spectrum of common human experience but maintains the particularity of an immediately active and experiencing "I."

As seen in the section on capitalization, the poet's nouns are on the whole both the most and the least substantial aspect of her verse. When capitalized, they occur with a deliberate, suggestively referential presence, but that distinctive prominence gives them a larger than life or symbolic undertone that detracts from a single referentiality. When mass or plural nouns are made singular and when adjectives and nouns are transposed, they lose as much specificity from the impossibility of literal reference as they gain from the suggestion that some new distinction of singularity or reference is possible. Nouns create the illusion of thingness in Dickinson's poems, but they do not direct us to particular events or things. They give, instead, the sense that the world is as mobile and flexible as her perception of it. The events of her brain are as concretely and substantially present as the events in her garden or those of her friends' lives.

Verbs

Critics tend to notice Dickinson's foregrounding techniques involving nouns more readily than they do her less ostentatious experimentation with verbs. It is true that Dickinson capitalizes primarily nouns; that nouns are the class of major focus in her contrasts of latinate and native, or polysyllabic and monosyllabic vocabulary; and that she coins far more nouns than verbs and experiments more with substitutions and transformations of nouns and adjectives than with verbs. Nonetheless, the poet does experiment with the forms of verbs in her poems; furthermore, she uses an unusually high proportion of verbs to nouns and adjectives.[41] Unlike her foregrounding of nouns, Dickinson's innovation with verbs sounds more ungrammatical than poetic or semantically significant: for example, she will drop or change a verb's marked features (its inflections of voice, tense, person, and mood) or alter the transitive and intransitive properties of verbs. This difference in her types of experimentation with nouns and verbs has both a semantic and a formal cause.

First, and obviously, Dickinson's interest in action corresponds to those aspects of meaning carried by a verb's inflection. She writes of how action is perceived, what its agent may be, what transformations it effects, and the process of change, or action, itself. Inflections mark the context, and thus generally the direction and boundaries, of a verb's predication. Second, in English verbs as a class tend to be less stable syntactically than nouns, although they are more flexible than nouns in incorporating other meaning. As we know from common usage, verbals operate syntactically as adjectives or nouns; adding the infinitive "to" or a participial or gerundive suffix transforms a verb grammatically into a substantive. Lindberg-Seyersted states that "the noun-class in English is capable of incorporating any part of speech" to explain why the largest number of Dickinson's neologisms belong to the category of the noun.[42] Josephine Miles apparently operates on this theory in her analysis of syntax in English and American poetry; she counts nouns used as adjectives in poetry as nouns, but verbs used as adjectives (that is, participial forms of verbs) as adjectives: the noun is syntactically more stable than the verb. Dickinson could easily have discovered from her own sensitivity to language that nouns lend themselves to greater syntactic play and verbs to greater stability in meaning. The verb provides the basis for most meaning; it lends itself to greater semantic than structural experimentation.

To take a familiar example, in

> Essential Oils — are wrung —
> The Attar from the Rose
> Be not expressed by Suns — alone —

"Be" at the beginning of the third line of this poem provides a sight rhyme with the *E* of "Essential" that begins the first line. The rhyming echo in this line-initial position calls attention to the unexpected form of the auxiliary "Be." In ordinary prose the sentence would read: Attar *is* not expressed by suns; "Be" is the infinitive or subjunctive or uninflected form of the expected, standard "is." Three other uninflected verbs occur in the poem's remaining five lines: the "Rose *decay*," "This *Make*," and "the Lady *lie*." Leaving these verbs unmarked for person, function, or tense suggests that they represent essential or primary process and activity. Without the restrictions of person and tense, the verb's action is unlimited; its reference is essential, not historical. "The General Rose" will always "decay," and both the capital letters of the substantives and the uninflected verb make the proposition more definitive.

Because Dickinson's use of uninflected verbs is among her most unusual language disruptions, critics have singled it out for comment. In early criticism the poet's uninflected verbs were generally assumed to be ungrammatical and therefore regrettable, or else a modified form of the subjunctive voice. Subjunctive verbs, like the ungrammatical verbs above, often take the form of the infinitive without its auxiliary "to." Dickinson frequently creates the subjunctive mood with the conventional change of the verb "to be." A few examples are: "As if my life were shaven" (510); "if there were / A time" (650); "Then 'Great' it be – if that please Thee –" (738); "If we had ventured less / The Gale were not so fine" (1175). The subjunctive mood contributes importantly to the speculative and qualifying tone of her verse. Because the subjunctive does appear often in Dickinson's poems in its standard form, a reader might be inclined to read questionable uses of "be" in particular as subjunctive—an option the poet doubtless intends. For the most part, however, there is a tonal and semantic difference between Dickinson's regular use of the subjunctive mood and her irregular use of uninflected verbs.

Grace Sherrer is the most persuasive proponent of the argument that most of Dickinson's uninflected verbs are grammatically regular, primarily as subjunctive verbs but also as colloquial or archaic forms well known to the poet and her contemporaries.[43] Because critics—informally if not in print—still deplore Dickinson's ungrammaticality or still defend her from claims of irregularity by trying to make her usage conventional, I will linger over Sherrer's argument longer than it alone would warrant. At times Sherrer reveals grammaticality that is helpful in understanding a poem. For example, in the lines ". . . 'Whatsoever Ye shall ask – / Itself be given You' –" (476), the addition of "shall" to the final line accounts for the poet's use of "be." The omitted auxiliary "shall" makes "be" sound ungrammatical, whereas

in fact it is not. Generally, however, Sherrer's claim for verbal regularity made more sense in 1935 than it does today. Sherrer was
working from an altered edition of Dickinson's poems (the only editions then available) and thus did not see many of Dickinson's irregular
verbs.

In the poem "You've seen Balloons set – Hav'nt You?" (700), for
example, Sherrer points out that "Crowd" in the line "The Crowd –
retire with an Oath –" may take the plural, in accordance with
common understanding of the noun as plural and with common usage.
In the next line of this poem, however, Dickinson uses an uninflected
verb with a noun that is not acceptable as a plural: "The Dust in
Streets – go down –". For Sherrer this verb creates no problem because
her text gives "dust . . . goes." The echoing "Crowd – retire" and
"Dust . . . go" lead me to see both verbs as unusual. "Crowd" and
"Dust" are mass or collective nouns and thus normally take singular
verbs. Making both verbs plural in this poem doubly emphasizes the
contrast between the tragic but "imperial" singularity of the poet/
balloon and the plural anonymity of the members of the crowd. Like
particles of dust, they have recognizable shape as an entity, they
assume importance, only when they are indistinguishable members of
a group. Particularly when repeated, the combination of mass noun
and plural or uninflected verb calls attention to a disparity, thereby
encouraging the reader to ask why these forms were chosen.

The question of correctness is generally irrelevant as a criterion for
judgment in reading Dickinson's work. If one could identify grammaticality with skillful use of language and ungrammaticality with
flawed or careless use (as one does in the speech of children), then
there would be some point in advocating grammaticality for its own
sake. With Dickinson, however, ungrammatical and grammatical uses
of language are equally intentional and manipulated with equal precision and skill. Assuming that the poet's unusual sounding constructions are conventional (even if only archaically) and therefore of no
special interest in fact hinders the reading of some poems. For example, Sherrer claims that the poet uses "Neighbor" colloquially, as
a plural subject, in the first stanza of the following poem:

> The Show is not the Show
> But they that go –
> Menagerie to me
> My Neighbor be –   (1206)

Sherrer would read the last line: "My Neighbor[s] be." Yet had the poet wanted to use the common plural form, she might have done so without disturbing her meter or any other reference of the poem; she has already used "they that go," and "Menagerie" is a mass noun. More important, seeing the poet's subject as plural detracts from the humor of her metaphor. With the singular subject, the speaker claims to see a collection of exotic animals, another whole circus, in the single person next to her (her neighbor). Identifying "Menagerie" with the entire crowd (all her neighbors) makes them less odd and the speaker correspondingly less amusing, if not less amused.

Unusual uses of language foreground themselves and their effects on the surrounding text. By speculating about these effects, a reader only follows the writer's cue. Consequently, even when a conventional explanation of apparently ungrammatical syntax is convincing, the reader should not be limited by its restrictive view of the poet's intentions from interpreting the construction in other ways, using the context of the poem and the rarity of the construction as guides. In "We will not drop the Dirk – / Because We love the Wound / The Dirk Commemorate – Itself / Remind Us that we died." (379), Sherrer reads "Commemorate" as an adjective participle and would insert "may" before "remind" (the commemorate dirk itself may remind us . . .). But despite its lack of inflection and thus ungrammatical form, "Commemorate" functions equally well as a verb in this sentence (we love the wound that the dirk commemorates; or we love the wound that commemorates the dirk). Furthermore, the assertive "We will not drop" at the beginning of the sentence makes it unlikely that the speaker would turn to the subjunctive mood for this statement at the end. The stark roughness of "Because We love the Wound / The Dirk Commemorate – Itself / Remind Us . . ." suits the painful speech of the (apparently) wounded speaker. Combining these readings, we see in this poem another instance of syntactic doubling—here unusually complex because "Commemorate" changes grammatical class (from uninflected verb to adjective) as well as function (from predicate to modifier of subject).

The subjunctive typically functions to connote either conditionality or universality. Interestingly, Dickinson critics tend instead to see it as connoting uncertainty and therefore read the poet's uninflected verbs as signifying doubt even when they are not strictly subjunctive. Lindberg-Seyersted, for example, accepts in modified form George Whicher's argument that uninflected verbs mark the poet's "chronic

trepidation"; "it is unquestionable," she says, "that in some poems
this idiosyncratic 'subjunctive' carries a strong element of uncertainty
and doubt."[44] Other critics, however, are more apt to interpret the
poet's use of uninflected verbs symbolically: it is an attempt to "uni-
versalize her thought"; the poet returns to "the basic stem" of verbs,
escapes "from all particularity . . . into the Absolute; she attempts a
verbal, and indeed a visual (for the inflections are visibly pared away),
correlative for the insight into essences at the core of meaning and
experience."[45] The suggestion that Dickinson escapes from particularity into the absolute gives insufficient recognition to her repeated
emphasis on the singular and the (especially domestic) particular. She
uses the particular, however, as David Porter observes, to reach its
essence. By using uninflected verbs Dickinson moves both out, to the
actual rose, and in, to essences; she brings the universal and the
personal into immediate play. She unhinges words and ideas from
conventional syntax and hence indirectly from a conventional concep-
tualization of the world, calling all rules into question.

"Essential Oils" thematically supports this interpretation of its
uninflected verbs. The uninflected *Be, decay, Make,* and *lie* embody
the process of transformation from time-bound Rose to essential Attar
that is the subject of the poem. These verbs present their root meaning
fully but leave their action universalized, unfinished, unspecified.
"Essential Oil" is continuously "expressed."

Uninflected verbs function similarly in another poem (515). It
begins:

> No Crowd that has occurred
> Exhibit – I suppose

There we stop. It should be "No Crowd . . . has exhibited," we
think. These past crowds seem still to exist. As befits a meditation
on resurrection, this poem repeatedly undercuts any clear sense of
time or of number. In twenty lines, Dickinson uses eight uninflected
verbs: "No Crowd . . . Exhibit," "Circumference be full," the "Grave
/ Assert," "The Dust – connect – and live – ," "Solemnity – prevail
– ," its "Doom / Possess," and "Duplicate – exist –". The atemporality
of these verbs is magnified by the even more unusual "All Multitudes
that were / Efface in the Comparison" (lines 10–11). What should
logically be either a reflexive or a passive voice construction (efface
themselves or were effaced) is instead intransitive, active, unmarked.

Singular "Dust" and plural "Multitudes" describe the same crowd of dead and take the same unrestricted verb form of active, continuing, timeless presence. Those crowds do still exist, and resurrection is not clearly an event of the future or of any other single time. It is ongoing, universal, like the poem's verbs. Authoritative pronouncements about the boundaries of the living and the dead do not hold in this poem.

In "To pile like Thunder," the uninflected form again opens a timeless, nonreferential space around the action. Here Dickinson's uninflected verb is a logically passive verb used intransitively, or transitively without a direct object, and with only an implied subject; "Experience either [Poetry or Love] and consume – / For None see God and live – ". "Consume" appears to be command, statement, and prophecy (depending on whether "Experience" is an imperative to the reader or a truncated form of "we experience" or "if you experience"). The logically passive "you will be consumed" appears active, a matter of your volition: [you] consume. There is no simple way to integrate that shifting of responsibility for the action of consuming easily into the rest of the poem. Thus the verb's ambiguous form leaves the effect of poetry (and love) uncertain.

Assuming a subjunctive mood in every truncated verb in Dickinson's poetry leads to a skewed perception of the poet. Dickinson writes several poems of hesitation or doubt and uses explicit and implicit questions as a major semantic and structural device. Her questions, however, are frequently rhetorical, and her speakers' doubts often have more to do with undercutting an established truth than with real doubt on the part of the poet. Regarding Dickinson's unusual verbs as uninflected allows the reader to respond to the unusual sound of the construction; the reader's interpretation may then be directed by its unexpectedness and by the context of the poem. The uninflected form, furthermore, corresponds to the poet's tendency to value process and continuation over specified event. Other language use in Dickinson's poetry makes one more apt to expect multiplicity and surprise from this poet than uncertainty and archaism, so why should expectations differ here? The verbs of "All Multitudes that were / Efface in the Comparison" and "Experience either [Poetry or Love] and consume" carry little hesitation and rich ambiguity, as do the poet's uninflected verbs generally.

The lines from these two poems reveal another of Dickinson's frequent experiments with verbs: the alteration of tense and mood. With "Efface" and "consume" the poet uses verbs that should logically be passive intransitively or as transitive verbs without a direct object. In other poems she moves from present to past tense, or from the indicative to the conditional mood without explanatory conjunctions or prepositions. As with the verbs discussed above, changes in the properties or tense of a verb may have the effect of stripping a verb of its inflections; making "consume" imperative or active and intransitive rids it of the need for marked inflection. Both forms of alteration create semantic ambiguity through a process akin to nonrecoverable deletion. Beyond this, however, the semantic effect differs. Where lack of inflection causes confusion with regard to person or number and tense, the uninflected verb takes on an atemporal, unhinging quality and the subject, by implication, tends to expand. Where lack of inflection makes a verb ambiguously transitive and intransitive or marks a change in tense within the poem, its effect depends more closely upon the context of change.

In the rhythmically experimental "Four Trees – upon a solitary Acre," the nonrecoverable deletion that results from using the transitive verb "Maintain" intransitively or without an obviously apparent direct object takes the form of syntactic doubling. Leaving "Maintain" (line 4) ambiguously transitive, Dickinson causes "The Sun" to serve doubly as the direct object of "Maintain" (four trees maintain the sun) and as subject of "meets" (the sun meets them):

Four Trees – upon a solitary Acre –
Without Design
Or Order, or Apparent Action –
Maintain –

The Sun – upon a Morning meets them –
The Wind –
No nearer Neighbor – have they –
But God –

The Acre gives them – Place –
They – Him – Attention of Passer by –
Of Shadow, or of Squirrel, haply –
Or Boy –   (742)

To some extent, however, "Maintain" may take not just the sun but the whole world as its object. The last stanza of the poem speculates indirectly along these lines:

> What Deed is Their's unto the General Nature –
> What Plan
> They severally – retard – or further –
> Unknown –

These trees may "Maintain" all Nature, themselves, or only a plan that has been discarded by the rest of the universe. Reading "Maintain" as an abbreviation of the passive voice "are Maintained" increases the possibilities: the trees may continue to live because some person tends them, that is, they may owe their existence to some individual's plan at the same time that they may structure some larger plan of Nature's or their own. Because one cannot know, they figure larger in one's imagination than obviously useful or tended trees would. As the speaker dramatizes by hypothesizing that their nearest "Neighbor" is God, the mystery of the trees' purpose leads as directly to all order and meaning as to nothingness.[46]

Familiarity with the conventions of English syntax makes a reader want to provide direct objects for transitive verbs. Consequently, a logically transitive verb used intransitively will almost always create syntactic and semantic ambiguity; the reader will attempt to find a direct object where there is none. This attempt tends to lead the reader to extreme interpretations: "consume" (1247), "Efface" (515), "Maintain" (742) seem to carry complete destruction or all being in their isolation.

In other poems Dickinson changes her verb tense or mood as shorthand for a point that is not ambiguous. In "My Life had stood," for example, Dickinson twice compares an action in the present tense to one in the past or present perfect:

> And do I smile, such cordial light
> Upon the Valley glow –
> It is as a Vesuvian face
> Had let its pleasure through –

> And when at Night – Our good Day done –
> I guard My Master's Head –
> 'Tis better than the Eider-Duck's
> Deep Pillow – to have shared –

In the first instance, the speaker/Gun compares her smile to the aftermath of a volcanic eruption. Her smile is not like the volcano's fire or threat but like its completed act: when she smiles it is as if a volcano had erupted.[47] The past perfect verb is more chilling than the present tense would be because it signals completion, even in the midst of a speculative ("as if") comparison; her smile has the cordiality of ash, of accomplished violence or death, not just of present fire. In the second instance, the speaker prefers guarding the master to having shared his pillow, that is, to having shared intimacy with him—primarily sexual, one would guess from the general structure of the poem. Again, the comparison contrasts action with effect rather than action with action (and when I guard . . . 'tis better than sharing . . .). As a consequence, the speaker seems ironically and almost condescendingly distant from the world of life (here, of potential life-creation or love). Shared intimacy, in her view, would bring nothing better than aggressive self-reliance does. Both uses of the perfect tense in this poem distance the speaker from humanity, perhaps as any skewed analogy would. Yet by allying herself with catastrophic power rather than sexual intimacy, she may also be indicating that the former seems more possible or safer to her; even the power of volcanoes may be known. The change in tense alerts the reader to the peculiarity and the importance of the comparisons.

Like most lyric poetry, Dickinson's poems are primarily in the simple present tense—what George Wright calls the "lyric present."[48] As Wright demonstrates, lyric poets' use of the simple present gives an aura of continuing and yet timeless action to their dramas. Wordsworth gazes at Tintern Abbey forever, and Dickinson's poet/gun continues to live "without the power to die." The use of simple present may create temporal ambiguity, however, when ongoing dramatic action is predicated of the reader ("you") rather than of the speaker. For example, the action of "He fumbles at your Soul" seems colored by both major uses of present tense. Simple present verbs portray habitual or repeated action (Jane takes piano lessons). According to this understanding, "He" would fumble at your soul repeatedly, by some unspecified schedule (every day? whenever some other unspecified event occurs?). Simple present is also used for verbs of sense and cogitation that have no clear beginning or end (Jane feels, sees, thinks, knows). In this sense they express timelessness: "you" are continuously touched in the poem. The moment of fumbling and of being scalped is existential: your condition is to suffer this blow. Or the experience is psychological, hence ongoing in the sense that it is consciously felt in suspended memory. The speaker's role in this reading would be prophetic: she knows that "you" cannot escape the described feeling or knowledge. The use of present tense here combined with the direct address to "you" prevents readers from distancing themselves from the poem. "He fumbles" now, as the poet speaks.

Even Dickinson's poems that begin in the past tense often conclude in the present. "One Blessing had I than the rest" (756), for example, ends with three indirect questions: "Why Bliss so scantily disburse – / Why Paradise defer – / Why Floods be served to Us – in Bowls – " and then "I speculate no more – ". The movement to the present tense typically involves a reevaluation of, or an attempt to improve upon, the past—either implicit, through questions as in this poem, or explicit. Examples of the latter occur in "It always *felt* to me – a wrong" (597), which concludes "Old Man on Nebo! Late as this – / My justice *bleeds* – for Thee!"; and in "I *cried* at Pity – not at Pain –" (588), which turns to "I *wish* I knew that Woman's name –" (italics mine). "It ceased to hurt me, though so slow" (584) uses the present tense to create a contrast between previous and present feeling: ". . . whereas 'twas Wilderness – / It's better – almost Peace –" (584). The change from past to present tense occurs only in poems with a first-person speaker. As she changes tense the speaker seems to draw a conclusion that disrupts what before had seemed clear; the change makes the speaker seem to be thinking aloud.

The first line of "This was a Poet – It is That" is confusing in its movement from past to present tense because the changing tenses carry nonspecific pronouns as subject and object. If what "was" a poet still "is" that (let us assume: a poet), then the second verb tense asserts that a poet—or at least this poet—does not die. What was a poet, what did "Entitl[e] Us" and so on, will always be one. Each reinterpretation of the pronouns "it" and "That," however, necessitates a new interpretation of the line's "is."

My favorite among Dickinson's multiple unexpected changes in verb tense occurs in the deceptively innocent "I started Early – Took my Dog – / And visited the Sea –" (520). Here the speaker presents

herself as walking quietly by the sea, seeing its landscape in childish
metaphors, until stanza 3 (italics mine):

> But no Man moved Me – till the Tide
> Went past my simple Shoe –
> And past my Apron – and my Belt
> And past my Boddice – too –
>
> And made as He would eat me up –
> As wholly as a Dew
> Upon a Dandelion's Sleeve –
> And then – I started – too –
>
> And He – He followed – close behind –
> I felt His Silver Heel
> Upon my Ancle – Then my Shoes
> *Would overflow* with Pearl –
>
> Until We met the Solid Town –
> . . . . .

The sudden introduction of the conditional "Would," however, gives
the speaker away. This auxiliary changes the mood of the verb and of
the poem: what seemed a single action in the past now seems to be
either a hypothetical or a customary, repeated action. The speaker's
tale becomes a sexual fantasy—repeated either in her imagining of
what it would be like to walk by what she sees as a masculine and
therefore dangerous sea, or in her imagination as she in fact walks by
the sea, or in her metaphorical representation of real dealings with
the world of men. The speaker teases the reader, and perhaps herself,
just as much as she does the sea/Man. She pretends to be entirely
innocent in her motives for going to the sea (walking the dog) and
then repeatedly lets it touch her to the point of mutual arousal before
she runs away to the "Solid Town." The last lines of the poem give
the sea dignity in his lovely but otherwise undignified chase and
underline the sexual content of the poem:

> Until We met the Solid Town –
> No One He seemed to know –
> And bowing – with a Mighty look –
> At me – The Sea withdrew –

As with Dickinson's mixture of past and present tenses in other poems, her combination of differing verb tense and mood in this narrative remove it from any simple, temporal context. The poet does not let us place her speaker easily, and the speaker is allowed her coy retreat to apparent innocence and safety.

Dickinson's gravitation toward the simple (habitual) present and toward the uninflected verb may suggest her overriding concern to escape the historicity of time, to make herself in some way timeless and thus safe from the forces of death and loss she feels so strongly, as Sharon Cameron argues. It seems to me, however, that these verb forms (and Dickinson's poems) point more toward a concern with ongoing process, revelation, continuous perception, and change than toward the lyric suspension exemplified by the dancers on Keats's Grecian urn or the predictable return of Wordsworth's "Lines Composed a Few Miles above Tintern Abbey." The teasing disappearance of Dickinson's verbs from any single time or person repeats itself in her experiments with other parts of speech, and in the narratives of her poems generally.

REPETITION

Like compression and disjunction, repetition is a defining feature of poetic language. Where drama and the novel depend on unities in their larger design (like Aristotle's, of time, place, and event), the poem grows in its smallest structural particulars from sets of unities: repetition of rhythm (meter), of words and sound (rhyme, alliteration, assonance, thematic repetition), and of structural and syntactic elements. Dickinson lived in a century that adored repetition in almost every form: think of the incantatory verbal and aural repetitions of Poe's poetry, the enormous prestige and popularity of orators like Daniel Webster, and Wagnerian *leitmotif*. It would be strange if Dickinson, in this context, did not structure her poetry through various repetitions.

Dickinson's use of repetition tends to reflect what was standard for the nineteenth century. Her thematic verbal repetition, syntactic and structural repetition, and use of alliteration and assonance do not distinguish her verse from that of other poets in the way her use of compression, disjunctive punctuation and grammar, and uninflected verbs (to mention only the most obvious) do. Dickinson's poetry is unusual, however, in its repetitions of a grammatical class of words. Rather than the expected adjectives and nouns, this poet tends to cluster function words, especially pronouns.

In the most unusual pattern of her repetitions, Dickinson deliberately overlaps nonspecific pronouns and definite pronouns without antecedents (that is, when they are indefinite), thereby creating a quality of timelessness and unspecifiable event analogous to that created by her uninflected verbs and changes of verb tense and mood. In Dickinson's poems, a pronoun may refer directly and specifically; it may operate as a grammatical subject ("it is summer"); the speaker may use "it" for "you," to refer to the person she addresses ("If it had no pencil / Would it try mine – ", 921), or for herself ("Why make *it* doubt – it hurts *it* so – ", 462, italics mine). Or "it" may be a blank around which the poet draws the boundaries for a phenomenon she cannot name, or a meaning not yet realized, even though the direction of its meaning is referential.[49] "It," "this," and "that" often mark a place in Dickinson's poems that receives no identifiable meaning. They stand for the kind of hole in knowledge that Dickinson tells us "a certain Slant of light, / Winter Afternoons – " may create: "We can find no scar, / But internal difference, / Where the Meanings, are – " (258).

"This," "It," and "That" in the first line of "This was a Poet – It is That" all function somewhere between the first, second, and fourth possibilities for meaning just listed: directly referential, as grammatical subject, and as unnamed blank in meaning. "This" may refer to the text of the poem, in a kind of synecdochic self-pointing that calls poem poet: this [poem] was a poet. Or it may refer to a figure unknown to the reader but present to the speaker. Or "It" and "That" may share a common reference that remains unspecified except in effect: it is that (the poet? the poem?) [which] distills. "That" may also carry as its antecedent the claim of the previous line: [the fact or recognition that] *this* was a poet distills. Or "That" may share the antecedent of "This": this was a poet, and it is *this* [that is, "That"] which distills. To choose any single reading leaves the reader unsatisfied, and much of the poem unaccounted for. More satisfying and more effective as an approach to the point of such ambiguity is to ask why the poet would chose to begin a poem on distilling "sense" with such non-sense.

Attention to Dickinson's nonspecific pronouns in "This was a Poet" immediately forces the reader to notice the enormous number of function words, especially pronouns, in the poem. In its 68 words, this poem includes 8 pronouns that are nonspecific or of indefinite reference, 6 definite pronouns, 9 prepositions, 5 articles, 2 adverbs of degree, and 1 conjunction, or a total of 31 function words, almost half the words in the poem. This figure does not include the large number of omitted (syntactically implicit) relative and definite pronouns (around 10, depending on the reader's reconstruction of several sentences). I repeat the poem:

> This was a Poet – It is That
> Distills amazing sense
> From ordinary Meanings –
> And Attar so immense
>
> From the familiar species
> That perished by the Door –
> We wonder it was not Ourselves
> Arrested it – before –
>
> Of Pictures, the Discloser –
> The Poet – it is He –
> Entitles Us – by Contrast –
> To ceaseless Poverty –
>
> Of Portion – so unconscious –
> The Robbing – could not harm –
> Himself – to Him – a Fortune –
> Exterior – to Time –

In the first sentence (stanzas 1 and 2), "that" occurs in metrically emphatic positions twice (end of line 1 and beginning of line 6), as does "From" (beginning of lines 3 and 5); "that" appears in the deep structure of the sentence in five places besides the two specified in the text. (In expanded form, the stanzas might read, "This was a poet. It is the fact that this was a poet *that* distills amazing sense from ordinary meanings and *that* distills attar *that* is so immense from the familiar species that perished by the door, *that* we wonder *that* it was not ourselves who arrested it before.") "It" is used three times and "this" once (all in positions of metrical stress), and the sentence concludes with two dashes isolating and foregrounding "– before –". The poem calls attention metrically and through repetition to its links between

present and past, known and other; it identifies "this" and "that." All
is connected with what precedes (comes "before," *was*) and follows
(comes "From," *is*), and everything blends into the ephemeral "Attar"
of poetic unity through the stated and omitted *that*'s and the ubiquitous, multireferential *it*.

The last two stanzas follow the same pattern, substituting multiple
of's, personal pronouns (He, Himself, Him) and *To*'s for *That, it* and
From of the first stanza. The proliferation of connective prepositions
and pronouns and the syntactic doubling ("It is He – Entitles us" and
"could not harm – Himself" share a subject) imply that what distills
the ordinary into essence is neither the poet nor his disclosed "Pictures"
of the world by our door but the interactions and transformations of
poet, world, and poem. The connecting interplay of *To, From, That,
Of* leads us to understand that, structurally as well as logically, the
poet is a part of his world and of his poems. At no point does "This,"
"That," or the poet exist independently of the rest.

The repetitive and heavily nominal syntax of the poem caused by
its repeated pronouns and prepositions affects it tonally as well. Despite the laudatory content of the poem, it is hard to take entirely
seriously a celebration of the poet that is so belabored. As the poem
becomes increasingly ceremonious and its syntax more disjointed and
convoluted, it begins to sound uncomfortably like Mark Antony's
ironic praise of Brutus. The hesitation, the choppiness of the poem's
initial and final lines, and the irregular syntax make us wonder if
Dickinson is not suggesting that this "Poet" is a Fortune only to
Himself. This is, I admit, only a suggestion: the poet of the poem
remains a distiller of "amazing sense"—no mean feat in the world of
dying roses. But the complex syntax and the repetitious function
words distract us from the poet, from the essence of roses, and point
to the structure, the dry sticks of the poem itself: unidentified "It" *is*
indefinite "That."

Poems in which the lack of reference for "it" or any pronoun takes
on thematic significance tend to work through repetitions of that
pronoun. Dickinson's most famous example of a repeated indefinite
"it" occurs in the following poem:

> It was not Death, for I stood up,
> And all the Dead, lie down –
> It was not Night, for all the Bells
> Put out their Tongues, for Noon.

It was not Frost, for on my Flesh
I felt Siroccos – crawl –
Nor Fire – for just my Marble feet
Could keep a Chancel, cool –

And yet, it tasted, like them all,
The Figures I have seen
Set orderly, for Burial,
Reminded me, of mine –

As if my life were shaven,
And fitted to a frame,
And could not breathe without a key,
And 'twas like Midnight, some –

When everything that ticked – has stopped –
And Space stares all around –
Or Grisly frosts – first Autumn morns,
Repeal the Beating Ground –

But, most, like Chaos – Stopless – cool –
Without a Chance, or Spar –
Or even a Report of Land –
To justify – Despair.   (510)

In this poem, explicit and omitted repetitions of "It was . . ." allow the speaker to attempt to mark the boundaries of that unnamed, powerful event. The repeated phrase "It was not . . . for" in the first stanzas make way for a description of the thing's qualities ("it tasted") in the third stanza, and then for elliptically parallel analogies: "As if my life were . . . / And . . . / And." The third "And," however, returns us abruptly from the speaker's feeling to that "it," now as though the speaker had been making positive instead of negative assertions about "it" all along: "And 'twas like" instead of "It was not." By presenting this statement as though it repeats a former speculation (and syntactic construction), the speaker implies that the poem presents only a fraction of the analogies she has tried and rejected in categorizing "it." At the same time, the speaker further weakens the negations of the opening lines with this "And" by implying that she has meant all along that "it" is like frost and fire—"some."

The poem ends with a final variation of this construction—"But, [it was] most like"—still not identifying "it" but positively identifying its effect and her feeling as "Despair." The poem appears to move toward greater certainty—from "It was not" to "'twas like" to "most, like"—but "it" is compared with increasingly indefinable things. The negative semantic emphasis at the end ("without" in lines 15 and 22, "Repeal," "Stopless") and the concluding acknowledgment that even her despair is unjustified also counteract the apparent increasing certainty of the repeated construction. The poem builds to a climax, but it only circles its central theme, the identity of "it." Like the repeated statements, the definition remains primarily negative, a hole in definable feeling and event. In another poem Dickinson writes:

> That Love is all there is,
> Is all we know of Love;
> It is enough, the freight should be
> Proportioned to the groove.   (1765)

In "It was not Death" she establishes the "groove" of *it*'s meaning as an alternative to naming its cause, the "freight" of *it*.

The ambiguous movement between nonspecific pronouns and definite pronouns used without antecedent is the primary structuring device of the following poem:

> We dream – it is good we are dreaming –
> It would hurt us – were we awake –
> But since it is playing – kill us,
> And we are playing – shriek –
>
> What harm? Men die – externally –
> It is a truth – of Blood –
> But we – are dying in Drama –
> And Drama – is never dead –
>
> Cautious – We jar each other –
> And either – open the eyes –
> Lest the Phantasm – prove the Mistake –
> And the livid Surprise
>
> Cool us to Shafts of Granite –
> With just an Age – and Name –
> And perhaps a phrase in Egyptian –
> It's prudenter – to dream –   (531)

In line 1, "it" is a nonspecific grammatical subject. In the following line, "it" may stand for the condition of being awake, as in the transformation: it would hurt us if we were awake: being awake would hurt us. Yet the reader hears in this "it" the suggestion of an ominous, unspecified tormentor as well. The suggestion increases in line 3, where "it" is still without antecedent but specific, and logically with the same reference as the preceding "it." The "it" that would hurt us is playing the game "kill us." By line 6, we are tempted to read "It is a truth – of Blood" as partial identification of the unspecified agent. "It" seems to be something absolute, like a god, like a "truth – of Blood." The ambiguous identification of grammatical "it" and unspecified agent "it" (inanimate and animate) repeats itself in the speaker's identification of our tombstones with our lives: "Surprise" may "Cool us" to "Granite." We become not corpses but monuments to our own death. "It" is the ubiquitous, unplaceable, and contentless subject of "it is good we are dreaming" and "It's prudenter – to dream – " and the equally ubiquitous and unplaceable but intentional agent of "it is playing – kill us." Grammatical subject eerily becomes akin to something like God.

"It" often acquires extraordinary significance in Dickinson's poems because it remains absolutely mysterious and absolutely feared or desired. In "I gained it so" (359), "it" is "the Bliss," "an instant's Grace" that makes the speaker forever unfit for her previous "Beggar's" contentment. She repeats, "I said I gained it – / This – was all – " but the repetition does not clarify. "This" may be inconsequential (as in the colloquial "this is the only thing I did") or everything (as in the literal "this was all"). Even the objective quantity of "it" remains unknown. Other poems present the *it* of dread: in "It struck me – every Day – " (362), *it* is lightning and fire; *it* blistered my dream, and sickened (me?) upon my sight. "[T]hat Storm – was brief – " the speaker nonspecifically thinks, "But Nature lost the Date of This – / And left it in the Sky – ". "This" "it" is impersonal, inescapable (there in dreams and upon awakening), unknown. The ubiquity of the pronoun in English as grammatical subject and definite pronoun makes it ideal for Dickinson's scenes of indefinite bliss and terror.

Dickinson manipulates this potential ambiguity in pronoun reference most frequently when her subject is a devastation that approaches death, or death itself. In the first three stanzas of the following poem *it* is again both personal and impersonal, and again collapses the distinction of "this" and "that":

If I may have it, when it's dead,
I'll be contented – so –
If just as soon as Breath is out
It shall belong to me –

Until they lock it in the Grave,
'Tis Bliss I cannot weigh –
For tho' they lock Thee in the Grave,
Myself – can own the key –

Think of it Lover! I and Thee
Permitted – face to face to be –
After a Life – A Death – We'll say –
For Death was That –
And This – is Thee –   (577)

In this necrophilic fantasy, the speaker imaginatively transforms her lover's corpse (appropriately "it") into "Thee" as soon as she has "it" safely to herself. She claims that "That" death and "This" are opposites, but if "it" is "Thee" then "That" and "This," or death and life, must also be identical. The speaker wants both to have her lover (dead or not) and avoid admitting to the perversity of her desire at its expressed extreme. "'Tis Bliss" even suggests that the corpse ("it") is her bliss as much as the fact of owning it is. The fantasy that her lover's living body is the corpse (death) and his corpse the personal "Thee" allows her to disguise the loss she faces: living or dead, he is not hers except in her fantasy, and there only as lifeless body—even though she concludes that to stroke his lifeless "Frost / Outvisions Paradise!" More abstractly, if death is whatever distances the speaker from her lover while "This" is what brings him near, "This" may also refer to the poem in which she claims him.[50]

Unlike "it," which seems to point to an absolute quantity or agent like God when of indefinite reference, indefinite "this" and "that" imply that the reader shares the speaker's perspective and therefore already knows what she points to. In "How soft this Prison is / How sweet these sullen bars" (1334), with its repeating "this repose," "Of Fate if this is All," "this" marks the speaker's private context but also appears to point to a "Prison" that the reader, too, can see—perhaps life itself, or whatever in each reader's life might be imagined as "Prison." "Let me not mar that perfect Dream" (1335) also points to the reader's experience without naming it; the poem seems to say that the reader knows what "that perfect Dream" is. Dickinson creates a

scene into which readers may place themselves and their own unspecifiable or secret objects and agents. Using demonstrative pronouns
and "it" ambiguously and indefinitely, she creates blank scenes of
desire and dread.

By foregrounding words of relation yet frequently omitting transitional phrases between sentences, Dickinson creates one of the most
curious and distinctive elements of her poetry. For this poet, things
(and people) gain significance as they affect oneself. This is not ego-
centrism (or anthropocentricism) but a recognition of how foreign
everything beyond the self must be. Just as she describes how "He"
approaches in "He fumbles at your Soul," or what "it" was "like" in
"It was not Death," or how she gained "it" in "I gained it so," rather
than "He" or "it" as independent agent, event, and object, she characteristically presents an event or a phenomenon through its effect on
her speaker. Consequently, although the overall progression of syntax
(and logic) may be disjunctive, establishing immediate connections is
crucial to the development of meaning. Repeated function words mark
the space around which Dickinson builds meaning and through which
she reveals relationship and effect.

Dickinson often begins her lines with function words, most often
with "And" but frequently with other conjunctions and with prepositions. To some extent this is predictable: iambic meter encourages
a weakly stressed syllable in the first position of the line, and the
phrase structure of English calls for function words at the beginning
of most phrases (articles before nouns, prepositions and pronouns
before their objects and predicates); furthermore, Dickinson's line
usually corresponds to a major phrase boundary (although she does
omit most of her line-initial articles). The overwhelming presence of
connectives and prepositions in this position, however, suggests the
poet's more than usual interest in relationship and effect.

By focusing unusual semantic as well as structural attention on its
function words, "The Service without Hope" (779) may serve as
example and explanation of Dickinson's use of function words. In the
first stanza of this poem Dickinson uses "without," "Because," and
"By" to establish and qualify the relation of service to hope. The
second stanza proceeds through "of," "of," "There," "like," "that,"
and "That" to absolute connection (or lack of connection), the substantive "Until."[51]

> The Service without Hope –
> Is tenderest, I think –

Because 'tis unsustained
By stint – Rewarded Work –

Has impetus of Gain –
And impetus of Goal –
There is no Diligence like that
That knows not an Until –

Most of one's life, this poem suggests, is lived within the boundaries
of motivation and impetus, of Hope, Gain, Goal (such as that represented by the normal use of function words, whether temporal—
before, after, as soon as—or logical—*in order to, because of, so*). The poem
praises, in contrast, action that is performed solely for its own benefit.
Linguistically represented, such action entails that its actor "know"
no function words. One acts without impetus only insofar as one never
has cause to attach such relational or functional qualifiers to meaning,
as long as one thinks and acts purely in absolutes. The nominalization
of "Until" objectifies this state and thereby dramatizes the possibility
of banning such a functional concept from the speaker's vocabulary
(and hence mind) as cleanly as one bans an object from one's life.

Yet the abundant function words of the poem, the repetitions and
internal rhymes (sustained/stint; impetus/impetus; that/that; no/
knows/not; an/un-til; *Dil*igence/Un*til*), the repeated negatives (without, unsustained, no, not), and the complex syntax suggest that
knowing no until is a difficult and delicate, perhaps impossible, task.
The connecting repetitions and rhymes of the poem and the apparent
impossibility of presenting any thought or action without marking
its relation to other thought and action implies that an "Until"
inevitably lingers in "Hope" behind every "Service," whether the server
recognizes it or not. Understanding requires the ability to draw
connections.

Dickinson also structures poems around clusters of verbs, most
frequently in her definition poems. These poems tend to proceed
syntactically through repeated relative pronouns and verbs, with the
syntax emphasizing literal action. Whereas definition normally takes
an A = B form and syntactically favors substantives (the first non–
function word of any A = B sentence will always be some form of
substantive), Dickinson's definitions most often take the form: A is
the B that ———, or else they make a noun (A) correspond to a

verbal or verb form (B) instead of to another noun. Examples of the latter are "Exultation" is *the going* / Of an inland soul to sea" (76) instead of the "sea" itself (italics mine); or "To see the Summer Sky / Is Poetry" (1472), where poetry is not "The sight" but the act "To see." Similarly: "To be alive – is Power – " (677); "To see her is a Picture – " (1568); and, in the skeptical subjunctive, "To pile like Thunder to its close / Then crumble . . . / While . . . / This – would be Poetry – " (1247).

When using a restrictive clause to define her subject as that which does a particular thing or behaves in a particular way (A = the B that ————), Dickinson typically uses a sequence of verbs to elaborate on the subject's action or effect for the rest of the poem instead of elaborating on nominal properties like visual or spatial features of the subject. For example, "Crisis" is a "Hair" that balances life or death and, in response to any variety of actions ("Let an instant push / Or an Atom press / Or a Circle hesitate"), may "jolt the Hand"

> That adjusts the Hair
> That secures Eternity
> From presenting – Here –   (889)

Similarly, "Exhilaration is the Breeze / That lifts us . . . leaves us" and "Returns us not" (1118); "Risk is the Hair that holds the Tun" and "Persuasive as Perdition, / Decoys it's Traveller" (1239); "Death is the supple Suitor / That wins" and "bears away in triumph" (1445); and "'Hope' is the thing with feathers – / That perches . . . sings . . . never stops . . . is heard," cannot be abashed, and "kept so many warm" (254).

The most extraordinary example of such repetition occurs in "The Love a Life can show Below" (673), where the last stanza is composed almost entirely of verbs. In the earlier stanzas of the poem, divine love is that which "faints upon the face of Noon – / And smites the Tinder in the Sun – / And hinders Gabriel's Wing – ". This, however, is not specific enough for the poet; divine love "hints and sways" in music, "Distils . . . pain," produces sunrise and sunset. Yet this, too, is insufficient to account for the force and ubiquity of divine love, so the poet retreats to a list of verbs, forcing readers to participate in her idea of that "diviner thing," and in the creation of the poem, by imagining their own direct objects—the human contexts—for its actions.

> 'Tis this – invites – appalls – endows –
> Flits – glimmers – proves – dissolves –
> Returns – suggests – convicts – enchants –
> Then – flings in Paradise –

The last line of the poem again supplies an object for love's action and thereby returns the reader to the world of particular actions; but Paradise is so magnificent and so unknown a quantity in comparison with the offhand, temporal "Then – flings in" that the event (like divine love) transcends everyday experience. Such love reveals itself by an overwhelming array of actions or active feelings that culminate, when least expected, in the effect of paradise. As the noun "love" is defined by cumulative verbs and a final object, love itself is defined only through its cumulative, somehow paradoxical, acts and effect.

To some extent the simultaneous emphasis on both verbs and function words, especially relative pronouns, is generally predictable; both characterize hypotactic syntax. Parallel, repeated *that*'s and conjunctions allow Dickinson to align verbs in a sequence of mounting action. Repeated function words even without repeated verbs may have an effect like that of verbs in keeping meaning active and unstable (as in the repeated prepositions and pronouns of "This was a Poet"), although more often the poet combines the repetition of function words and verbs. In "To pile like Thunder," words of relation dominate the structure of the poem more clearly than verbs do because of their line-initial position. Six of the poem's eight lines begin: To, Then, While, This, Or, For. The only idea-carrying or thematic word beginning a line is the verb "Experience," as a warning or command. On the right-hand margin, at the end of these lines, however, we find: hid, come, prove, consume, live. This 40-word definition poem contains nine notional verbs:

> To *pile* like Thunder to it's close
> Then *crumble* grand away
> While Everything created *hid*
> This – would be Poetry –

Or Love – the two coeval *come* –
We both and neither *prove* –
Experience either and *consume* –
For None *see* God and *live* –

Poetry lies in acting with cataclysmic effect in a world that is equally active (or reactive). Without this interaction of event and audience there would not be a poem—"Or Love." Similarly, the poem tells us that there is no way to hold the experience of poetry or love; it cannot become stable or be fully known. To "Experience either" is to lose oneself—to "consume" (or be consumed)—in the same kind of subjectless, objectless unknown that love and poetry come from, "For None see God and live." A clap of thunder reveals the poet's feelings of extraordinary power and transcience in experiencing the greatest facts in her world: Poetry, Love, God. But these facts (and nouns) as such are less the point than the meshing and differentiating commotion that reveals and identifies them. Repeated line-initial conjunctions and line-final verbs allow this succinct conflation.

As in "To pile like Thunder," Dickinson frequently changes the construction and tone of her final stanza from what preceded it. The change is particularly noticeable in two-stanza poems, where a pattern is barely established before it is set aside, and it is usually marked by a change in syntactic construction, often involving the repetition of different classes of words. In the poem just quoted, function words— especially conjunctions—dominate the first stanza while verbs without inflectional marking dominate the second. (Although most of the verbs in this stanza have the correct grammatical form, because they are imperative or in simple present tense with plural subjects, there is no inflectional marking.) A similar pattern occurs in "Essential Oils," where the first stanza of the poem contains repeated forms of "to be" (twice as auxiliaries of the notional verbs "wring" and "express"), and the second stanza contains only uninflected notional verbs. Moving from passive voice and copular forms to uninflected notional verbs here has the effect of strengthening the claims of the second stanza. The cool certainty of the passive voice and copular forms— "are wrung," "Be not expressed," and "is the gift of Screws"—carries through to the notional (and therefore less absolutely assertive) verbs that follow: the General Rose "decay," while this "Make Summer" and the Lady "lie / In Ceaseless Rosemary."[52] The thematically resonant statements of the first stanza lend thematic force to the narrative claims of the second.

SYNTAX

Much of the previous discussion involves Dickinson's use of particular syntactic constructions and ways in which readers must recreate deleted portions of her syntax in order to interpret a poem. In this section I look at syntax as an umbrella category that combines several of the features already mentioned, focusing on the more complex or hypotactic elements of Dickinson's syntax. Although much of Dickinson's syntax is conventional, disruptions of the conventional occur frequently enough to keep the reader cautious and to keep the writer's attitude toward these (and other social) conventions ambiguous.

Dickinson's unconventional syntax, like her experiments with other aspects of language, functions primarily to draw the reader into the poem. A poem will remain partially blank until the reader becomes engaged in filling it out. More specifically, her irregular syntax may be structurally symbolic, or imitative of a poem's sense. For example, in "Further in the Summer than the Birds" (1068) the unusual use of the opening conjunction, omitted words and phrases, and syntactic inversions help create a sense of the delicate momentary Grace the speaker finds it so difficult to describe. The poem begins:

> Further in Summer than the Birds
> Pathetic from the Grass
> A minor Nation celebrates
> It's unobtrusive Mass.
>
> No Ordinance be seen
> So gradual the Grace
> A pensive Custom it becomes
> Enlarging Loneliness.

In the last two stanzas inverted phrase order, the omission of several words, form/class substitution, and uninflected verbs make the poem even more difficult to decipher.

Antiquest felt at Noon
When August burning low
Arise this spectral Canticle
Repose to typify

Remit as yet no Grace
No Furrow on the Glow
Yet a Druidic Difference
Enhances Nature now   (1068)

We might suppose that the poet means something like: "This custom
or grace is felt to be oldest at Noon, when the August sun is burning
low and this spectral canticle arise(s), typifying repose; up until this
moment, no grace has been remitted and the glow remains unfurrowed
(unblemished); yet a druidic difference enhances nature now." There
are other ways to reconstruct the syntax here, however, and one must
take into account the puzzling "Yet," Dickinson's unmarked verbs
(arise and remit), and the general lack of connection regardless of how
one finally reconstructs it. There is no causal or temporal relation, for
example, between the August noon and the verb "Arise," and there
is no clear subject or agent for "Remit." These verbs take the action
of the poem out of a temporal frame of reference; the canticle of
crickets apparently may "Arise" and "Remit" (or not remit) grace at
any point in time. The speaker's almost religious feeling on hearing
crickets at noon in late summer is a grace so delicate that she can
only name it through metaphor and through fractions of conventional
meaning. It is a moment between definable, known states, and the
syntax is correspondingly suspended from particular connection and
reference.

Such obscurity is relatively rare, though, in Dickinson's syntax;
usually her inversions and omissions are readily understood. One sees
the relative accessibility of her syntax by comparing it with the
virtually unrecoverable syntax of a twentieth-century poet—for example, Charles Olson in an early section of his *Maximus Poems*:

The seedling
of morning: to move, the problems (after the night's
presences)

the first hours of
He had noticed,
The cotton picks easiest

As my flower,
after rain, wears,
such diadem

As a man is a
necklace
strung of his own
teeth (the caries
of 'em[53]

Here it is much more difficult, if not impossible, to reconstruct consecutive whole sentences that are logically connected than it is from Dickinson's sentence fragments. Olson omits all but a few words of a sentence, whereas Dickinson provides all but a few. Olson's fragments are not logically connected, while with Dickinson we do not doubt that things connect, that relationships do hold.

Dickinson's poetry is generally more concerned with the individual person or psyche in moments of relationship than with universal or ultimate principles of connection. The abundance of function words and the irregularities of syntax call attention to bonds of relation but also stress the fragility of these bonds. Words and speakers lean toward connection in the poems, but stop short of what would seem irrevocable or conventionally natural relationships. Mid-sentence dashes, inversions, ellipses, and unexpected analogies or metaphorical juxtapositions prevent connection from being more than temporary and tenuous.

Dickinson's syntax tends to follow one of three patterns. First, it may be paratactic, juxtaposing short sentences without connective explanation or through simple conjunction, most often with the use of "And" ("And now We roam . . . And now . . . And every time," 754). Second, it may be hypotactic, that is, containing subordinate qualifying or restrictive clauses. Although Dickinson uses frequent self-embedded constructions, most often her complex syntax is right-branching, often depending on parallel restrictive clauses as in her definition poems: "'Hope' is the thing with feathers – / That perches . . . sings . . . never stops . . ." (254), or "Faith – is the Pierless Bridge / Supporting what We see / Unto the Scene that We do not . . ." (915). As these examples demonstrate, such sentences frequently include the copular "be" as their primary verb, although in the poem's development the copular assertion is typically overwhelmed by the action of the clauses that precede or follow it. Finally, Dickinson's syntax may be patterned by contrast: she links short statements with the conjunctions "or," "but," "yet" and with repeated negations.

Hypotaxis

In her study of the syntax and vocabularies of English and American poets, Josephine Miles suggests that clausal (verb-dominated) syntax typically emphasizes connection, rational process, and the perceiving mind. Miles finds a correspondence between a poet's style and that poet's interest in either natural facts and substance or conceptual relationships, drawing the lines of the distinction between a predominantly phrasal and a predominantly clausal (usually hypotactic) syntax. Dickinson, Miles affirms, has an unusually clausal syntax for the age in which she was writing.[54] As Miles would anticipate, her poetry is discursive. Whether paratactic or hypotactic, the poems are process or thinking poems, riddles of relationship.

To speak of Dickinson's verse as primarily discursive or conceptual is misleading, however, without further qualification. Again, a comparison of Dickinson's verse with that of another poet interested in the complexities of relation in language helps clarify what is distinctive in her syntax. Shelley's "Mont Blanc" abounds with self-embedded or branching clauses and ambiguous relations between pronouns and their immediate antecedents, but the phrases flow together as powerfully and smoothly as the water of the "Dizzy Ravine" he addresses. For example, in one passage (lines 34–48) we find:

> Dizzy Ravine! and when I gaze on thee
> I seem as in a trance sublime and strange
> To muse on my own separate fantasy,
> My own, my human mind, which passively
> Now renders and receives fast influencings,
> Holding an unremitting interchange
> With the clear universe of things around;
> One legion of wild thoughts, whose wandering wings
> Now float above thy darkness, and now rest
> Where that or thou art no unbidden guest,

> In the still cave of the witch Poesy,
> Seeking among the shadows that pass by
> Ghosts of all things that are, some shade of thee,
> Some phantom, some faint image; till the breast
> From which they fled recalls them, thou art there!

Shelley draws the complexity of the world into each sentence; modifying words, phrases, and clauses lap back repeatedly to qualify or expand upon what has already been presented. One easily loses track of the simple sentence outline. The complexity of Dickinson's sentences, on the other hand, tends to be semantic; it mirrors the logic of her conception rather than a multifarious world. Next to Shelley's lines, even her hypotactic syntax seems skeletal. She uses fewer self-embedded phrases; her branching constructions tend to be prepositional or relative clause transformations and are short; and she uses far less phrasal parallelism or descriptive echoing (as in Shelley's "my own separate fantasy, / My own, my human mind," or "some shade of thee, / Some phantom, some faint image"). Dickinson's modifying clauses are also primarily restrictive instead of additive in meaning; they qualify or narrow the subject on which they depend. For example, Dickinson's definition of *escape* in the following poem identifies the action with a basket used for a particular purpose in particular circumstances:

> Escape — it is the Basket
> In which the Heart is caught
> When down some awful Battlement
> The rest of Life is dropt —   (1347)

The restrictions of "In which . . ." and "When . . ." make sense of what would otherwise be a ludicrous definition (escape is a basket). This stanza of "Escape is such a thankful Word" is altogether typical of Dickinson's poetry. Even with the repeated subject (Escape — it), the hypotaxis, and the inversion in the last two lines of this stanza, the syntax does not confuse. The poem's complexity is conceptual.

The hypotaxis of another poem shows more clearly the differences between Shelleyan and Dickinsonian complexity. The first stanzas follow:

The Angle of a Landscape —
That every time I wake —
Between my Curtain and the Wall
Upon an ample Crack —

Like a Venetian — waiting —
Accosts my open eye —
Is just a Bough of Apples —
Held slanting, in the Sky —   (375)

In these stanzas, despite the double suspension of predicate from subject (The Angle . . . is just a Bough, and That . . . Accosts my eye), the syntax remains easily decipherable. "Accosts" is the only verb that could complete the suspended relative clause, and the phrases that intervene between subject and predicate are all parallel and exactly a line long. The construction of the poem is very neat:

Subject (NP)$_1$ [Angle]
   Relative clause (NP)$_2$ [That] + Relative clause$_2$ [every time . . .]
      Prepositional phrase$_1$ [Between; modifies Angle]
      Prepositional phrase$_2$ [Upon; modifies Angle]
      Adverbial phrase$_3$ [Like; modifies Accosts]
   Predicate of relative clause (VP)$_2$ [Accosts]
Predicate (VP)$_1$ [Is] . . .

In abbreviated form and restoring normal syntactic order, the sentence might run: "The Angle of Landscape that Accosts me like a Venetian every time I wake is just a Bough of Apples." The wonderful pun on Venetian (even though we are told the window has curtains rather than blinds), the ambiguity as to whether the Venetian is waiting "Between my Curtain and the Wall" or the speaker is accosted there, and the suspense before the speaker finally reveals what "Accosts" her eye in concluding the sentence are exhilarating (although they are apparently beside the point of the rest of the poem—which tells us that the bough in the poet's morning "Picture" changes with the seasons, while the "Chimney," "Hill," and "Steeple's finger" do not). This self-embedding creates the artful suspense of hidden object or cause later mastered by Henry James in prose, not the dense layering of natural and psychological detail of Shelley's embedding. It is the mark of a confident writer who plays with her audience by withholding what the rules of syntax promise she must finally give.

Dickinson's hypotaxis works differently in a philosophical poem of unknown date. Here progressive restrictive and adverbial clauses proceed without suspense or hesitation to reveal what would be the consequences of the poem's opening condition. The poem contains just one sentence, as though nothing more could be said beyond it.

> Did life's penurious length
> Italicize its sweetness,
> The men that daily live
> Would stand so deep in joy
> That it would clog the cogs
> Of that revolving reason
> Whose esoteric belt
> Protects our sanity.   (1717)

In simplified form, this poem might read: if life's brevity italicized its sweetness, men would go mad with joy. There are no syntactic inversions or modifying descriptive phrases here; the poem's lucid compression moves us to its conclusion as directly as possible. Yet the extended metaphor and qualifying clauses of the sentence slow its movement to the conclusive "sanity" that is as necessary to the poem's sentence as to Dickinson's metaphor of revolving belt and inner sanctum. Here, although the syntax is complex, the difficulty of the poem lies in the density of its metaphorical predications. The poem states that "daily" living men stand so deep in joy that the cogs of their belts of reason become clogged. This statement in turn implies that some men do not live "daily"; that reason revolves like a belt; that joy is like a pool or mire one stands in; and that joy endangers sanity. Sorting out the ideas of life, joy, and reason implicit in the poem's metaphors requires far more mental exercise than following the syntax of the poem. Because even in her complex sentences Dickinson's individual noun and verb phrases tend to be short (often consisting of a single word), because modifiers are few or similarly brief, and because Dickinson so often breaks her lines and sentences typographically into phrasal or single-word units, her syntax attracts less attention to itself than do her individual (especially metaphorical) words. We are lost between words in Dickinson's poetry more often than among them.

Hypotactic syntax is supported by a semantic emphasis on active relationship in the definition poem "The Province of the Saved."

The Province of the Saved
Should be the Art – To save –
Through Skill obtained in Themselves –
The Science of the Grave

No Man can understand
But He that hath endured
The Dissolution – in Himself –
That Man – be qualified

To qualify Despair
To Those who failing new –
Mistake Defeat for Death – Each time –
Till acclimated – to – (539)

This poem consists of three sentences, the first two linked by the syntactic doubling of the phrase in line 4 that closes the first sentence through apposition (Skill / The Science of the Grave) and that begins the second sentence as an inverted direct object (No Man can understand The Science of the Grave). That sentence then seems conclusive, "But" the next line modifies "No Man" to the kind of man who can understand: He that hath endured dissolution. "That Man," we then learn, is able or "qualified" to lead others to his understanding, his endurance. In simplified paraphrase: the province of the saved should be the art to save through a skill learned only by he who has endured dissolution himself. The art of saving is obtained only by enduring the sense of difference or distance from one's self and from the world that becomes extreme and literal (physical) in the "Grave." Or, perhaps, this Art can be learned only by dying.

The poem's connections between life and death, saving and being saved are established and explained by its repeated function words and verbs. Repeated *to*'s in the poem's last sentence—foregrounded by positioning at the beginning of lines 9 and 10 (To qualify . . . To Those) and isolated by dashes as the last syllable of the poem (acclimated – to –)—hark back to the emphatic "To" of the first stanza (the Art – To save). The repeated copular linkage and infinitive verb in the first and last stanzas (Should be . . . To save; be qualified / To qualify) serve as guides to the fundamentally active premise of the poem's claim. Syntactically, "To save" in line 2 is a noun phrase used as a modifier. However, by capitalizing "To" instead of "save" or both words, Dickinson gives more prominence to a formal criterion of the verb than to the line's (substantive) syntax or to the (semantic) content of the verb "save"; she reverses the normal relationships between grammar and syntax, and grammar and "sense" in language. "To" used before a verb marks the infinitive form; it contributes nothing to the sense of the word. The "Province of the Saved" is actively "To save"—to be involved in the ongoing process or action of the infinitive verb, not passively to have suffered a single, time-bound act of salvation. Assuming that the "Man" who "can understand" is saved, then the saved are those who have obtained skill, have endured dissolution, are qualified to qualify (despair), and who use these accomplishments "To save."

The last stanza of the poem elaborates this definition of salvation by telling us that those who are not saved, who do not qualify experience, mistake defeat for death; they mistake a temporary setback for a permanent loss of self. Again the syntax is hypotactic: one knows the unsaved by what they do. By "failing" to sense their essential division from the world and the corresponding division within themselves (body/soul? defeated/saved?), they are forced to "Mistake" each experience of defeat as an absolute division from the world, or death.

Up to this point in the poem, the conditions of being saved and not being saved appear to be separate from each other. The last line of the poem, however, returns to the spatial metaphor of the first line, undercutting the apparent differences. Those who presently fail become saved as they become "acclimated" to defeat. Logically, then, the saved are acclimated to defeat. The province of the saved is in the fact the same as the province of those who are not; the difference lies only in one's relative sense of comfort in that climate. "Should" in the first stanza and "failing new" in line 10 now make sense. The poet proposes that the saved be those who save—that the verb define its participial noun and its passive voice in a new way. Similarly, the passive "to be qualified" (to have met certain requirements) "should" be at one and the same time actively "to qualify" (modify) experience for others and "to qualify" (fit) others for experience, that is, to join in the process of saving and qualifying. Dickinson proposes in this poem that one wholly, not just grammatically, identify a condition with its verbal root: the saved are those who save; the qualified those who qualify (both as transitive and intransitive verb). There is no passive or static possibility for salvation or meaning.

Dickinson's discursive arguments and definitions are as apt to take the form of copular statement or metaphor as to use notional verbs.

"Be" in particular often functions as the primary verb in her sentences and thus carries the primary weight of predicative meaning. Dickinson's two most obvious uses of the verb "to be" are for what Elizabeth Perlmutter has called "existential" statements (There is a . . .) and as a copular or linking verb (as in definition poems: A is the B that . . .). Both uses are essentially assertive; things exist and one can make clear sense of them. As Perlmutter argues, any "A is the B that . . ." statement logically includes the implicit assertion that A exists.[55] Asserting something's existence, however, does not necessarily lead to a set conception of that thing or a simple syntactic construction. Dickinson's use of the copula is often negative or conditional and generally introduces a hypotactic series of modifying or defining clauses. Ernest Fenollosa calls "to be" the "dead white plaster" of language,[56] but Dickinson uses the enormous potential of this verb to establish multiple tactics of assertion and identification.

To return to some familiar examples, Dickinson's definition of poetry qualifies its primary (copular) assertion through temporal adverbs and the conditional voice: "To pile like Thunder . . . / Then . . . / While . . . / This – would be Poetry – / Or Love – ". As in "Essential Oils – are wrung – ", the creation of poetry requires more than the isolated natural act (suns or a peal of thunder) and, even with all the conditions the definition demands, the result remains uncertain: "This *would be* Poetry – / Or Love – ". "It was not Death, for I stood up" marvelously exemplifies the poet's use of copular multiplicity through repeated negative assertions: "It was not . . . It was not . . . It was not . . . And 'twas like . . . " and so on. The speaker feels that something has happened or something exists, but her attempts to name "it" only dance painfully around the thing itself, concluding with a "Despair" that seems to refer to the impossibility of finding a single-word name as much as to the aftermath of the experience. The poem, on the other hand, does "name" the experience through its qualifying negations and assertions; what "it" was cannot be said more simply.

Like the paratactic "and" and nonspecific or indefinitely referring "it," "to be" is a vehicle Dickinson uses to move from an expected sequence of logic or reference or assertion to an unexpected one. It provides the basis for several of the poet's most striking images and speculations on phenomena of the world or of feeling. Statements that begin simply—"Exultation is the going" (76), "There's a certain Slant of light" (258), "Nor would I be a Poet – " (from "I would not paint

– a picture," 505)—do not remain simple. "Exultation" is "going" in a particular landscape and direction: "the going / Of an inland soul to sea, / Past the houses – past the headlands – / Into deep Eternity – ". A "Slant of light" is known by its effects, which may change at different moments: it is the slant "That oppresses, like the Heft / Of Cathedral Tunes – "; "'Tis the Seal Despair . . . When it goes, 'tis like the Distance / On the look of Death – ". The speaker who would not "be a Poet" prefers the "privilege so awful" of being both the "Enamored – impotent – content – " audience and the Jove-like poet: "What would the Dower be, / Had I the Art to stun myself / With Bolts of Melody!" The poem ends with an exclamation rather than a question, perhaps because the speaker knows "the Dower" would be unpayable—"For None see God and live," as Dickinson concludes in another poem. To be one's own audience, to hear one's own poetry, is as devastating as to be hit by any other thunderbolt.

The copula also blurs the distinction between personal feeling and natural fact or law. In "There's a certain Slant of light," for example, the poet uses her own response to a kind of winter light to declare that this "certain Slant" affects everyone identically; the description is not based on her feeling but asserted radically and generically: this light *is* heavy, depressing, like "the Distance / On the look of Death."[57] Whether Dickinson begins with the deceptively flat "is," as in these examples, or concludes there, as in "It is the gift of Screws," the link between subject and subjective complement is generally ambiguous and complex.

Hypotaxis allows Dickinson to specify the relations that analogical juxtaposition or use of metaphor may imply. Furthermore, it allows the poet to predicate a world of inextricably interrelated causes and effects, actions with their multiple possibilities for further action. Although Dickinson's speaker may be caught in narrative stasis at the end of a poem—"With shackles on the plumed feet" (512), or subsisting solely on "that White Sustenance – / Despair – " (640)—her syntax seems to allow for ever further transformations and complexities.

Negation and Contrast

"'No' is the wildest word we consign to Language," Dickinson writes to her suitor Otis Lord (L 562). Perhaps this is so because, like disjunction generally, *no* creates space and therefore potential for new seeing and new meaning. *No* opens the doors that normal definitions close.[58] Negation keeps the poet honest to her own sense of a changing world and experience, and it allows her to create her own boundaries of definition and meaning.

Repeated assertion and negation, or description and contrast, have two major effects in Dickinson's poetry. As in paratactic constructions, repeated coordinate conjunction may give a tone of impulsiveness to a poem. The speaker seems to be working things out as she goes along, here by juxtaposing alternative or contrasting hypotheses and explanations rather than compiling them as she does with *and*. Dickinson also uses repeated *not* or *but* to create a kind of negative definition or reverse catachresis, what she describes in "There's a certain Slant of light" as the hole of "internal difference, / Where the Meanings, are — " (258). A catachresis fills a blank, naming a concept that previously had no linguistic description. Dickinson's "difference" instead makes us aware of the blank; she creates absence instead of providing a new name or concept for it. Such negative definition illuminates the subject of a poem by specifying what it is not, or by contrasting it with more easily named experiences and phenomena. It expands categories of meaning by providing a plethora of alternative or analogous contexts for the subject. Instead of labeling her subject with a name, in these poems Dickinson uses her whole poem as a name or definition; the poem fills the hole it creates by outlining the boundaries that no word has yet been designed to fill.

We see both a definitional and a dramatic use of contrast in "To pile like Thunder":

> To pile like Thunder to it's close
> Then crumble grand away
> While Everything created hid
> This — would be Poetry —
>
> Or Love — the two coeval come —
> We both and neither prove —
> Experience either and consume —
> For None see God and live —   (1247)

As noted earlier, in the first stanza of the poem Dickinson uses adverbial connectors to narrow her definition of poetry: "To pile like Thunder . . . Then crumble . . . While Everything . . . hid / This

– would be Poetry – ". The poem then proceeds with the unexpected coordinate conjunction and new definitional term: "Or Love – ". This second choice of subject for the definition is particularly disruptive because "Poetry" carries all the traditional marks of closure in a poem: it logically completes the sentence, and it is a rhyming word at the end of a metrically normal line and the end of the stanza. "Love," in contrast, occurs at the beginning of a new stanza (where we anticipate a new sentence and a change in subject), and breaks that new stanza's first line unusually early, after the first foot.

The syntax of the second stanza of this poem is choppy, breaking after the first iamb, at the end of the first line, and again at the end of the second: "Or Love – the two coeval come – / We both and neither prove – ". The internal sight-rhyme of "Love" / "prove" (a rhyme closer than any of the end-rhymes of the stanza) further disrupts our sense of the stanza's movement by making "Or Love" seem to carry the weight of a whole line by itself, which then rhymes with what seems to be the third line of the stanza: "We both and neither prove." In the drama of the poem, "Or Love" appears to be an afterthought, as does the "both and neither" of the following line. It is as though the speaker's sudden realization that poetry and love are analogous causes her to stumble momentarily in her definition, and then to conclude far from the crescendoing description with which she began. Although Dickinson's poems do not often change course this dramatically, they frequently give the impression that the speaker learns about her subject through the process of articulating her contradictory thoughts.

A more typical negative definition occurs in the poem "It was not Death, for I stood up" (510). The speaker here muses: "It was not Death . . . It was not Night . . . It was not Frost . . . Nor Fire . . . And yet, it tasted, like them all . . . And 'twas like Midnight, some . . ."

> But, most, like Chaos – Stopless – cool –
> Without a Chance, or Spar –
> Or even a Report of Land –
> To justify – Despair.

The "it" of this poem is the premier subject of Dickinson's description and definition poems: it is not anything that we know a name or analogy for, "And yet" it is like any number of things. Still, even when finally identifying the feeling "it" gives her, the speaker relies on repeated negatives: stop*less, without* "a Chance, or Spar – / Or . . . Report" to justify her despair. Dickinson repeats this pattern of contradictory and negative exploration in earlier and later poems. In an early poem ("It cant be 'Summer'! . . . It's early – yet – for 'Spring'! . . . It cant be 'Dying'! . . .") she ends inconclusively: "So Sunset shuts my question down / With Cuffs of Chrysolite!" (221). In a short poem probably written circa 1866, the poet writes:

> It was not Saint – it was too large –
> Nor Snow – it was too small –
> It only held itself aloof
> Like something spiritual –   (1092)

Dickinson uses the word *not* more often than any words but articles, a few prepositions, and *and, it, is,* and *that*.[59] Her pattern of repeated negative assertion suggests that the poet's attention is most captivated by the things and moments of her life that can be known only indirectly or through multiple, competing perceptions: "not Saint . . . Nor Snow"; "This – would be Poetry – / Or Love."

Even when she can name her "it" (the initiating phenomenon), Dickinson's interest in it as subject lies in its indefinable qualities or effect. She begins with "a certain Slant of light" in poem 258, for example, but the effect of the slant—perhaps the particular angle of slant—is without a name. We can no more find a "scar" marking its presence in language than we can find one in that urn of "internal difference, / Where the Meanings, are – ". In another poem, she describes the "Druidic Difference" created in the moment of late summer when crickets sing. "Further in Summer than the Birds" (1068) uses asymmetrical comparatives ("Further," "Antiquest"), participial adjectives ("enlarging," "burning"), and highly elliptical syntax to contribute to the uncertainty of the explicit negatives. The "Mass" is "unobtrusive"; "No Ordinance be seen"; it (or the moment?) "Remit as yet no Grace / No Furrow on the Glow"—and "Yet," as we come to expect at the conclusion of these poems, "a Druidic Difference / Enhances Nature now."

Dickinson's use of "Difference" here and in "There's a certain Slant of light" uncannily anticipates Jacques Derrida's idea of *différence* and of negative or deconstructive interpretation. Using Derrida's language, one might say of Dickinson's poems generally and of these poems in particular that they do not acknowledge a center of meaning. The discourse of these poems remains on the periphery of definition ("not Death," "not Saint," or "like the Distance / On the look of Death"). Because there is no semantic or linguistic center, no focal word of origin or meaning (and in particular no Christian "Word" that explains all), there is expansive play of language and of analogy, which is to say of the mind.[60] In a number of poems, Dickinson's speaker threatens the world with a power she will never disclose; she pictures herself as outside of all central structure and relationship (outside the feast, without "Him"—as lover or God). As these metaphors suggest, however, the poet does tend to work from a narrative center. She sees herself oppositionally, defining her position in the world negatively, by distance from some social structure or law.

Jane Eberwein speculates that Yankee women generally were "more likely to use freedom in making negative choices" than in acquiring things or asserting themselves. Excluding rather than expressing desires offered a woman protection from criticism and provided some power, insofar as the process of discriminating and rejecting was the woman's own.[61] As with her language, however, the negations or exclusions of Dickinson's life reveal a center by what they do not claim. By defining her margins, Dickinson reveals what she does not have, that is, the unnamed meaning she will illuminate. At the same time, by choosing marginal or indirect, nonauthoritative expression, the poet allows herself a greater range of choices and of potential meaning than any central choice of language or law could provide. Negation has the linguistic function of making room for the expression of new perception by breaking away from what has already been established, and the narrative (or structurally symbolic) function of maintaining the poet's independence by reasserting her oppositional stance to authority. Like her questions, her negations have a constructive and assertive role.

Dickinson's use of *but* reinforces the sense of contrast and negation in her poems, although the conjunction functions more to mark a moment of reversal or difference than to define outlines for the as yet indefinable. This conjunction also contains an assertive element. Since *but* requires a common topic in both of its conjuncts, it simultaneously negates a part of what has preceded and qualifies its negation with something like the "And yet" Dickinson makes explicit in "It was not Death" and "Further in Summer."

The pattern of developing contrast occurs in small in "Essential Oils – are wrung." This poem twice opposes the natural or "General" rose to the rose of Attar, although the first time only implicitly. We learn negatively that "Attar . . . Be not expressed by Suns alone" before receiving the positive: "It is the gift of Screws." The second stanza begins with a positive statement, made only to be countered: "The General Rose – decay – / But this – in Lady's Drawer / Make Summer." This sentence then concludes with a third point of comparison instead of elaborating on either of the previous two: " . . . When the Lady lie / In Ceaseless Rosemary." We see attar or poetry through its difference from ordinary roses and its difference from, but also resemblance to, the Lady (poet?) herself. We cannot know what is essential except by contrast with the natural, untransformed parts of the world.

In other poems the pattern of assertion and contrast reveals a more complex aspect of the speaker's relation to her subject and her audience. In the following poem, for example, each stanza contains a proposition and a contrasting proposition or statement.

> Sunset at Night – is natural –
> But Sunset on the Dawn
> Reverses Nature – Master –
> So Midnight's – due – at Noon.
>
> Eclipses be – predicted –
> And Science bows them in –
> But do one face us suddenly –
> Jehovah's Watch – is wrong.   (415)

The first stanza of this poem presents a simple contrast: sunset is natural at night "But" not, one infers, at "Dawn." The second stanza's "But" is more complex. By line 6, the speaker has marshaled the forces of "Nature," astronomy, and "Science" behind her and her expectation that day or "Noon" follow "Dawn" rather than the "Sunset" and "Midnight" that "we" have apparently received. Instead of contrasting prediction with lack of prediction or science with some other force, though, the speaker then simply accuses the "Master" she speaks to: "Jehovah's Watch"—that is, by metonymy, the Master himself— "is wrong." He is unnatural, unscientific, above all unfair to "us"—the comfortingly nonspecific community that Dickinson's persona so often speaks from when confronting a "Master." As the poem's break in logic shows, the speaker has no real argument except that "he" is "wrong." "But" serves to introduce what she has wanted to say all along rather than to provide a step in a dialectical or logical argument.

Similarly, in "Suspense – is Hostiler than Death – " (705), "But" marks the point of a change in direction rather than pointing a direction of change (lines 4–8):

> Suspense – does not conclude –
>
> But perishes – to live anew –
> But just anew to die –
> Annihilation – plated fresh
> With Immortality –

The disjunctive effect of the repeated *But*s and the dashes of line 5 reflect the speaker's surprise at encountering anew the "Suspense" she thought had died. Its hostility is in its unpredictability and in its ability to return. The richness of *but* lies in its similar unpredictability and potential for infinite repetition: "But perishes . . . But just anew . . ." Like repeated *not,* repeated *but* keeps a reader circling the poet's subject.

SPEECH

The elements of language that characterize Dickinson's style are also those said to characterize speech. Spoken language is paratactic more than hypotactic in its connections; it tends to be disjunctive, and to rely on sentence fragments. It contains more questions and exclamations than does written language and often contains pauses in mid-sentence, such as those represented by various slanting marks in Dickinson's manuscripts and marked typographically in printed texts by dashes. Speech typically uses both frequent repetition and frequent ellipsis.[62] Lindberg-Seyersted finds speechlike syntax and diction to be the single most important aspect of Dickinson's language; the poet's voice gives the illusion of informal and personal speech. As this critic demonstrates at length, particularly Dickinson's use of colloquialisms and her direct address to an audience make the poems seem more like acts of discourse than icons of art.[63]

Colloquial Idiom

The speechlike accents of Dickinson's poetry are more easily heard than described. Listen, for example, to the opening lines of poem 376:

> Of Course – I prayed –
> And did God Care?
> He cared as much as on the Air
> A Bird – had stamped her foot –
> And cried "Give Me" –

In these lines we hear informality in the opening "Of Course," the quick scorn of the abrupt rhetorical "And did God Care?" and in the impatient immediacy of the response, with its slight inversion of syntax and its omission of "if" ("as [if] on the air") and of the reduced (repeated) noun phrase "And [as if a Bird had] cried . . ." Together these elements create a dramatic portrait of the speaker difficult to surpass in as few words. Short sentences, a contraction, and common or rural analogies contribute to the effect of informality in other poems: "I went to Heaven – / 'Twas a small Town –" (374) and "A Toad, can die of Light – / Death is the Common Right / Of Toads and Men –" (583). Informal expressions mark some poems as spoken: "Don't tell! they'd banish us – you know!" (288) or "The Lingering – and the Stain – I mean –" (307). The poet's frequent use of all-purpose words like "thing," "kind" (as a noun), and "so" also gives the flavor of speech. The second stanza of poem 583, for example, begins: "Life – is a different Thing – / So measure Wine –". In "I play at Riches," both *thing* and *done* are used with a common but pointed imprecision: "For often, overbold / With Want, and Opportunity – / I could have done a Sin / And been Myself that easy Thing / An independent Man –" (801). Calling "an independent Man" a "Thing" belittles him, or his condition ("it") in two ways: the colloquialism shows the speaker's lack of respect, and the objectification repeats and emphasizes it.

In "I met a King this afternoon!" (166), we hear informality in the poem's unpoetic and redundant uncertainty as well as in the colloquial "kind" and "'Twas." The excessive exclamation marks add to the effect: "And he was barefoot, I'm afraid! . . . And sure I am, the crest he bore / Within that Jacket's pocket too! . . . 'Twas possibly a Czar petite – / A Pope, or something of that kind!" In other lines, this poem contains the colloquial phrases "If I must tell you," "not at all," and emphatic *such* twice: "And such a wagon!" and "Another such a vehicle." Nominal *kind* appears in the phrases of other poems: "A Kind behind the Door –" (335); "And though I may not guess the kind –" (561); "A kind of *plummet* strain –" (663); "Of no corporeal kind" (1634). As in the poet's use of indefinite and nonspecific pronouns, her uses of indefinite nouns like "thing," "kind," "whatever" ("Whatever it is – she has tried it –", 1204) allow her to explore a subject without naming it, or to define a state that has no proper name, and to play humanity and objectification off against each other. Such words signal that she claims no authority for her own conclusions. Like her (also implicitly informal) audience, she is trying to figure out various aspects of her experience in the familiar terms of ordinary speech. The use of colloquialisms prevents hierarchical distance between speaker and audience in the poems and reduces the foreignness caused by the less familiar or easy aspects of the poet's language.

Feminine Diction and Syntax

When speaking of the "feminine" in language, critics apparently assume a common understanding of that word, yet its implications may be widely differing. As Bonnie Costello says in introducing her essay "The 'Feminine' Language of Marianne Moore," the word may suggest restraint, humility, "ladylike . . . 'chastity,'" or a preoccupation with daily life, with the "surfaces" of things (the quality of "genuineness" that T. S. Eliot and others attribute admiringly to Moore while distinguishing it from "greatness"). "Femininity" in writing may correlate with minimal "intellectual interest," a selfless love of others, "natural" feelings (woman as child), and a leisurely—that is, digressive or merely unaggressive—style. Or the "feminine" may inhere, as Costello herself argues of Moore's work, in a poet's focus on particular "virtues and manners" considered stereotypically feminine (for example, modesty) and, as she implies, in the poet's elusive, oblique, self-abnegating but highly conscious style.[64]

In regard to Dickinson, the most frequent current claims for her "feminine" language and aesthetic stem from her use of domestic and stereotypically feminine imagery. Jean McClure Mudge presents at length the evidence for Dickinson's vision of the home from the perspective of one at repose inside it. Her perspective is typical for a nineteenth-century woman, Mudge argues: "Interior house imagery may . . . be read as quintessentially feminine."[65] Sandra Gilbert argues that Dickinson structured her "life/text around a series of 'mysteries' [romance, renunciation, domesticity, nature, and women's nature] that were distinctively female." Dickinson "explore[d] and exploit[ed] the characteristics, even the constraints, of nineteenth-century womanhood so as to transform and transcend them."[66] Gilbert's argument, as she indicates by choosing *female* instead of *feminine* to describe the poet, involves Dickinson's cultural and historical sphere, a larger arena than the poet's use of gendered cultural stereotypes. She bases her argument, however, on Dickinson's deliberate manipulations of patterns of femininity (for example, dressing in white) and the poet's continuous reference to the work and objects of women's sphere. Like Gilbert, I find that Dickinson exploits cultural patterns of female behavior and that she extends this exploitation to a use of language patterns stereotypically associated with the feminine. She uses at least to some extent a "women's language," that is, a language that American culture associates with the feminine, and therefore usually with women.

"Feminine" vocabulary or "virtues and manners" are relatively easy to identify because they stem from tasks or the sphere traditionally dominated by women: talk of the kitchen, household, nursery, of sewing or homemaking is thought to be "feminine." For example, the author of a poem that personifies the sunset as a careless housewife seems feminine in imagination, as in the first lines of the following poem:

> She sweeps with many-colored Brooms –
> And leaves the Shreds behind –
> Oh Housewife in the Evening West –
> Come back, and dust the Pond!

> You dropped a Purple Ravelling in –
> You dropped an Amber thread – . . .   (219)

In another of Dickinson's poems, the masculine wind begins a storm by kneading, a feminine action often considered to induce tranquillity but here run amok:

> The Wind begun to knead the Grass –
> As Women do a Dough –
> He flung a Hand full at the Plain –
> A Hand full at the Sky – . . .   (824)

In other poems, memory is a "sacred Closet" waiting to be swept with "reverential Broom" (1273); the spider's merit "as an Artist" is "certified / By every Broom and Bridget" but evidently not by those arbiters of taste who are not involved in daily cleanings (1275). The poet likens madness to split seams and then to escaped balls of yarn: she tries to "match" the "Cleaving in my Mind . . . Seam by Seam . . . But Sequence ravelled out of Sound / Like Balls – upon a Floor" (937). She compares anguish to the feeling pincushions must have when one pushes needles into them: "the Grief – that nestled close / As needles – ladies softly press / To Cushions Cheeks – / To keep their place –" (584). Women's clothes appear frequently in descriptions of the seasons or the day; sewing recurs as a metaphor for poetic creation ("Dont put up my thread & Needle –," 617; "A Spider sewed at Night," 1138) and as an analogy for any number of other things, for example:

> The Months have ends – the Years – a knot –
> No Power can untie
> To stretch a little further
> A Skein of Misery –   (423)

Or, "A Frost more needle keen / Is necessary, to reduce / The Ethiop within" (422). In all, a substantial number of Dickinson's analogies draw on typically feminine activities.

Elements of language beyond diction that mark a voice as feminine are less easily categorized. Linguists provide persuasive evidence that there is no single "women's speech" or "women's language" as such. Language use depends on the factors of class, social status, education, and immediate audience and context as well as gender. Yet despite the importance of these factors, some kinds of language choices do seem to be gender-linked. Equally important for cultural studies, women and men of all economic and social strata will not hesitate to categorize certain types of language as sounding feminine or masculine. People hear gender in language, even though the perception may be based on differences in two speakers' presentations or the listeners' own expectations, not on differences in language use.[67] Furthermore, although empirical studies do not agree in categorizing any specific language patterns as inherently gender-marked, studies do show that certain types of language are more apt to be used by women than by men.[68] For instance, women are more likely to use questions and exclamations than their male contemporaries and to speak in sentence fragments—both leaving their own sentences unfinished and completing the unfinished sentences of other speakers.[69] Particularly in all-female groups, women's speech tends to be communal: there are more interactive expressions or comments and more noninformational signals (tag questions, expressions like "you know," "you see"), more explanations of authority for a statement's claim (for example, "——— says," "I think," "I've heard"). A study of conversational interaction also shows that, when talking to men, women tend to do more of the work of maintaining the conversation than their conversational partners, for example by interjecting encouraging words and asking leading questions.[70]

Although for obvious reasons there are no empirical studies of gender and speech in the nineteenth century, advice books to women on proper behavior include frequent instructions on language use, tonal inflection, and manner of speaking. A woman's voice is to be above all soft and gentle. In *Recollections of a Southern Matron,* Mrs. Gilman instructs that "the three golden threads with which domestic happiness [every *true woman*'s goal] is woven" are "to repress a harsh answer, to confess to a fault, and to stop (right or wrong) in the midst of self-defense, in gentle submission."[71] Like Mrs. Gilman's, most nineteenth-century instructions to young women on speech and conversation have a moral rather than an aesthetic or grammatical basis. A woman is never to lie but "Always Conciliate"—the first commandment in "Rules of Conjugal and Domestic Happiness" (*The Mother's Assistant and Young Lady's Friend,* 1843).[72] She governs by "persuasion . . . The empire of woman is an empire of softness . . . her commands are carresses" (*The Lady's Amaranth,* 1839).[73] She is never to say anything in word or tone that might hurt or offend a listener.

It is difficult to translate patterns of speech difference into generalizations about gender difference in written language because the rules for written English are much stricter than are those for speech; consequently, there tends to be less variety in writing than in speech. Furthermore, training for writing is much more homogeneous for both women and men than is the highly context-oriented and informal training for speech. Nonetheless, particularly in popular and relatively informal writing, we may see the lines of gender difference that underlie stereotypes of gender and language. To take a current example, while compiling a study of language difference between women's and men's popular magazines (based on magazines published in 1983 and 1984), I encountered striking stylistic similarity between both the language of women's magazines and empirical findings on women's speech, on the one hand, and the patterns of Dickinson's language use, on the other. The language of women's magazines tends to use far more direct address (the reader is always "you"), more questions and exclamations, more quotation of authority and less claim for authority or expertise on the writer's part, and greater use of the present tense than does that of men's magazines.[74] Because the writers for women's and men's magazines are by no means all, respectively, women or men, these language differences appear to stem from editorial policy, not natural language use.[75] The assumption of editorial boards of women's magazines seems to be that women respond more favorably to or are more comfortable with language that is personal, direct, relatively intimate, largely based on active and present-tense verbs, and nonassertive (in its repeated bows to outside—not the journalist's—authority and deemphasis of the propositional statement) than they would be with language that included fewer of these features. Consciously or not, that is, they assume that these language features are particularly suited to women.

The repeated claim that women's spoken and written language is indirect seems only logical from a historical perspective, given the nineteenth century's strictures on propriety and manners and its limitations on women's sphere of action.[76] With Dickinson, we see indirection in her extreme ellipticism and metaphoricity as well as in her reticence in speaking about herself referentially—even while writing poem after poem in the first person singular and in writing countless letters to friends.[77] Dickinson's disclaimer to Higginson of identity with her poetic speaker is well known: "When I state myself, as the Representative of the Verse – it does not mean – me – but a supposed person" (L 268). The poet also disguises her personal involvement in the poems by speaking of herself in the third person or in the plural: "Why make it doubt – it hurts it so –" (462); or "A Doubt if it be Us / Assists the staggering Mind" (859). She often objectifies aspects of her mind, not just in classical debates of the Heart and Soul, but as things: "My syllable rebelled –" in "I could suffice for Him, I knew" (643) or, to take a familiar example, the speaker is a "Loaded Gun" in "My Life had stood – a Loaded Gun" (754).

Highly metaphorical representations that guard the speaker from having to assert herself in open opposition to existing powers or ideas also tend to characterize female more than male speakers and writers. Dickinson's predominantly metonymic figurative structures (which are more indirect than metaphor per se) may link her with a history of women's use of language. Referring to Jakobson's distinction between the processes of selection and combination in language, Cora Kaplan argues that women tend to prefer the selective or metonymic process, the process of deciding between elements that may occur in each others' place. "Metonymy," she writes, "is a dominant trope in women's poetry, since it is a way of referring to experience suppressed in public discourse."[78] Kaplan refers back to Jacques Lacan's hypothesis that metonymy provides a way "to bypass the obstacles of social censure"; through its indirection, metonymy allows veiled or disguised statement. Roland Hagenbüchle demonstrates most persuasively Dickinson's use of metonymy and its ambiguous indirection, associating the poet's use of asymmetry, ellipsis, and polysemantic and hypothetical language with the metonymic base of her tropes.[79] Although he does not talk about the protective function of metonymy, Hagenbüchle stresses its effect in creating indeterminacy and in undercutting polarized oppositions (the realm of metaphor). Whether or not it can be proved that women generally choose metonymy over other types of figurative language, Dickinson clearly exploits its potential for indirection in ways that support the explanations of Lacan and Kaplan.

As the different studies of gender in speech and in writing suggest, there may be different reasons for women in various contexts to choose the language patterns they do. The overlap in styles of speech and writing associated with women, however, indicates that women may be more comfortable with certain characteristics of language in a broader range of circumstances than men are. This is not to say that no men ask questions, present themselves indirectly, grant more authority to others' than to their own claims, or address their readers directly and informally, but rather that women tend to share conversational habits that incline them to greater uses of these language patterns in speech and writing. Although it is unlikely that Dickinson means to identify herself with conventional notions of femininity, her vocabulary, immediate intimacy, indirect claims for personal authority or grandeur, and her more widespread indirection in speaking of her life, as well as her wide use of question and exclamation marks and the dash, all correspond to features of language that have been associated with the feminine. It is perhaps merely another sign of her general colloquialism that Dickinson speaks in the voice of her everyday life, therefore in the voice of a woman. It is also, perhaps, one more indication that this poet wants to give a new voice to poetry, and that she identifies this voice in some ways as a woman's.

THREE

Reading the Poems

Omissions are not accidents.
Marianne Moore

T HE PRECEDING chapter interpreted the function of particular
language features by sketching their effect in isolated lines of
the five sample poems. This chapter develops those sketches
into full readings of the poems, combining the interpretive linguistic
readings of the grammar with information about Dickinson's life and
previous analyses of the poems.[1] Because literary criticism over the
years has read the basic plot of Dickinson's poems in a fairly predictable pattern of change, I will review the history of critical response
to "He fumbles at your Soul" but not for the other poems.

"HE FUMBLES AT YOUR SOUL"

> He fumbles at your Soul
> As Players at the Keys
> Before they drop full Music on –
> He stuns you by degrees –
> Prepares your brittle Nature
> For the Ethereal Blow
> By fainter Hammers – further heard –
> Then nearer – Then so slow
> Your Breath has time to straighten –
> Your Brain – to bubble Cool –
> Deals – One – imperial – Thunderbolt –
> That scalps your naked Soul –

113

When Winds take Forests in their Paws –
The Universe – is still –

   5. Nature] substance   12. scalps] peels
   9. time] chance   13. take] hold
  14. Universe – is] Firmaments – are[2]

Predictably, the earliest readings of "He fumbles at your Soul" were biographical and romantic: the poem is "an account of a love declaration"; or the poem describes the Reverend Charles Wadsworth's manner in the pulpit and Dickinson's response to him (for years Wadsworth was the critics' favorite candidate as the object of Dickinson's frustrated love).[3] In other readings, and as in almost every other poem she wrote, "He fumbles" is later seen as expressing Dickinson's fear of masculinity and of masculine power, here embodied in the hell-fire preaching minister, or a lover, or God Himself.[4] In the next, more abstract stage of critical readings, Weisbuch reads in the poem the ongoing anguish of dying consciously; suffering becomes the fulfillment of a divine destiny.[5] Kher sees in the "Soul" and "He" a willing reader and powerful poet, but also a possibility that the speaker is the poet. In other contexts she writes that terror and beauty are one for Dickinson, and that "Terror is the womb that crystalizes the experience of poetry," implying that the speaker requires the tormentor to be able to write.[6]

Following these archetypal tendencies but returning to the circumstances of Dickinson's life, Rich sees the poem as a drama between the poet and her own power, given external and masculine form: "Since the most powerful figures in patriarchal culture have been men, it seems natural that Dickinson would assign a masculine gender to that in herself which did not fit in with the conventional ideology of womanliness."[7] Porter also notes the link in this poem between the speaker and her gender, seeing the connection, however, in the internal violence of the imagery rather than in the speaker's relation to patriarchy as a cultural institution. Porter cryptically notes that the violence of this poem's images is "inverted in the way we are beginning to see is a woman's perspective"; the "disarmingly soft," even sensual opening lines conceal "the terror of the assault" for the female speaker.[8] The range of the responses to this poem—from biographical to psychobiographical to structuralist and archetypal to gendered readings—typifies that of Dickinson criticism generally in this century and reflects the importance of the critic's predisposition in thematic readings of Dickinson's poems.

In my reading, "He fumbles at your Soul" dramatizes a moment of anticipation and ambiguous fulfillment. Its contrasting metaphors and adjectives make the experience it relates seem both ecstatic and terrible: you are played like "full Music"; your "brittle" self is thunderstruck; you are taken or held like trees in wind. "Fumbles" with its echoing "Paws" gives the experience a sensual edge, as the variant "hold" does, while "Blow," "Hammers," and the scalping "Thunderbolt" make the experience violent. The action of the poem is simple: He fumbles at your soul, stuns you, prepares your nature, and deals one thunderbolt. Less simple are its mixture of sensuality and violence, its present-tense address to an unidentified speaker, its syntactic doubling in line 8, and its peculiarly tangential coda, or unrhymed concluding couplet.

The speaker's use of simple present tense in this poem makes its drama seem both repeated and continuous. The poem's unidentified "He" and "you" complicate a reading of the drama as repeated act by making the repetition one of type rather than of particular event. If its event is repeated and its characters are archetypal, the poem describes what occurs whenever "your" (anyone's?) soul is aroused and, metaphorically, scalped. "He"—be it lover, attacker, a promised or threatened event of any kind, God—toys with "you" and then strikes. The particulars of who "He" is and how he plays on you may change, but the outline of initial uncertain touch, extraordinary "degrees" of preparation, and "imperial" blow do not. As ongoing event, the poem's drama might reveal an archetypal existential condition, as Weisbuch argues; as ongoing narrative, however, it may also reveal the speaker's state of mind. Although the "I" plays no active role in the poem's text, the poem is spoken; an unidentified speaker addresses a generalized "you." As narrative event, the poem may reveal the speaker's attempt to outlive an overwhelming experience by articulating it in a universalized verbal and pronominal form: this happens to "you," not (just?) her. The present tense may imply that she continuously relives the sequence even while trying to distance herself from it by representing it as universal, or prophetic of someone else's life.

Because of the ambiguous identity of the speaker and verb tense, the event of the poem is indeterminate: it might have happened to the speaker or to all women, or all people, once or repeatedly, as recurring particular event or in numerous forms.[9] This indeterminacy repeats itself in other elements of the narrative. Singular "He" is like plural "Players" who drop full music. He perhaps represents a whole culture of powerful beings (patriarchy personified?) that offers the speaker ambiguous fulfillment or punishment. Later, mid-poem and mid-line, the phrase "Then so slow" syntactically modifies both what "you" hear and his blow, obscuring the difference between you and Him. The victim—"you"—is utterly passive up to this point in the poem. We know her sensations only through the quality of metaphor she gives His actions: "you" are an instrument whose "substance" or "Nature" has been opened to bare its soul; "you" are listening—an anticipatory act. After "Then so slow," however, your and His rhythms coincide: as you listen to the "so slow" hammers, He "so slow" deals his thunderbolt. The leisure on both sides gives your "Breath" and "Brain" time to become calm. From the evidence of the syntactic merging, "you" seem to meet the blow, to have made your own preparations, to have cleared your soul of its debris in just the time He allots you so that it awaits "naked" what will befall. The climax is as ecstatic as it is devastating; the tension of the poem resides in its perfect commingling of the sensations of breathless anticipation and terror.

Characteristically, Dickinson does not explain her poem's context in its final lines. The couplet's lack of rhyme reflects its lack of explicit congruence with what preceded. Yet the act of winds taking or holding forests clearly provides an analogy for the earlier event: perhaps your soul has been touched to its uttermost by a thunderbolt as forests are taken up by winds; what follows either occurrence is a motionless silence of annihilation, or peace. Or winds "hold" forests as He has imperially met your "naked Soul"—with an Emersonian suspension of giving and receiving ("If there be omnipotence in the stroke, there is omnipotence of recoil").[10] Or the stillness may be analogous to the anticipation preceding the thunderbolt; there is utter stillness when winds hold forests just as there is when you are held in the suspense of His sensuous, then unmistakably powerful touch. In all cases the closing analogy, like the body of the poem, allows us to interpret His approach as both fulfilling and devastating. The duality is especially strong when we consider both variants: winds take and hold, as storms destroy and cleanse, as silence may be of despair or peace. The poem does not distinguish the feelings and effects of ecstasy from those of terror.

The increasing terror or anticipation of the poem is also created through the progression of its tropes. In the opening analogy "you" are an object of His touch, but the touch is limited and culturally viable if not outright approved. Players at the keys of a piano make music only in conjunction with the instrument; there is a balance and harmony here. As the poem continues, however, "He" becomes more and more elemental. "Stun" and "prepare" may still be acts of a professional or craftsman, and "Hammers" may refer back to the piano, but with these words the focus shifts from playing to the striking of blows. Concluding this sequence with a thunderbolt gives "Blow" its most primitive form: soul and tormentor have left the drawing room or concert hall for the primeval world of scalping and of unharnessed power from which there is no protection. This line of development helps explain Dickinson's choice of scene for the poem's closing analogy. The victim takes the final step here from being naked or unprotected object in nature to being part of nature itself: "your" experience is like that of forests as well as like that of pianos. The poem opposes forces within nature rather than distinguishing human from elemental or physical experience; its progression from cultured to elemental drama collapses distinctions between the violence of the civilized and the natural worlds. The fumbler at a piano is seen as analogous in relative power to the instigator of nature's storms.

Thinking of Dickinson as the author and perhaps speaker of the poem underscores the psychological balance of attraction and terror. In the poem, the speaker gives herself "naked" to His power. Dickinson never gave herself to anything—including the power of her own poetry—with such abandon. Yet as member of a Christian community and as woman, abandonment of the self, especially of skeptical self-consciousness, should have been her role. The poem may dramatize the conversion experience Dickinson never underwent, or a romantic falling in love—here imagined as an aggressive act from the outside, as it commonly was in medieval and Renaissance stories featuring Cupid or hunt scenes. "His" blow may be sexual, and the soul's nakedness a figure for the body's more obvious vulnerability and readiness.[11] The poem is perhaps a dramatic rehearsal of what Dickinson partly hopes and largely fears may happen to her in the sexual and religious worlds. As she wrote to Sue in anticipatory dread of marriage in 1852, perhaps as many as ten years before writing this poem, using the analogy of female flowers longing for the sun that scorches them instead of the soul and thunderbolt (L 93):

> You have seen flowers at morning, *satisfied* with the dew, and
> those same sweet flowers at noon with their heads bowed in

anguish before the mighty sun; think you these thirsty blossoms will *now* need naught but — *dew?* No, they will cry for sunlight and pine for the burning noon, tho' it scorches them, scathes them; they have got through with peace — they know that the man of noon, is *mightier* than the morning and their life is henceforth to him. Oh, Susie, it is dangerous, and it is all too dear, these simple trusting spirits, and the spirits mightier, which we cannot resist! It does so rend me, Susie, the thought of it when it comes, that I tremble lest at sometime I, too, am yielded up.

In her imagination, Dickinson accepts and moves to meet this moment of almost literal consummation; she is touched with flame. In her life, however, she absolutely resists being overwhelmed by any more powerful force or figure. Both the desire or need to give herself up in ecstatic union and the desire to remain separate and intact are real to her. Their balance creates the tension of this poem.

"THIS WAS A POET — IT IS THAT"

This was a Poet — It is That
Distills amazing sense
From ordinary Meanings —
And Attar so immense

From the familiar species
That perished by the Door —
We wonder it was not Ourselves
Arrested it — before —

Of Pictures, the Discloser —
The Poet — it is He —
Entitles Us — by Contrast —
To ceaseless Poverty —

Of Portion — so unconscious —
The Robbing — could not harm —
Himself — to Him — a Fortune —
Exterior — to Time —

Like "Essential Oils – are wrung," "This was a Poet" compares poetry to perfume, although here using the process of distilling rather than expression through screws as the metaphor for creation. The Poet "Distills amazing sense" from the "familiar species" of experience that we have not "arrested" for ourselves. Also as in "Essential Oils," the stanzas outlining the analogy between perfume and poetry are easier to interpret than those that follow. In this poem, the poet changes roles after stanza 2. At first the contrasts of "amazing" and "immense" with "ordinary," "familiar," and the past tense "perished" make him seem a kind of magician; he creates "Attar" with such apparent ease that we "wonder" we haven't done so ourselves previously. As the poem proceeds, the poet no longer distills sense but discloses "Pictures" and possesses a fortune so innate or so huge that robbing cannot harm it or him. Unlike the maker of "sense," the poet of stanzas 3 and 4 hoards his riches. He is a fortune "to Him[self]," not to the world, and although we may see his "Pictures" he "Entitles Us" only to "ceaseless Poverty." The change in metaphors establishes a contrast between the poet as he first appears and his character in the concluding stanzas.

The fragmentation and inversion of syntax and the unusually prominent repeated function words of this poem also undercut its opening metaphor. The disjunction between celebrating the poet for his "amazing" and invaluable gift to the world and implicitly belittling him through the use of objectifying and fussily redundant syntax suggests that Dickinson is not at ease with some aspect of her subject. For example, the poet comes uncomfortably close to the status of a thing in the copular linkages "This was a Poet – It is That" and "It is He." Here object pronouns (this, it) and indefinite equations (*what* is or was he?) reduce the poet's humanity: we expect at least "This was a Poet – It is *He* [not *That*]" for a human agent and would find "the poet discloses pictures" far more cordial a construction than the objectifying participal "The Discloser – It is He." The poet's lack of humanity is further suggested by his peculiar invulnerability in the last stanza: "a Fortune – / Exterior – to Time – " is glorious as a description of immortal poems but somewhat mechanical and materialistic as a description of a man. We are poor, capable of "wonder," within "Time," while He is alone, "Exterior" to our world, knowable only "by Contrast."

Referring again to "Essential Oils" is useful in understanding the mixed tone of this poem. In that poem the "Lady" is entirely private;

she exists without social context except for that implied by her honorific title ("lady," not "woman"), and her poetry/perfume takes the metaphorical form of a sachet, hidden in her "Drawer." The Poet of "This was a Poet," on the other hand, is a public figure presented in contrast to a community which includes the poem's speaker—"We." This causes no problems even within the context of Dickinson's other poems on poetry as long as we interpret this differentiation to mean that the poet is distinct from the crowd. To the extent, however, that the speaker is also a poet, as she by simple logic must be, this claim loses its edge. The poet/narrator who speaks in Dickinson's poem considers herself a part of the admiring, ordinary crowd rather than separate from it. Her stance indicates that not all poets share "His" isolation from community. Again, in "Essential Oils," the Lady's solitary life and death reflect and contrast with the distorting creation of the poem. Like the "General Rose" or any part of the natural world, she will "decay"; but the essence of her "Drawer" will "Make Summer" endlessly. She seems to be at the same time Rose, operator of the screw-driven press, and wearer of Attar, or subject, creator, and reader of the poem; she makes summer through the process of expressing her own painful experience and even in death. The "Poet" of "This was a Poet" instead creates effortlessly, without sacrifice. Although he begins by distilling Attar, he becomes a "Discloser" of "Pictures"— an operation that requires no personal giving, much less pain. Far from requiring secrecy for his art or finding it in his death, this poet is "unconscious" of his wealth of poetic power. Despite the shared metaphor of "Essential Oils" and "This was a Poet," the latter's "Poet" seems to create poetry by a process closer to that of the former's "Suns" than to the Lady's process of "Screws." This poet is like no "Rose" or member of a community; "Exterior – to Time," he is like no living thing.

As I have indicated, Dickinson's awkward syntax and use of "We" manifest her ambivalence about this practitioner of her craft. Once we look at her life and at the themes of other poems, reasons for such ambivalence may be seen. As fellow poet, Dickinson must admire any distiller of "amazing sense." As younger sister of a favored son and as a consciously female poet, however, Dickinson might well differentiate herself with some resentment from the poet who creates unconsciously and with ease, the man of ceaseless, inherited cultural wealth.[12] Evidently during the time when she wrote or at least copied "This was a Poet" for her own safekeeping, the contrast between herself as artist and the world was particularly vivid.[13] In the fascicle where she binds this poem, Dickinson precedes it with two poems on similar differences. In the first, "It would have starved a Gnat – / To live so small as I – " (612), the speaker brags that she can live on even less than a gnat, and without his privileges to fly to more sustaining places or to die. In the poem immediately preceding "This was a Poet," the speaker is a "Girl" poet "shut . . . up in Prose –" by uncomprehending adults, whom she escapes "easy as a Star" by willing herself to be free (613). Later in the fascicle Dickinson includes "It was given to me by the Gods" (454), a poem about another "little Girl" far richer with her handful of "Gold" than anyone could guess and richer than anyone else is: "The Difference – made me bold –", she confides. These are poems of difference and of strength, whether these qualities stem from unique starvation or mysterious wealth. When the difference stems from wealth, however, it is usually only temporary and at times not even that. In "The Malay – took the Pearl" (452), which follows "This was a Poet" in fascicle 21, the "Jewel" the speaker covets goes instead to her rival, the unselfconscious and therefore successfully active "Swarthy fellow."

"This was a Poet" begins with what appears to be shared wealth but ends with the speaking poet's "ceaseless Poverty." Perhaps in 1862 Dickinson ambivalently imagined the creation of poetry to be a natural process, more or less along the lines of diving to reach a "Pearl" as the healthy "Malay" does (452). The Poet enters nature as "that" which distills sense and discloses pictures, leaving the human world of loss, death, and time behind. "Essential Oils – are wrung," probably written during the following year (1863), may be her revision of the earlier poem. This poem's change of analogy, from distillation to expression, for the making of perfume epitomizes the difference between the two poems. In distilling, one begins with liquid and obtains a more concentrated or purified form of that liquid by evaporating its water; in expressing, one begins with (in this case) petals and obtains a concentrated liquid by crushing them into pulp—a greater transformation and a more physical process. In "Essential Oils – are wrung," "Attar" is not the "gift" of wealthy poets who disclose pictures or distill essence but of poets who learn the slow, painful process of expression or "Screws."

Although Dickinson admires and may even envy poets of natural brilliance and ongoing fortune, she considers her own verse of economically hoarded, largely hidden power to be the greater. Nonetheless, because her claims for greatness and demonstrations of power remain veiled, the poet's envy remains unallayed. The ambivalence between admiration and ironic disdain finds expression in the uneven syntax of "This was a Poet."

"MY LIFE HAD STOOD – A LOADED GUN"

My Life had stood – a Loaded Gun –
In Corners – till a Day
The Owner passed – identified –
And carried Me away –

And now We roam in Sovreign Woods –
And now We hunt the Doe –
And every time I speak for Him –
The Mountains straight reply –

And do I smile, such cordial light
Upon the Valley glow –
It is as a Vesuvian face
Had let it's pleasure through –

And when at Night – Our good Day done –
I guard My Master's Head –
'Tis better than the Eider-Duck's
Deep Pillow – to have shared –

To foe of His – I'm deadly foe –
None stir the second time –
On whom I lay a Yellow Eye –
Or an emphatic Thumb –

Though I than He – may longer live
He longer must – than I –
For I have but the power to kill,
Without – the power to die –

   5. in] the –   18. stir] harm
  16. Deep] low   23. power] art

"My Life had stood" is beyond question the most frequently and extensively explicated of Dickinson's poems. Better than any theoretical pronouncement, the continuing variation and richness of its explications demonstrate the multiplicity of meaning that may result from Dickinson's compression, parataxis, textual variants, and densely compacted metaphor.[14]

In my reading, "My Life had stood" is an adolescent fantasy about coming of age that breaks down before what should be its happy conclusion—powerful adulthood—revealing the flaw in its initial fiction but perhaps also the extreme limitation the speaker feels in her life choices. Although she escapes her Corner, the speaker is left in a limbo that promises none of the constructive power of adulthood. The poem may also be a terrible fantasy of adult womanhood—that condition which allows none of the privileges of childhood but few of the privileges of male adulthood in their place.

At the beginning and end of this poem, the speaker's "Life" is in stasis. At first, like most nineteenth-century girls, she waits to be "carried . . . away –" to her life; she waits for an "Owner," a "Master" to serve and guard. At the end, she apparently hopes for some return to a condition without an "Owner," but without having conceived of any alternative to the loaded gun fiction or role to restructure her existence. To return to her initial state would be to exist indefinitely in a state between life and death that allows consciousness but prevents action or choice. Having imagined herself as a gun, the speaker now appears to be trapped in that fiction.

In the middle stanzas of the poem the speaker lives out her fantasy, gaining some autonomy of action and tremendous power, but at a cost. Like the speaker of "The soul has Bandaged moments" (512) who "dances like a Bomb, abroad," this speaker's action takes only apocalyptically destructive forms. She is a gun; her smile is volcanic. Her aim and shot are so deadly that none of her victims rise "*the* second time" (my italics)—the unidiomatic definite article suggesting the second coming and the beginning of eternal life. The speaker imagines that she can kill beyond God's power of resurrection. Still, she has no power over her own life or choices.

The paradoxical power and powerlessness of the poem's speaker follow necessarily from the poem's opening metaphor: a gun cannot shoot itself. A woman/gun or poet/gun, by analogy, cannot stimulate her own activity or fulfill the purpose of her creation. This inability is seen as natural or normal in a woman's life; as with a gun, she is supposed to be directed and stimulated by an "Owner." Unlike a gun, however, the woman is also supposed to be creative, not destructive, and receptive, not explosive. Dickinson's gun/woman fits uneasily into any normal category. She needs her owner to "speak," but she does not say at all what is expected of her as owned object. She also becomes curiously independent of her owner: she aims with her own "Yellow Eye," pulls her own trigger, and chooses to guard her Master rather than share his bed. In these ways she is less his instrument than she is the independent expression of his enmity and power. Nonetheless, her independence is limited. The gun's target remains "foe of His," and its sole named target is "the Doe"—the only distinctly female creature of the poem. As Gelpi writes, in killing the Doe the speaker kills the feminine aspect of herself, sacrificing her natural female role in order to take on the male roles of independent speech and power. The paratactic *and*s linking hunting with smiling and guarding ("And now . . . And now . . .") suggest that all the speaker's actions with her Master are repeated variations on this single one: she destroys herself in being "carried . . . away" with and by his ownership, or in using his power. In a paradox characteristic of Western culture, and particularly of the American tradition whose canonized texts so monolithically portray nature as feminine, the female speaker who destroys nature indirectly destroys herself.[15]

The repetition "foe . . . deadly foe" emphasizes the speaker's lack of self-control in her killing. As gun, she directs all antagonism and anger outward, toward the world, rather than toward herself or Him. With a kind of hysteria, the speaker adopts His perspective on allies and enemies; where he hates, she kills. Much the same emphasis and differentiation occur with the repetition of "longer" and "the power to" in the last stanza of this poem:

> Though I than He – may longer live
> He longer must – than I –
> For I have but the power to kill,
> Without – the power to die –

The repetition of the comparative "longer" suggests the speaker's concern with longevity even before we learn that—as inhuman gun— she cannot die. Parallel uses of "longer" and "the power to" stress "must" in the first grouping and "Without" in the second. Together and singly, these words reveal the speaker's desperate frustration: though she "may longer live," he "must" outlive her, she insists in fear that he will not; she has "but" one "power" and is "Without" the greater. The poem concludes with what she cannot do instead of what she can. As the next two lines indicate, she has consigned ultimate power over herself to him. Just as he activates her "Life," he may provide her only possibility for dying. She is "deadly foe" to all others, but does not have "the power to" die. The paradox reveals the trap she is in: having killed her own natural life and ally (the doe) in the desire to speak for him, she will have nothing but another corner, if that, should he cease to "own" her by dying himself; yet this virtual death can only be prevented by her actual death, through his act. In other words, with or without him she in some way dies, and literal death seems preferable to the metaphorical or lasting, conscious one. The power of killing, then, is secondary to the power of dying. With the latter lost (or given away), the former proves of little value. Power in this poem becomes a parody of itself. As heroes from the stature of King Lear to this anonymous speaker of a twenty-four-line lyric have come to recognize, even deadly power over others is as nought in face of the realization that one is powerless to affect one's own living.

Power is at the heart of this poem for its writer as well as its speaker. The speaker fantasizes about a level of destructiveness imaginable only to one who has felt her (or his) potential for explosion but never expressed it. I am so powerful, she in effect says, that my mere smile would emit the fire of Vesuvius; I kill beyond death, and all I value in myself is my capacity to destroy (not the tender qualities of the "Doe" or the connubial sharing of the matrimonial bed). Yet this "Life" of the speaker's anger is too dangerous for her to express on her own, and so she waits with it "In Corners" until someone else will "own" the anger for her, and thereby release her to express herself. By calling them "His" foes and herself "His" possession, she may shoot without guilt or anxiety at what she most dislikes in the world or fears in herself. The dream of expressed power becomes a nightmare, however, as the speaker begins to contemplate the frustration of living only in this limited form. Dickinson's hesitation between "art" and "power" to describe the act of killing sharpens the correlation between her life as poetic speaker and the "Life" of the gun/speaker of the poem. To the extent that the ruling fiction of her life is of life as "Loaded Gun," she must either stand in corners or kill because killing is her only "art," her only form of expression.

In spite of the identification of art and power as forms of action, and art and violence as forms of expression (therefore also of power), the poem makes little sense as strict autobiography. Probably 32 or

33 when she wrote "My Life had stood" (ca. 1863), Dickinson had written hundreds of poems and had made the major decisions of her life. She had become reclusive, had seen a few of her poems in print, and had initiated her correspondence with Higginson; moreover, she had had the assurance as both artist and adult to ignore Higginson's criticism of her work while continuing to correspond with him in spite of his failure to understand her achievement. A biographical reading of "My Life had stood" would mistakenly suggest that the poet was deeply uncomfortable with her art, in spite of her enormous productivity in the preceding five or six years. In the fiction of the poem, either she can say nothing or her speech devastates; she has too much power to touch others without destroying their lives and not enough to control her own.

From a broader perspective, however, it is no cause for wonder that this mind of extraordinary capacity in its life of strict—even though chosen—limitation occasionally felt itself capable of nothing but paralytic stasis or devastation. What writer has not felt blocked and longed to possess in language the power and accuracy of a well-aimed, loaded gun? It would also be no wonder if the poet maintained her initial mood of unholy glee in shooting foes and being owned, therefore killing without responsibility, even when her target was a creature uncomfortably like herself. Dickinson wrote Higginson in 1862 that her poems "relieve" a "palsy" (L 265); perhaps in this poem she is saying they also fulfill a desire to shoot. But the poem does not rest there. Even in creating its fantasy, the poet's mind is larger than her metaphor. The crescendoing violence of the first half of the poem finds no echo in the musing conundrum of its final stanza. Like the concluding couplet of "He fumbles at your Soul," this stanza leaves the speaker and reader suspended in a stillness partly the result of ignorance and partly the result of mature reflection: What *can* happen now? The speaker has played this fantasy to its end, and it does not take her anywhere.

"TO PILE LIKE THUNDER TO IT'S CLOSE"

> To pile like Thunder to it's close
> Then crumble grand away

> While Everything created hid
> This — would be — Poetry —
>
> Or Love — the two coeval come —
> We both and neither prove —
> Experience either and consume —
> For None see God and live —

In "To pile like Thunder" Dickinson again voices her belief that the expression of creativity, or love, or deeply religious experience of any kind involves the release of potentially destructive power. Here, however, instead of being the victim of the power as in "He fumbles," or the anonymous deprived crowd as in "This was a Poet," or the mere instrument of destruction as in "My Life had stood — a Loaded Gun," the poet imagines herself as the entire event: she is not the thunder wielder or bolt or struck object but the act of thunder piling and crumbling while "Everything created" responds. She imagines what it would be like if she *were* the act of poetry, or love, or God.

As stated earlier, according to Dickinson poetry inheres largely in the effect it has on its reader. She wrote to Higginson: "If I read a book [and] it makes my whole body so cold no fire ever can warm me I know *that* is poetry. If I feel physically as if the top of my head were taken off, I know *that* is poetry" (L 342a). This may be true of all major experiences or phenomena. For example, we "know" love by the way it makes us feel; reason does not explain or define it, and no one can learn the effect of the experience before it has occurred; it cannot be taught. The conclusion of Dickinson's poem, however, suggests that one cannot "know" these things at all. The poem links poetry and love with the impossible experience of seeing God, implying that they, like divinity, stand above human knowledge. Poetry and love have all the force of divinity; to know them is to "consume." As in the pagan myth of blind intercourse with Zeus, to see the god's power is in some sense to die. Poetry and love, then, become matters of faith, just as God is. One can only believe they exist, encouraged in the belief by epiphanic glimpses or sensations of their reality and their power. Dickinson articulates what is almost an Emersonian view of the human relation to God in this poem: through the most profound human actions (writing poetry, loving) one unites with the divine Oversoul, and the poet reaches farthest toward the upper range of human power. For Dickinson, however, in contrast to Emerson, the elements of terror and impossibility in this venture remain strong.

"To pile like Thunder" represents the poet as balancing power and vulnerability: the poet wields thunder but will "die" if her creation succeeds. There is a balance as well in the poet's relation to her own art. On the one hand, she is divine creator; on the other, she is as ignorant of her creation as a reader—or, in the analogous act, as one struck unexpectedly by love. She is a poet but also a member of the community of impoverished observors Dickinson writes about in "This was a Poet." Unlike that poem's fabulously wealthy and controlling "Discloser" of "Pictures," this poet does not own the power she wields. Creation is as devastating to her as to anyone else. The metaphor Dickinson uses to portray the relationship of poet and audience or initiating and receiving love in this poem also returns us to the drama of "He fumbles at your Soul." The earlier poem, from the perspective of this later use of "Thunder[bolt]," becomes more a story of the poet responding to the effects of her own creativity than a story of fear: the poet, like any good reader, releases herself to the poem and it transfixes or "scalps" or "peels" her "naked Soul" with its "Thunderbolt." She has both piled "like Thunder" and "hid"; she is forest and wind. The difference between reader and poet, this reading of these poems implies, is that the latter calls out a power that she herself has created, or at least has participated in creating.

The special joy of being ravished by one's own creativity is the subject of another of Dickinson's poems. In "I would not paint – a picture" (505), "Nor would" the speaker "be a Poet" because it is a greater experience to be reader and poet simultaneously. As in "He fumbles at your Soul" and "To pile like Thunder," the metaphor for this merging is implicitly sexual, albeit through the formal guise of legal engagement. The speaker exclaims:

> What would the Dower be,
> Had I the Art to stun myself
> With Bolts of Melody!

Poet and audience are a bridal couple; to read one's own poetry, accept one's own thunderbolts, is to enter into marriage with one's own powerful soul. In its balance of giving and receiving, Emerson's stroke and recoil, poetry feels indistinguishable from love: both demand full engagement and offer ultimate expression or release. Perhaps the speaker's experience is primarily ecstatic rather than terrifying in "I would not paint – a picture" and "To pile like Thunder" because poetry is the explicit subject of these poems. Stunning oneself with "Melody" maintains the suggestion of harmony and civilization that appears only at the beginning of "He fumbles at your Soul." The two poems on poetry may also contain less ambivalence at the prospect of such devastation because their speakers assume or imagine positions of greater control. In "To pile like Thunder" especially, although poet and reader become inseparable and the inevitable effect of being either is to "consume," the poem begins with the fantasy of elemental power and action—piling thunder.

In emphasizing the poet's activity, "To pile like Thunder" also presumes human responsibility for the creation of love. Moreover, the creation of both forces occurs repeatedly: poetry and love "coeval come." Had Dickinson used the past tense, "came," here the line would suggest that both are primal forces of equal longevity, that they were born into the universe simultaneously. With "come," however, Dickinson implies that the birth of one always entails the birth of the other. Repeatedly, for example with the creation of every new poem, love also "comes." The sexual connotation of "coming"—with its literary resonance of both divinity and death—strengthens the identity of poetry, love, and religious epiphany in ecstatic consummation. As in "He fumbles at your Soul" and "Essential Oils – are wrung," suggestively sexual imagery represents an experience of mingled pleasure and pain, anticipation and dread, or just gain and loss: differing elements release themselves and merge, giving way to a universal stillness ("Everything . . . hid," or "Winds hold Forests," or "Ceaseless Rosemary") that perhaps most resembles death. In Renaissance uses of this metaphor, one may "die" several times in a single night; in Dickinson's use, the climax seems more irrevocable. The present tense of "come" with its suggestion of repeated event and the assertion that we do "prove" both poetry and love (at the same time that we prove neither), however, tempers the poem's apparent linking of the pure experience of divinity in any form with abrupt and complete loss of life. Both the poem and love will come again, but they can only be known in the instant of contact and in that instant one also "consume[s]."

The uninflected verb "consume" may further temper the poem's suggestion of ultimate human vulnerability. So far I have read the line "Experience either and consume –"as though the second verb is the threatened effect of the first: if you experience you will (be) consume(d). The two verbs may, however, represent parallel directions: "Experience either and consume (either poetry or love)." Consume, in this reading, specifies what happens when you "experience": to taste of either poetry or love is to devour either. Any taste entails complete consumption because neither gift comes partially; furthermore, experience of either may bring consumption of the other because they are ultimately inseparable. Reading "consume" as a transitive verb also substantiates the human involvement in capturing these experiences and brings that involvement back down to the level of the world. One eats or ingests a poem, as it were; one completely takes the poem in.

As Dickinson's own use of poems in letters suggests, to give poetry is to communicate most intimately, to love. In offering love, however, the poem implies that one also offers death. Death, then, must be the transformational experience that follows consumption or consummation (both possible extensions of "consume") of any kind: sexual union, the communication of love, the devastation that attends any complete relinquishing of the soul to something greater than itself. Perhaps in this poem's analogies Dickinson reveals more clearly than in any other poem the role of creativity in her own life. To be a poet is to love in a kind of absolute way—not to choose a partner or object for reciprocal involvement but to express love fiercely, to cherish the world through power. It is, furthermore, to participate in the divine. The poet does not become God, but the gift of her art is indistinguishable from the revelation of divinity. Although the world has long separated God from poetry, for Dickinson there is no separating poetry from the experience of God. In a sense, poetry provides her access to and her expression of both love and religion.

FOUR

Names and Verbs:
Influences on the Poet's Language

Books are the best things, well used; abused, among the
worst. What is the right use? . . . They are for nothing but
to inspire. I had better never see a book than to be warped
by its attraction clean out of my own orbit, and made a
satellite instead of a system . . . One must be an inventor to
read well.

Ralph Waldo Emerson, "The American Scholar"

THE PRECEDING chapters have examined Dickinson's language
use in individual poems and in the context of her belief in the
power of the written word. In this chapter I present a case for
various stylistic, theoretical, and thematic influences on Dickinson's
writing, examining probable models or sources for the most striking
of her language techniques and ideas. Dickinson read widely and
passionately. By the number of her references to books and quotations
from them, it is evident that the Bible was her best known text—
although, like Melville, she seems to have regarded it more as a
"lexicon" of "certain phenomenal men" and mysteries than as an
orthodox spiritual guide.[1]

Biblical style, in its King James version and as modified by seventeenth-century writers and Americans generally, provided a model
for the extreme compression, parataxis, and disjunction of Dickinson's
style. Contrary to the assumptions generally underlying scripturalism,
however, Dickinson believes both that language is essentially fictitious
or arbitrary and that language's potential for meaning exceeds the
individual's control of it and its application to any single circumstance.
For her, language is simultaneously inadequate and too powerful. It
is, therefore, primarily a tool for delineating moments of epiphany or

change, not the tool of Adamic naming or for inscribing command-
ments in stone; it does not reveal eternal truth. This belief and its
concomitant linguistic tendencies toward fragmentation and emphasis
on the verb rather than the noun find partial support in the work of
two New Englanders, Emerson and Noah Webster. In her fifth letter
to Higginson, the poet claims "[I] never consciously touch a paint,
mixed by another person –" (L 271). Like every poet Dickinson helps
herself to colors, but the mix is unmistakably her own.

THE LANGUAGE OF THE BIBLE

To be familiar with the Bible was as unquestioned a part of nineteenth-
century New England life as eating, and in some minds as necessary
a part. The Bible was a primary text in schools, including Amherst
Academy and Mount Holyoke Female Seminary, where Dickinson
studied, respectively, from the ages of 9 through 16 and for ten
months of her seventeenth year (two terms). Written into the Academy
by-laws was the stipulation that "the instructors should be persons of
good moral character . . . firmly established in the faith of the
Christian religion, the doctrines and duties of which they shall in-
culcate as well by example as precept . . . The Preceptor shall open
and close the school each day with prayer. All the students shall
uniformly attend upon the public worship of God on the sabbath."[2]
Mount Holyoke prided itself on its piety and its conversion of non-
believers, and the Bible heads the list of textbooks circulated by its
principal (*Life* II, 362, n. 19). Thus Dickinson was under considerable
pressure to convert while at Mount Holyoke, and this caused her some
concern. There were other students who, like her, refused to "give up
and become a Christian" (L 23), but she felt herself to be in the erring
minority.[3] Waves of religious revivalism swept New England and
Amherst during Dickinson's girlhood and youth, and all her family
and close friends eventually joined the church. Scripture was common
idiom among them. At the age of 14, for example, in a playful letter
informing her friend Abiah Root that she is not at school this term
and is about to learn to make bread, Dickinson writes (L 8; September
1845):

> So you may imagine me with my sleeves rolled up, mixing
> flour, milk, salaratus, etc., with a deal of grace. I advise you

if you don't know how to make the staff of life to learn with
dispatch. I think I could keep house very comfortably if I knew
how to cook. But as long as I don't, my knowledge of house-
keeping is about of as much use as faith without works, which
you know we are told is dead. Excuse my quoting from the
Scripture, dear Abiah, for it was so handy in this case I couldn't
get along very well without it.

Writers of popular and scholarly literature also apparently "couldn't
get along very well without" quoting or paraphrasing the always
"handy" Bible. For cultural and familial reasons, then, as well as for
her own spiritual and aesthetic ones, Dickinson knew her Bible well.

Although critics frequently refer to the Bible as Dickinson's primary
literary source, discussion has focused on her use of particular biblical
passages, ideas, and myths. Even Johnson's extreme claim that the
poet's "words and phrases . . . are absorbed from the Bible" and "have
passed through the alembic of the King James version of biblical
utterance" retreats at once to note which books the poet quotes most
frequently.[4] Yet the stylistic correspondences of Dickinson's language
to the Bible's are easily isolated and identified.

The language of the Bible is characteristically conjunctive, highly
economical, and often organized in parallel sets or binary pairs, variously thematic, syntactic, and lexical. James Kugel describes the
biblical sentence as "highly parallelistic . . . usually consisting of two
clauses, each clause stripped to a minimum of three or four major
words."[5] For example, the following lines from Dickinson's favorite
gospel author move in terse, heavily conjunctive syntax organized in
repeating sequences and pairs:

> And in them is fulfilled the prophecy of Esaias, which saith,
> By hearing ye shall hear, and shall not understand; and seeing
> ye shall see, and shall not perceive: For this people's heart is
> waxed gross, and *their* ears are dull of hearing, and their eyes
> they have closed; lest at any time they should see with *their*
> eyes, and hear with *their* ears, and should understand with *their*
> heart, and should be converted, and I should heal them. But
> blessed *are* your eyes, for they see: and your ears, for they
> hear.   (Matthew 13:14–16)[6]

The passage begins with balanced pairs of affirmation and denial: ye
shall hear and not understand, and shall see and not perceive. The

sequence then becomes longer, at first through plain addition of evidence: hearts are gross, and ears are dull, and eyes are closed. The *and*s here are symmetrical; the order of the phrases may be changed without altering the meaning of any unit. In the clause beginning "lest at any time they should . . ." the first *and* (linking *see* with *hear*) is simply conjunctive, but the sequence then becomes asymmetrical and misleadingly simple: the *and*s preceding *understand* and *heal* substitute for what should logically be a subordinating conjunction or conjunctive phrase. In rough paraphrase, the sentence might run: "this people's heart, ears, and eyes are closed lest they should see and hear, *which would lead them to* understand, and *which would make it possible that* I heal them." The work of the reader in following this sentence consists in filling in the blanks created by these *and*s. To interpret "and I should heal them," the reader must construct a phrase to replace *and*. Particularly in "and I should heal them," *and* is more disjunctive than conjunctive; it does not belong in the same sequence as "see . . . and hear . . . and understand." Because the parallel sequence of verbs allows the repeated subject (*they*) to be omitted, "should heal" appears parallel to "should understand" and the other verbs preceding it; however, "heal" has a different agent of action (*they* see, *I* heal). The unexpected and syntactically disguised move from *they* to *I* creates a masterful rhetorical effect: Jesus' healing seems as inevitable a result of opening one's eyes as actual seeing is.

The conjunctive parataxis of this passage is complex in its intent and effect.[7] It creates suspense and builds to a surprising but apparently inevitable climax—the perfect combination for representing the simple effectiveness of God's grace if you but "see and hear" it. At its conclusion the passage returns to what Kugel calls the most characteristic biblical mode, the parallel double clause, here repeated so that its figure is doubled twice: in the deleted repetition "but blessed are your eyes . . . and [blessed are] your ears . . ." and within each clause: "your eyes, for they see . . . your ears, for they hear . . ." The extreme compression of Dickinson's poems and that of biblical text are strikingly similar. In both cases the compression stems from frequent use of ellipsis, parallel and short syntactic structures linked paratactically or by simple conjunction, and apposition.

Compact and conjunctive or paratactic syntax occurs in biblical passages less artful than the one just quoted. In Genesis, for example, the story of Babel begins:

And the whole earth was of one language, and of one speech. And it came to pass, as they journeyed from the east, that they found a plain in the land of Shinar; and they dwelt there. And they said one to another, Go to, let us make brick, and burn them thoroughly. And they had brick for stone, and slime had they for mortar. And they said, Go to, let us build us a city and a tower, whose top *may reach* unto heaven; and let us make us a name, lest we be scattered abroad upon the face of the whole earth.   (Genesis 11:1-4)

At the conclusion of a psalm from which Dickinson quotes in a letter, we find:

Keep back thy servant also from presumptuous *sins*; let them not have dominion over me: then shall I be upright, and I shall be innocent from the great transgression. Let the words of my mouth, and the meditation of my heart, be acceptable in thy sight, O Lord, my strength, and my redeemer.   (Psalm 19: 13-14)

First Corinthians contains the more extreme but not atypical passage:

Therefore let no man glory in men. For all things are yours; Whether Paul, or Apollos, or Cephas, or the world, or life, or death, or things present, or things to come; all are yours; And ye are Christ's; and Christ *is* God's.   (1 Corinthians 3:21-23)

In each of these passages there is a rhythmical sameness of tone. Sentences or clauses are short, and connections between them are coordinate rather than subordinate, the most frequently used being *and*. Often there is no linking conjunction or adverb, which causes a momentary lapse in the reader's progress forward. In the lines "Keep back thy servant also from presumptuous *sins*; let them not have dominion over me," for example, the antecedent for "them" is not immediately clear, nor is the role fearfully ascribed to *sins* in the servant's life. "Dominion" in the second clause thematically echoes the opening clause's possessive *"thy* servant" to mark the difference between welcome and unwelcome servitude. But the two are not given equal syntactic weight: God's dominion is presumed and receives merely the possessive "thy"; sin's dominion is feared and can only with God's help be avoided. Linking the sequence of pleas "Keep back thy servant . . . let them not" is the unarticulated assumption that God controls all, but also that any contact with "presumptuous sins" would give them "dominion" over even God's servant. The second clause explains why the plea of the first clause is necessary. As in so many of Dickinson's poems, the logical connecting work of the syntax is left to the reader and is only clear on repeated readings.

Kugel, too, concludes that the point of biblical parallelism is to make the reader discover the connection between "two apparently unrelated parallel utterances."[8] "A is so and B is so" or "A is so and B is not" will make sense as a complete statement only when we understand A and B in relation to each other. We see the similarity between the Bible's and Dickinson's suggestive use of paratactic juxtaposition most clearly in comparing its proverbs to her aphorisms. For example, the proverb "A good name *is* better than precious ointment; and the day of death than the day of one's birth" (Ecclesiastes 7:1) may be interpreted multiply. The reader must imagine and order the array of possible relations between its halves, between ointment and birth, and a good name and death. Remember the similar gap between subjects at the end of Dickinson's poem "He fumbles at your Soul": "Deals – One – imperial –Thunderbolt / That scalps your naked Soul – / When Winds take Forests in their Paws – / The Universe – is still – ." Like the thematic lapses created by parataxis in Dickinson's poems, the blank space (or the space filled with a coordinate conjunction) in biblical texts becomes a focal point of meaning; the text is transparent only when a sentence or clause is isolated, and then the transparency is misleading. The Bible's word, like the New Testament's Word incarnate, carries the greatest meaning when it links apparently discontinuous or separate realms: the literal and the figurative, the personal and the universal, earth and heaven.

Dickinson uses parataxis, repeated conjunctions, and parallel syntax less frequently than the Bible does. Even poems as markedly paratactic and conjunctive, respectively, as "It was not Death" and "My Life had stood" appear sparing in their juxtapositions in comparison with the biblical passages just quoted. Recall the opening lines of the former poem:

> It was not Death, for I stood up,
> And all the Dead, lie down –

It was not Night, for all the Bells
Put out their Tongues, for Noon.

It was not Frost, for on my Flesh
I felt Siroccos – crawl –
Nor Fire – for just my Marble feet
Could keep a Chancel, cool –

And yet, it tasted, like them all . . .   (510)

In these lines we hear biblical sparseness and see an overlapping balanced effect in the repeated "It was not . . . for" clauses and in the qualifying coordinate clauses "for I . . . And all . . ." of lines 1 and 2. Dickinson, however, repeats few besides function words, and her syntax is generally less repetitive than the Bible's: here she repeats the initial structure of balancing clauses only in the first two stanzas, and with considerable variation.[9]

In both biblical prose and Dickinson's verse, the short clauses and rapid progression from one unit to the next give a feeling of inevitability to the narrative's progression. The paratactic linking of phrases "And now we roam . . . And now we hunt . . . And do I smile" of "My Life had stood – a Loaded Gun," like Paul's "All is yours, and ye are Christ's, and Christ is God's," collapses hierarchies of importance and precedence at the same time that it builds toward a climax. Individually every action or conclusion—like every soul or "sparrow" in New Testament theology—holds equal weight, yet all gain their importance from their existence within the whole, be it Dickinson's poem or the Christian God. When the linked actions form a sequence, it seems equally inevitable. In a poem about what the heart asks, Dickinson's speaker seems to move from childhood to old age, although the process of decreasing demands could as easily happen in a single night as in the course of a lifetime:

The Heart asks Pleasure – first –
And then – Excuse from Pain –
And then – those little Anodynes
That deaden suffering –

And then – to go to sleep –
And then – if it should be
The will of it's Inquisitor
The privilege to die –   (536)

Regardless of which time scheme is primary, the sequence (combined with the poem's opening definite article—*The* Heart) implies that no heart continues to ask for pleasure and that every heart will eventually have received enough pain to desire its own death.

SEVENTEENTH-CENTURY STYLISTS

Compression, (disjunctively) conjunctive syntax, and parallelism characterize other modern writing besides Dickinson's—much of it, like hers, influenced by biblical style. Morris Croll describes "baroque" or early to mid-seventeenth-century prose in terms easily convertible to both Dickinson's and the Bible's language. The similarities have a logical basis on both sides: Montaigne, Burton, Pascal, Sir Thomas Browne—Croll's major examples of baroque stylists—were extremely familiar with the Bible and biblical texts, and Browne and George Herbert were among Dickinson's favorite writers. In fact, the resemblance between Dickinson's and Herbert's poetry was so strong that Millicent Todd Bingham published two stanzas of his "Matin Hymn" that Dickinson had copied out and stored with her verses as Dickinson's own.[10] The seventeenth-century sentence, Croll tells us, is "exploded." It uses either loose coordinating conjunctions, or has "no syntactic connectives . . . In fact, it has the appearance of having been disrupted by an explosion within" (209). In both its "loose" and "curt" forms, this style portrays "not a thought, but a mind thinking" (210); the sentence's movement is spiral, not "logical" or straight. Rather than adopting the Bible's balanced parallelism, this style tends to be asymmetrical, to break a parallelism as soon as it has been established: ". . . out of the struggle between a fixed pattern and an energetic forward movement" the baroque style creates its "strong and expressive disproportions" (226).

According to Croll, "curt" baroque prose tends to begin with a complete statement of its idea, much like a proverb in style and tone; the rest of the paragraph or section (or poem) provides new apprehensions or varying imaginative aspects of that logically exhaustive initial statement. Abrupt changes in subject and changes from one mode or style to another (from literal to metaphoric, or from concrete to abstract form) characterize the following imaginative exploration of the kernel idea. Croll gives an example from Browne's *Religio Medici* (which Dickinson owned):

> To see ourselves again, we need not look for Plato's year: every man is not only himself; there have been many Diogenes, and as many Timons, though but few of that name; men are lived over again; the world is now as it was in ages past; there was none then, but there hath been some one since, that parallels him, and is, as it were, his revived self.   (218)

Browne's prose anticipates, and Croll's anatomy describes, the progress of several Dickinson poems: first the aphoristic statement of the theme, then brief varying elaborations of its idea. "Essential Oils – are wrung" announces its theme immediately. Other poems begin: "Life – is what we make it" (698); "Impossibility, like Wine / Exhilarates the Man / Who tastes it; . . ." (838); "Perception of an object costs / Precise the Object's loss – " (1071); "To disappear enhances" (1209); "The Rat is the concisest Tenant" (1356). An even more extreme example of curt baroque prose is Herbert's "Prayer, I," which consists of numerous fragmentary representations of prayer, beginning:

> Prayer, the Church's banquet, Angel's age,
> God's breath in man returning to his birth,
> The soul in paraphrase . . .

and ending:

> Church-bells beyond the stars heart, the soul's blood,
> The land of spices, something understood.

The poem contains no complete predicate. Much of Dickinson's poetry, like baroque poetry and prose, moves by a sequence of "'points' and paradoxes reveal[ing] the energy of a single apprehension in the writer's mind" (218–219).

"Loose" baroque style, usually intermingled with the "curt" style, differs only in its greater use of participals and subordinate conjunctions, according to Croll. Its subordinate conjunctions, however, are used so loosely as to have the effect of coordinate conjunctions: individual clauses maintain great autonomy, and there is no tightly logical or single means of advance from one member to the next. Look, for example, at the Herbert stanzas that Dickinson copied out (stanzas 2 and 3 of Herbert's "Matin Hymn"):

My God, what is a heart?
Silver, or gold, or precious stone,
Or star, or rainbow, or a part
Of all these things, or all of them in one?

My God, what is a heart,
That thou shouldst it so eye, and woo,
Pouring upon it all thy art,
As if that thou hadst nothing else to do?

Although the second of these stanzas is considerably less paratactic than the first, its connectives remain loose. "That" refers back to the preceding (repeated) question "What is a heart," and thus carries the weight of the whole preceding stanza. *Eye, woo,* and *pour* (thy art) may present the same action of God with increasing specificity, or "pouring . . ." may be a less direct, more general action, as its less active (participial) form suggests. Herbert's descriptions of God's actions overlap one another, as do his speculations about the substance of the heart in the previous stanza. Each embedded or branching clause repeats part of a previous idea and leads in a new direction; the progress of the sentence continues to seem spontaneous and to offer multiple directions for interpretation.

Because Dickinson's poetic mode anticipates that of twentieth-century poets, particularly the Modernists with their revived interest in the metaphysical poets, her poetry sounds less strange to the twentieth-century ear than it did to her century's. A glance at Longfellow's verse, which Dickinson greatly admired and referred to frequently, illuminates the gulf she created between her own and her contemporaries' work. This does not mean there were no similarities between her poetry and, for example, Longfellow's; like Dickinson, Longfellow experimented with rhyme, meter, and the rhythms and diction of speech. In "The Jewish Cemetery at Newport" his language is colloquial: he uses relatively simple syntax, leaves sentences incomplete, and uses frequent exclamations and colloquial phrases ("all this moving"). Yet the long lines, the repetitive, highly adjectival phrasing, the heavily right-branching parallel syntax, and the lack of metaphorical complexity give this poem an entirely different character from Dickinson's poetry. The first stanza runs:

How strange it seems! These Hebrews in their graves,
Close by the street of this fair seaport town,

> Silent beside the never-silent waves,
>   At rest in all this moving up and down!

In "My Lost Youth" Longfellow writes in shorter, rhythmically and syntactically looser lines, but the contrast with Dickinson's economy and ellipsis is still striking. The last stanza of this poem follows:

> And Deering's Woods are fresh and fair,
>   And with joy that is almost pain
> My heart goes back to wander there,
> And among the dreams of the days that were,
>   I find my lost youth again.
>   And the strange and beautiful song,
>   The groves are repeating it still:
>   "A boy's will is the wind's will,
> And the thoughts of youth are long, long thoughts."

Longfellow's poems are readily accessible on the levels of narrative and intent as neither Herbert's nor Dickinson's are. His verse, and most nineteenth-century American verse, works through extension and repetition, whereas Dickinson's works through compression and juxtaposition.

THE HYMNS OF ISAAC WATTS

From the Bible and from Herbert's poems and Browne's prose, Dickinson would be familiar with tersely conjunctive syntax, sentences that progress asymmetrically or through apposition and paradox, and paradoxical or cryptically metaphorical rather than extended logical developments of an idea. Closer to home, the psalms and hymns of Isaac Watts, as familiar to many New Englanders as the Bible itself, offered her these same characteristics in a meter she adopted for almost all her poems. Emily's mother, Lavinia Norcross Dickinson, owned *Watts' Hymns,* and the family library housed copies of his *Church Psalmody* and *Psalms, Hymns, and Spiritual Songs of the Reverend Isaac Watts.*[11] Although the poet does not mention Watts by name, she was undoubtedly familiar with several of his hymns, and she quotes from one of them.[12] Her use of hymn meter (often called the common meter) for all but a few metrically experimental poems is widely attributed to her reading, and singing, of Watts.

In addition to being part of the common New England vocabulary of rhythm and verse, Watts may have held special attraction for Dickinson because of his frequent use of irregular rhymes and harsh-sounding phrases (usually involving vocabulary considered neither poetic nor religious), and because of the extraordinary variety of sounds and themes he used within a simple rhythmical frame. [13] Watts's hymn 632, for example, uses a common conjunctive parallelism and irregular rhyme in stanza 5:

> And must my body faint and die?
> And must this soul remove?
> O, for some guardian angel nigh,
> To bear it safe above!

Watts rhymes *men* with *vain, fell* with *miracle, haste* with *test, throne* with *down* (hymns 347, 438, 632, 648), or, in hymn 352 alone, *lies* with *ice, stood* with *God, sea* with *away.* In lines unusually vivid and metaphorical, Watts's hymn 630 uses the polysyllabic "abominable" with an art anticipating Dickinson's. It begins: "My thoughts on awful subjects roll, / Damnation and the dead," then recounts the "horrors" a "guilty soul" imagines on her deathbed:

> Then, swift and dreadful, she descends
> Down to the fiery coast,
> Among abominable fiends,
> Herself a frighted ghost.

> There endless crowds of sinners lie,
> And darkness makes their chains;
> Tortured with keen despair, they cry,
> Yet wait for fiercer pains.

A darkness so tangible it "makes" chains; a soul in herself "dreadful" or in "dreadful" flight; sinners keenly despairing "Yet" waiting for "fiercer pains": these images and ambiguities would appeal to Dickinson's imagination.

Dickinson's own rhythms, loose rhymes, and abbreviated (therefore often cryptic) metaphors of description sound less unusual when placed beside Watts's hymns than when compared with the work of her contemporaries. Listen, for example, to the similarities in meter, rhyme, use of polysyllables to fill a line (her "possibility" and "Cordiality," like Watts's "abominable"), and vivid substantiation of the insubstantial between Watts and Dickinson in a poem she writes on the soul's near escape from death:

> That after Horror – that 'twas *us* –
> That passed the mouldering Pier –
> Just as the Granite Crumb let go –
> Our Savior, by a Hair –
>
> A second more, had dropped too deep
> For Fisherman to plumb –
> The very profile of the Thought
> Puts Recollection numb –
>
> The possibility – to pass
> Without a Moment's Bell –
> Into Conjecture's presence –
> Is like a Face of Steel –
> That suddenly looks into our's
> With a metallic grin –
> The Cordiality of Death –
> Who drills his Welcome in –   (286)

Like Watts, Dickinson uses common meter here; lines coincide with clause or phrase boundaries, and stanzas form complete syntactic and metaphorical units; abstractions gain concrete properties (his darkness forms chains; her thought has a profile); and rhyme is consistent but not perfect (note her *Pier* with *Hair, Bell* with *Steel*). Dickinson's poem compacts more metaphors, and her primary metaphor for the soul's meeting with death is far more chilling than Watts's, but her familiarity with his dramatic and loosely irregular verse may have cleared a way for Dickinson to her own extraordinary poems.

THE AMERICAN PLAIN STYLE

In a still broader sense of influence, the American idiom itself, in both its literary and daily forms, may have contributed to Dickinson's use of a style that is biblical in origin.[14] By the mid-nineteenth century Puritan "plain style" had become the language of self-expression, the trusted idiom in America, although—or perhaps because—it had lost its bolstering doctrinal and political contexts. According to Perry Miller's "An American Language," the plain style's demand that one speak from personal knowledge and as comprehensibly as possible made it the natural mode of discourse for a people living "in the wilderness" and, by the late eighteenth century, attempting to form a democracy.[15] All American writers, he claims, have had to deal with the consequences of this wholesale adoption of the principles and techniques of plain style (214). Because of its pervasiveness, Dickinson would inevitably have used language to some extent within its dictates. For epistemological reasons also, Dickinson may have felt some affinity for this style. Miller describes the plain style as inherently "defiant"—a style that both proclaims authority for the word and places the word's authority in individuals' articulate examinations of the truth; the style encourages practical discourse on theoretical or spiritual truths. Hence, it can as easily be turned against the idea of an authoritative God as it can be used to support that idea. Authority of language lies with the "plainest" (that is, apparently most artless yet still most commanding) speaker. The Puritans kept the style's implicit defiance in check by subordinating their word to God's Word; the latter was the law which theirs attempted to interpret and reflect. Emerson, Miller claims, partially maintained this check on defiance through his romantic belief in Nature as the origin of language, while Thoreau released the defiance of this style in his prose, "glory[ing] in his participation in the community of sin" (226).

More covertly than Thoreau, Dickinson does the same. Her very disguise of defiance, however, may also stem in part from inherent characteristics of the plain style, which demands the simplicity reflected in its name but paradoxically also a kind of reticence that may prevent its complete message from being articulated. Ideally, the plain speaker "convey[s] the emphasis, the hesitancies, the searchings of language as it is spoken" (232); plainness lies in the apparent artlessness of the speaker's or writer's use of the word. Partly as a consequence, writers in the plain style leave much unsaid, and they claim that their discourse says even less than it does. Using words sparingly leaves much to implication, and making modest claims for a text may disguise the authority its author in fact feels. Thus the plain style frequently underplays its own importance and seriousness;[16] even when it most anarchically expresses the perception of the individual, it maintains the guise of saying little, and that only matter-of-factly.

Hence, while speaking "plain" truth, an individual may confound every doctrine that the Puritans held true and believed the plain style must express. As Miller puts it: "The forthright method [plain style] proved to be . . . the most subversive power that the wicked could invoke against those generalities it had, long ago, been designed to protect" (220). Through reticence, indirection, and disguised claims for the authority of her word, Dickinson manipulates characteristics of the plain use of language in poetry that contradict Puritan convictions about the individual's relation to God and His Word. The style that affirms God's truth for the Puritans, and denies that God's power is the only good (while still celebrating it) for Thoreau, becomes ironic with Dickinson: while appearing to affirm or naively question, she denies the trustworthiness of any superhuman power.

Although biblical style, particularly in its King James translation, has been widely influential, the Bible has influenced ideas of language at least as profoundly as it has actual language use. In the Bible, language is authority: "And God said, Let there be light: and there was light" (Genesis 1:3); or as John redescribes this moment: "In the beginning was the Word, and the Word was with God, and the Word was God" (John 1:1). Adam's name giving is a second creation; he brings into the human world of language what God's Word has made. For Moses, the word is law to be preserved in stone. Language in all these cases is transparent; it has an immediate relation to things and principles and reflects their essential nature. By knowing the proper names, one may know the world. For American Puritans, this idea of language led to the belief that an individual's power to articulate depended on his or her spiritual condition. Those who had been converted were expected to manifest their condition of grace and to demonstrate their obedience to God through the quality of their understanding as represented in their use of words. What one knew one could, and must, express.

This notion of language depended on the inherent "truth" of the word; no word could be ambiguous or ironic and still manifest the essential truth of God. By the same logic, lying—that is, abusing the word by distorting or obscuring its meaning—diminished a person's ability to know the world and, through it, God. Hence, lying was a grave sin. William Ames preached that "the frequent use of obscene speeches seemeth to be more hurtful to piety, than the simple act of fornication," while proper or "plainly" eloquent speech ideally would be so powerful "that an unbeliever comming into the Congregation of the faithful . . . ought to be affected, and as it were digged through with the very hearing of the Word, that he may give glory to God."[17] According to this philosophy, the most economical style is also the most efficacious. Regardless of the speaker's immediate audience, all language is directed ultimately to God, and "God's Altar needs not our pollishings," as the compilers of the 1639 preface to the *Bay Psalm Book* proclaim. Flourishes at worst confuse meaning, but even at best they hinder a statement's force: "The efficacy of the Holy Spirit doth more clearly appear in a naked simplicity of words, then in elegance and neatness . . . So much affectation as appeares, so much efficacy and authority is lost."[18] Authority and utility are the twin supports of this system.

The idea that language should adequately define and name things had a broad secular base as well in nineteenth-century America. In his essays "On Candor" and "On Language," James Fenimore Cooper lists an increasing lack of directness in expression as one of the greatest flaws of American English.[19] Fearful of the vulgarizing effect of democracy even while he extols its virtues, Cooper laments that Americans pervert the significance of words by using them inappropriately and inexactly. The original meaning of a word is its proper meaning; to transfer its use to a different context or to use it more broadly constitutes a misuse of the word, not to mention a "misapprehension of the real circumstances under which we live" (112). Believing that a word may be misused and thus cause a "misapprehension of the real circumstances" of life presupposes that the proper use of language leads to accurate or proper apprehension of the world. Language delineates and labels the facts of nature. The word Cooper chooses as an example reveals the social roots of his anxiety about language change: the broadening misuse of the word "gentleman" does not make a tramp into a gentleman, he insists; it only weakens the proper meaning of the word and confuses the "natural" distinctions between types of men. Without saying so explicitly, and like the Puritans, Cooper would have language be unironical, immediately and unambiguously connected to the equally "plain" facts of the world.

It is in her attitude toward language and toward communication itself as much as in her characteristic manipulations of the word that Dickinson differs from her contemporaries and predecessors who wrote in plain style. Like them, she emphasizes the bare force of the word, eschewing elaborate syntax, modifiers, and extended conceits. Like them, she tends to stress the word's direct mediation between the individual and the world (for them, God). Like them, but to an unusual extreme, she makes small claims for her writing: her poems are "a letter to the World"; she is often a girl, or (like) a daisy, bird, spider, or gnat. Even when she has volcanic power, she generally appears harmless and unimportant: "A meditative spot – / An acre for a Bird to choose / Would be the General thought –" (1677). Dickinson, however, senses a different need for both plainness and reticence from those who believe in a natural or divine law of language. The word has two faces for her. Its effect may be epiphanic and it may come to her as a "gift," revealing "That portion of the Vision" she could not find without the help of "Cherubim" (1126). This is the language of poetry, of pure communication, "Like signal esoteric sips / Of the communion Wine" (1452), or a "word of Gold" (430). At other times the word is all but meaningless—an "Opinion" (797), an empty term. In a letter to Bowles she writes: "The old words are *numb* – and there *a'nt* any *new* ones – Brooks – are useless – in *Freshet- time* –" (L 252). Her trick as poet is to make the old words new. To do this, she trusts "Philology," not God or Nature, and when she succeeds in doing this she feels that she has been lucky.

To Dickinson's mind, success in speaking plainly, in creating a word "that breathes" (1651), does not prove spiritual salvation or make her a candidate for fame, partly because her sense of moral superiority depends on overthrowing the notion that God or the world can save her. The economical use of the words of ordinary life gives language its power. Speaking indirectly or subversively disguises the poet's usurpation of moral judgment from divine or human law, and thus saves her to speak again. As Perry Miller suggests, in Dickinson's poetry the pull between plainness and reticence subverts the whole idea of plainness. Because her meanings are not plain, they cannot be expressed plainly despite her use of simple words; her plainest speech *is* that of indirection.

As this conception of language implies, for Dickinson there is no stable relation between spiritual truth, the facts of existence, and the terms of language. Names are not adequate to things, and the function of language is not primarily to name. Things are perceived and understood through their relations to the rest of the world and by the process of cumulative, even contradictory, definition rather than by categorization or labeling. Dickinson has greater affinity with the lexicographer, the scientist of language seeking to clarify each word's various meanings, than she does with the Romantic *Ur*-poet Adam. Her language stresses the relation between object and its effects or relations in an active world; meaning, for her, is not fixed by rules or even by her own previous perception of the world. The principles of Dickinson's world do not have to do with immutable properties and distinctions.

Dickinson manifests her belief in the flux or instability of relationship in the narratives of her poems more obviously than in her use of language. For example, the figures of her poems often change positions relative to each other, or prove to be undifferentiable rather than separate identities. In "The Moon is distant from the Sea," first "She" is the moon and "He" the water, then she becomes "the distant Sea –" and his are the ordering "Amber Hands –" of light (429); the "single Hound" attending the Soul proves to be "It's own identity." (822); in an early poem, she and her playmate Tim turn out to be "I – 'Tim' – and – Me!" (196). In a late poem, desired object, self, and "Messenger" are indistinguishable in both their presence and their absence; in a mockery of simplicity, all have the same name:

> We send the Wave to find the Wave –
> An Errand so divine,
> The Messenger enamored too,
> Forgetting to return,
> We make the wise distinction still,
> Soever made in vain,
> The sagest time to dam the sea is when the sea is gone –
>   (1604)

Although this poem may be read as an elaboration of a truism—that one must give to receive, or that some losses cannot be prevented— it also ironically suggests that distinguishing present and absent sea (loved "Wave" from our own) is "vain." The "wise distinction" persists in failing to recognize the absurdity of damming what is not there and cannot be kept anyway. We attempt to conserve only what we have already lost.

Similarly, in "The Sea said 'Come' to the Brook" (1210), the grown Brook takes the same form and title as the Sea that wanted to keep it small, as if to prove that the existence of one sea does not prevent the growth of innumerable physically indistinguishable others. In the last stanza it is not immediately clear which "Sea" is which:[20]

The Sea said "Go" to the Sea –
The Sea said "I am he
You cherished" – "Learned Waters –
Wisdom is stale – to Me"

In countless other poems, unspecified and multiply referential "it" or "this" is as meaningful a subject for speculation as any clearly delineated event or object. Metaphor serves as the primary tool of definition and explanation because it allows for the greatest flexibility in its reference to fact.

EMERSON'S THEORIES OF LANGUAGE

To the extent that language does reflect the world for Dickinson, her conception of language is closer to Emerson's than to the Puritans'. The Amherst poet was familiar with the Concord poet's works from at least 1850 on. In that year, she received "a beautiful copy" of Emerson's 1847 *Poems* (L 30). In 1857 Emerson lectured in Amherst, eating and sleeping at the Evergreens, where Emily may have joined Austin and Sue in entertaining him. She told Sue that he seemed "as if he had come from where dreams are born" (*Life* II, 468). In 1876 the poet gave Mrs. Higginson a copy of *Representative Men*—"a little Granite Book you can lean upon" (L 481). She also quotes or paraphrases five of Emerson's poems in her letters and poems, most notably his "Bacchus" in her "I taste a liquor never brewed" (214) and "The Snow Storm" in her "It sifts from Leaden Sieves" (311).[21]

Emerson writes at length of language as an ideal system of meaning in his essays "Nature" and "The Poet." His use of language in his own prose, however, contradicts his theories. In theory, Emerson's notion of language stems from Puritan ideas of the word as an extension of the Oversoul, or God. For him, as for the Puritans, language in its pristine or original state is transparent: "Words are signs of natural facts."[22] Similarly, for Emerson, speech that derives from an accurate perception of nature "is at once a commanding certificate that he who employs it is a man in alliance with truth and God" (*Works* I, 36). In its ideal form, language translates and interprets spiritual truths as for the Puritans, but now through the mediation of nature. Because of this mediation, at its plainest and most authoritative language is "picturesque"; it is "poetry." Words stand for (name, signify) facts of nature, which are in turn "emblematic" of spiritual facts. Language, then, is both referential (transparently reflective of nature) and metaphorical. Human language derives from nature, which is in turn "the organ through which the universal spirit speaks to the individual" (*Works* I, 66). Ideally there would be a one-to-one correspondence between the facts of nature, the words of speech, and the facts of the spirit; that is, human language would exactly reproduce the language of the universe.

Because of its base in nature, according to Emerson, language is also both fixed or universal and constantly undergoing change. The laws of the spirit or Oversoul, the ultimate referent of language, do not change, but their forms in nature may. Natural objects "furnish man with the dictionary and grammar of his municipal speech" (*Works* I, 37); when these objects are altered so are the meanings of our language. Each age requires its own interpreter or poet to keep language true to nature (and to read nature's new forms), but each interpreter expresses the same truths, albeit in different forms. Because the laws of nature are fixed, the primary act of language making is naming and the principle word is the noun. Emerson traces the development of language through that of the individual: "Children and savages use only nouns or names of things, which they convert into verbs and apply to analogous mental acts"—a necessary stage in language making, he implies, but a departure from language as pure poetry (*Works* I, 32). Verbs provide, as it were, the transitional form in the desired transformation of language from directly referential (noun to fact) to symbolic (noun to spiritual fact). Language translates perceived nature into human speech and thereby assists in the transformation of nature into spirit. It is not itself stable, but it leads from the world of nameable things to the sphere of immutable spirit.

Emerson never develops the implications of this philosophy for the use of a particular syntax or parts of speech. Were he to do so, the poet or premier language user would logically be Adamic, a pronouncer of names. The ceaseless contradictions and qualifications of Emerson's prose, however, suggest otherwise. Although he preaches about natural laws, he sees nothing but change, and he bases all knowledge and all language on what may be seen (the inner eye interpreting through the outer). While at one minute in "Self-Reliance" he commandingly and absolutely propounds: "Trust thyself: every heart vibrates to that iron string" or "Whoso would be a man must be a nonconformist," in the next he questions: "Suppose you should contradict yourself; what then?" (*Works* I, 47, 50). In a longer passage from the same essay, Emerson characteristically combines highly embedded syntax replete with parallel modifiers and self-referring phrases with paratactically juxtaposed aphorisms as pithy as any that Dickinson coins: "In this pleasing contrite wood-life which God allows me, let me record day by day my honest thought without prospect or retrospect, and, I cannot doubt, it will be found symmetrical though I mean it not and see it not. My book should smell of pines and resound with the hum of insects. The swallow over my window should interweave that thread or straw he carries in his bill into my web also. We pass for what we are. Character teaches above our wills" (*Works* I, 58). Emerson's essays move by associative elaboration of a central idea—often first presented in metaphorical form—not by formal, logical stages or steps. He uses language as if its meaning were less certain or clear than he describes it as being.

Certainly Dickinson recreates the full force of Emerson's perception that all nature, and thus all language, is in constant "flux" in her definition of nouns. Recall, for example, her use of repeated verbs and restrictive clauses in her definition poems: "Revolution is the Pod / Systems rattle from / When the Winds of Will are stirred" (1082); "Escape" is "the Basket / In which the Heart is caught / When down some awful Battlement / The rest of Life is dropt –" (1347); or "Bloom – is Result –" of a process requiring some thing or someone "To pack the Bud – oppose the Worm – / Obtain it's right of Dew – / Adjust the Heat – elude the Wind – / Escape the prowling Bee / [and] Great Nature not to disappoint . . ." (1058). To repeat earlier and more extreme examples, the love "diviner" than that "a Life can show Below" can only be defined by its cumulative acts and effects. In this poem's final stanza, the subject-noun is almost lost in the barrage of its verbs:

> 'Tis this – invites – appalls – endows –
> Flits – glimmers – proves – dissolves –
> Returns – suggests – convicts – enchants –
> Then – flings in Paradise –   (673)

Similarly, Dickinson defines the nominalized verb "saved" by its relation to the act or art of saving: "The Province of the Saved / Should be the Art – To save – " (539). An abstraction, like an object, stems from or stimulates action, and hence it can be known. Ernest Fenollosa, a later pupil of Emerson's, articulates the philosophy that seems to underlie Dickinson's definitions: "Fancy picking up a man and telling him that he is a noun, a dead thing rather than a bundle of functions! A 'part of speech' is what it does . . . one part of speech acts for another . . . 'Farmer' and 'rice' are mere hard terms which define the extremes of the pounding. But in themselves, apart from this sentence-function, they are naturally verbs. The farmer is one who tills the ground, and the rice is a plant which grows in a special way . . . a noun is originally 'that which does something,' that which performs the verbal action."[23] By Fenollosa's logic, land apart from their "sentence-function," Dickinson's action-oriented nouns are "naturally verbs."

Dickinson's poems typically conceptualize action instead of presenting it, or they make the action itself conceptual, epistemological. Even in poems about action or change in nature ("A Route of Evanescence" or "Further in Summer than the Birds"), the poet emphasizes process, causality, and relationship more than temporal acts; the flight of her hummingbird receives its effect from reflected light and the bush it touches. The poem is full of action, but there is only one verb (*Adjusts*):

> A Route of Evanescence
> With a revolving Wheel –
> A Resonance of Emerald –
> A Rush of Cochineal –
> And every Blossom on the Bush
> Adjusts it's tumbled Head –
> The mail from Tunis, probably,
> An easy Morning's Ride –   (1463)

Revolving, Resonance, Rush, tumbled, and *Ride* refer to aspects of the bird's movement but do not present it. The poet's use of nouns and participial adjectives suggests that the bird flies so fast and so effortlessly that the act itself cannot be perceived; we know the act by what it touches and by what we can surmise ("the mail from Tunis").

For Emerson, the whole end of nature is to be interpreted; things are "characters" to be read, and "every object rightly seen, unlocks a new faculty of the soul"; language and the world and language and the soul are one (*Works* I, 31, 36, 41). For Dickinson, nature is not transparent and language is not an organic adjunct (or reflected image) of its processes. We "consign" words to language instead of allegorically perceiving them in nature's great poem. As though in response to Emerson's maxim that "Words are signs of natural fact," Dickinson finds language's greatest power in abstraction, in what cannot be found in nature. "Dont you know that 'No' is the wildest word we consign to Language?" (L 562), she questions; and her "Essential Oils" of meaning are "wrung," "not expressed by Suns – alone –". To enliven language, this poet makes it less instead of more natural; she distorts grammar, inverts syntax, and represents words as produced or conventional units which she can reproduce for her own purposes. Powerful words are blades, swords, and distilled attar—things created by human civilization for human use. In their less powerful aspect, words are arbitrary labels and may be tossed aside: "If the Bird and the Farmer – deem it [a tree] a 'Pine' – / The Opinion will do – for them –" (797).

Emerson expresses the idea that language is inadequate and primarily conventional (not organic) in the ceaseless reexaminations and shifting balances of his prose and in his numerous references to the fallen state of humanity and language in the contemporary world. Dickinson holds the same belief but does not find it a reason to despair. The impermanence of meaning and language liberates her to speak as she might not otherwise dare. Emerson's search for meaning is directed toward nature: his poet is always in part the scribe of what he sees. Dickinson's search most often occurs within "Philology" (1126, 1651), not nature. Her dictionary is her "companion," and she ranges freely in her explorations of meaning there.

NOAH WEBSTER AND LEXICOGRAPHY

Dickinson may have found support for her semantic emphasis on the verb or change and for her belief in the constant changes of language in her family dictionary. Temperamentally and philosophically, she was suited to lexicography. Unlike understanding that stems from archetypes or symbols, lexical understanding works from context and always provides alternative shades or directions of meaning. Lexicography encouraged both Dickinson's scientific and her fanciful tendencies: speculating on the connections of a word's various definitions or possible etymologies might lead to the profound, or it might lead to the ludicrous.

Dickinson may also have felt a special affinity for the lexicographer Noah Webster. In opposition to almost all grammarians and philologists of his day, Webster was convinced that language stems etymologically from verbs, not from nouns. In an introductory essay to his 1841 *American Dictionary of the English Language,* Webster theorizes that the "ordinary sense" of all words in any language may be expressed by thirty or forty verbs and that these radical verbs originate as modifications of the primary sense "to move."[24] These verbs are then modified into the "appropriate" or "customary" significations that we now recognize as entries in our modern dictionaries. The "principal radix" of a family of words may be a noun or an adjective instead of a verb (as *just* is the radix of *justice* and *justly*); that primary word, however, would always theoretically be traceable back to a verb (as Webster traces *just* back to "setting, erecting" and the adjective *warm* to Latin *ferveo*—"I boil"). Webster states in another essay: "Motion, action, is, beyond all controversy, the principal source of words."[25]

Given Dickinson's interest in language and in her dictionary (an 1844 reprint of Webster's 1841 edition), there can be little doubt that she read Webster's introductory essay. In 1862 she wrote Higginson that "for several years, my Lexicon – was my only companion –" (L 261), and she speaks in a poem of "Easing my famine / At my Lexicon –" (728). Even taking hyperbolic self-posing into account, we can assume that the young poet spent a lot of time reading her dictionary. A family connection between the Dickinsons and the Websters may also have encouraged her interest in the family dictionary. Webster lived in Amherst from 1812 to 1822 and served with the poet's grandfather on the first Board of Trustees for Amherst Academy; Emily Dickinson later attended the Academy with the lexicographer's granddaughter, Emily Fowler. Although she may not have been influenced by Webster's theory, Dickinson would at least have found scholarly support there for her own probably unarticulated interest in the verb's role in meaning.

NINETEENTH-CENTURY WOMEN WRITERS

Dickinson was influenced in establishing the techniques of her style by writing which states or implies both that language is primarily an instrument of naming and that language primarily expresses the boundaries of motion, of interactive meaning. Although it is not the focus of this study, Dickinson's use of narrative is also an element of her style. The poet tends to tell a story in her poems, to present ideas or feeling through a plot. The Bible's use of parables—in fact, the Bible itself as an encyclopedia of stories—may have encouraged her propensity to write in tales. Her plots, however, resemble those of popular writers of the period, particularly women writers, suggesting that they may well have influenced this aspect of her style. Certainly Dickinson's most common plot closely resembles the base plot of several women writers.

The Dickinson family subscribed to *The Atlantic Monthly, Harper's New Monthly Magazine,* and *Scribner's Monthly* along with *The Springfield Republican* and two other newspapers—all of which published at least occasional current fiction, poetry, or literary criticism. Emily, Lavinia, Austin, Sue and their friends also bought books on a regular basis and exchanged them with one another. The poet's letters are full of references to what recently published story or book she is reading or that someone has recommended that she read. Although the most frequently repeated references are to authors famous at the time and now (Emerson, Longfellow, both the Brownings, Eliot, and so on), the poet also speaks highly of a number of American women writers, mostly less well known at present: among others, these include Helen Hunt Jackson, Harriet Beecher Stowe, Rebecca Harding Davis, Francis Prescott Spofford, Elizabeth Stuart Phelps, and Marcella Bute Smedley. In a letter of her early twenties (L 85; 1852), for example, Dickinson writes Sue how "small" her "catalogue" of reading has been of late and then goes on:

> I have just read three little books, not great, not thrilling – but sweet and true. "The Light in the Valley" [a memorial of Mary Elizabeth Stirling, who died a few months previously], "Only" [by Matilda Anne Mackarness] and A "House upon a Rock" [also by Mackarness] – I know you would love them all – yet they dont *bewitch* me any. There are no walks in the wood – no low and earnest voices, no moonlight, nor stolen love, but pure little lives, loving God, and their parents, and obeying the laws of the land; . . . I have the promise of "Alton Lock" [by Charles Kingsley] – a certain book, called "Olive," [by Dinah Maria Craik] and the "Head of a Family," [also by Craik] which was what Mattie named to you.

Dickinson's debt to British women authors as role models is much greater than her debt to Americans, but in terms of plot her response to the two groups is largely indistinguishable. Gilbert and Gubar attribute not only her primary romantic plot but also the forms of her daily life to Dickinson's familiarity with the plots of British and American women's novels and poetry: "The fictional shape Dickinson gave her life was a gothic and romantic one, not just (or even primarily) because of the family 'rhetoric' of exaggeration but because the gothic/romantic mode was so frequently employed by all the women writers whom this poet admired more than almost any other literary artists." In her poems, they argue, she articulates variously the details of the plot she has constructed for her reclusive and eccentric life.[26]

The most common plot of Dickinson's poems involves a speaker who is the victim of some monstrous power, usually ambiguously sexual or romantic and usually specifically male. Several poems involve courtship (about which the speaker is ambivalent). For example, death is a courteous gentleman who "kindly stopped for me –" (712) or "the supple Suitor / That wins at last –", bearing his bride away to "Kinsmen as divulgeless / As throngs of Down –" or, in another variant, "as responsive / As Porcelain." (1445). A bee and rose act out the drama of courtship in a number of poems; for example, in "A Bee his burnished Carriage / Drove boldly to a Rose –", she "received his visit / With frank tranquility" and then, as he flees, "Remained for her – of rapture / But the humility." (1339). Another poem (239) seems to give the withholding lover both feminine and (implicitly) masculine roles; in the middle of the poem, "Heaven" is first a seductress but then a Conjuror—a term usually reserved for male magicians:

> Her teasing Purples – Afternoons –
> The credulous – decoy –
> Enamored – of the Conjuror –
> That spurned us – Yesterday!

Heaven teases without giving what she promises and, in what Dickinson usually makes the masculine role, spurns the already enamored. "I cannot live with You" (640), like any number of poems written to "you" or "him," rests on the same premise as "'Heaven' – is what I cannot reach!" (239): relationship here is impossible (except in the cases where it is not desired, as with death) and so the speaker is left with "that White Sustenance – / Despair –".

Haunted houses or ghosts appear in several poems, the most famous of which are well known: "One need not be a Chamber – to be Haunted," with its gothic chase through an "Abbey" and with "Assassin hid in our Apartment" (670); and "The Soul has Bandaged moments," where a "ghastly Fright come[s] up / And stop[s] to look at her –" (512). Ghosts appear as everything from "Eternity's Acquaintances" (892) to the "Emerald Ghost –" of a storm that cannot be shut out in "There came a Wind like a Bugle" (1593), and figures in these and other poems are frequently haunted.[27] Dickinson once wrote to Higginson that "Nature is a Haunted House – but Art – a House that tries to be haunted" (L 459a). Gilbert and Gubar claim that this comment's "frank admission of dependence upon [gothic] metaphors . . . tells us that the self-hauntings of (female) gothic fiction are in Dickinson's view essential to (female) art."[28] At the very least, the metaphor shows Dickinson's conscious and theatrical use of popular gothic and domestic metaphor.

In most of Dickinson's plots the speaker feels herself besieged or unjustly tormented. One might speculate, of course, that Dickinson writes of suitors, unrequited love, and goblins or specters because these are her primary day-to-day concerns, but this seems unlikely. What we know of her life suggests rather that these story elements are a literary coin she trades in to give her thoughts currency and drama. The poet's twisting and even mockery of the stock gothic plot in several poems (for example, where ghosts are not the "superior spectre" one need fear; 670) also suggest its distance from the larger concerns of her life. She does not live as a heroine and probably does not believe that heroines as such exist, but she knows how to dress her speakers, and to some extent her public self, in that garb.

In her study of nineteenth-century American women poets, Cheryl Walker accumulates evidence that the commonly held nineteenth-century stereotype of the poetess also provided material for Dickinson's themes and plots and may have contributed to the molding of her life (especially her reclusiveness, dressing in white, and repeated assertion of extreme sensitivity). Focusing on the expressions of feeling that the pose of poetess invites, Walker sees less irony in Dickinson's manipulation of that common plot than I do. The poet assumed a role in and out of her poems, Walker argues, partly for convenience, as protective camouflage, but partly because the role fit, and perhaps also because the paucity of roles for a woman poet left her relatively little choice: "Sometimes it is hard to distinguish the true feelings of these women poets from those dictated by the role they assumed to satisfy public expectations. For a woman like Dickinson the sense of difference from others, the intense feelings, were certainly real. But it is also important to remember that one's self-conception is determined in part by the social vocabulary of one's culture. Still, the poetess was more than a social norm. She was an accessible image for a literary self." According to Walker, Dickinson's frequent reference to or use in her poems of "intense feeling, the ambivalence toward power, the fascination with death, the forbidden lover and secret sorrow"—all major features of expression and plot in the "women's tradition" in poetry—mark her familiarity with this tradition if not its influence on her. Although her language itself (and thus ultimately the poetry) is at great variance from that of her contemporary female and male poets—Walker herself admits that the poet "certainly . . . ignored [this tradition's] stylistic conventions"—Dickinson's topics and sentiments are often indistinguishable from those of her sister poets.[29]

Judging by a contemporary writer's characterization of typical feminine and masculine styles, Dickinson shares more with the latter than with the former. Mary Abigail Dodge, whose sketches Dickinson almost certainly read in the *Atlantic Monthly* in the late 1850s and 1860s and who chose her pen name "Gail Hamilton" because it allowed her to write with a "sexually indeterminate pen," brags of her ability to keep her gender unknown by demonstrating her mastery of both masculine and feminine styles:

> I inform you that I could easily deceive you, if I chose. There is about my serious style a vigor of thought, a comprehensiveness of view, a closeness of logic, and a terseness of diction, commonly supposed to pertain only to the stronger sex. Not wanting in a certain fanciful sprightliness which is the peculiar grace of woman, it possesses also, in large measure, that concentrativeness which is deemed the peculiar strength of man. Where an ordinary woman will leave the beaten track, wandering in a thousand little by-ways of her own,—flowery and beautiful, it is true, and leading her airy feet to "sunny spots of greenery" and the gleam of golden apples, but keeping her not less surely from the goal,—I march straight on, turning neither to the right hand nor to the left, beguiled into no side-issues, discussing no collateral question, but with keen eye and

strong hand aiming right at the heart of my theme. Judge thus of the stern severity of my virtue.[30]

When writing of women's digressiveness, Hamilton's prose becomes every bit as "flowery" and "airy" as that of the writers she describes. This sentence uses embedded and parallel descriptive clauses, repeated right-branching constructions, and a profusion of adjectives. The style of the "stronger sex," in contrast, is to the point, as typified by the first two and last sentences above. More than Hamilton, Dickinson writes with what might in her age be called a "masculine" "terseness of diction" and "concentrativeness." Although the speech of the poems may resemble women's more than men's speech, the poems' language does not for the most part resemble nineteenth-century women's written language, especially prose. Hamilton openly disproves the accuracy of her stereotypes of masculine and feminine writing by combining what she considers the best features of both in her own prose. Nonetheless, the stereotypes basically hold as descriptions of nineteenth-century prose. American women's writing did tend to be more adjectival, "flowery," and digressive than men's writing—although a twentieth-century reader of popular nineteenth-century men's writing might well describe it using the same adjectives. What Dickinson takes from this writing is its indirection (leaving the straight "beaten track" for a more ambiguous goal), its primary story elements, and its feeling—not its form.

The claims of influence on the work of any writer must be tenuous. My purpose here has not been to argue that Dickinson writes as she does *because* of her familiarity with the Bible, or with Emerson's writing and philosophy, or with Webster's theory of the origins of language, or because of any other sources. Rather, I present this chapter's evidence as a way of reiterating that all language has a supporting context. The syntactic, structural, semantic, and narrative aspects of Dickinson's poems echo writers and texts the poet knew well. She did not manufacture her style out of thin air any more than she lifted it full blown from other writers' pages. Her seclusion from the world was not, in short, a seclusion from language. In delineating stylistic similarities, I have described some of the affinities between Dickinson and the writers who provide the closest models for her language use. In the following chapter I explore theoretical answers as to why Dickinson may have chosen these strategies of language manipulation as the basis of her style.

FIVE

The Consent of Language and the Woman Poet

> For masterpieces are not single and solitary births; they are
> the outcome of many years of thinking in common, of
> thinking by the body of the people, so that the experience
> of the mass is behind the single voice . . . For we think
> back through our mothers if we are women. It is useless to
> go to the great men writers for help, however much one
> may go to them for pleasure. Lamb, Browne, Thackeray,
> Newman, Sterne, Dickens, De Quincey—whoever it may
> be—never helped a woman yet, though she may have learnt
> a few tricks of them and adapted them to her use.
>
> Virginia Woolf, *A Room of One's Own*

IN PREVIOUS CHAPTERS I have characterized Dickinson's language use from the biographical perspective of her intent in communicating with an audience, from the analytical perspective of interpretive linguistics, and from the historical perspective of stylistic influence. Together, these views reveal that, contrary to earlier prevailing beliefs about this reclusive poet, Dickinson means to communicate through her poems. Moreover, her language use, however peculiar, is not unique either in most of its particulars or in its design. Nonetheless, the voice of Dickinson's poetry is uniquely her own in the extremity and compression of its various borrowed techniques, in the density of its metaphorical and metonymic predications, and in its overall disruptiveness.

Disruption is a conscious strategy of Dickinson's poetry, and the primary strategy that differentiates her work from what are otherwise its closest models. For example, George Herbert's poetry, like Dickinson's, is characterized by structural and syntactic compression, intensely personal questioning, paratactic immediacy and impatience, and direct address to an audience (usually God). Both poets could be said to write in the Christian tradition of combined pragmatic and mystical self-examination, a tradition of intimate conversation with the soul through meditations addressed to God (for Dickinson, most often to an unnamed Him). Yet neither Herbert's poetry nor this Christian tradition contains the extreme fragmentation of Dickinson's work or the broad use of doubling that characterizes her syntax, address to the audience, and tone. Nor, in spite of the disjunctive qualities of compression and parataxis generally, do they explain the several forms of disruption in Dickinson's poems: analogies that do not hold, a subversively ironic tone, frequent negation and qualification, repeated use of conjunction with *but,* and the several plots that stem around the challenging of authority. Speculative descriptions of women's writing do account for these aspects of Dickinson's writing, as well as for the repeated antagonistic stance of the speaker in several narrative poems. In strategy and in its combination of stylistic elements, Dickinson's poetry more closely resembles theories of what feminist writing, or a woman's writing, an *écriture féminine*, would be than it resembles the actual work of other—even women—writers. One may go further. In several characteristics and in dominant strategies, Dickinson's language could almost have been designed as a model for several twentieth-century theories of what a woman's language might be.

I refer here to feminist theories of language and gender inclusively, even though it has become standard to regard feminist theory as fundamentally divided between Anglo-American and French perspectives and to acknowledge the many differences of theory within those broad groupings. These are useful and necessary distinctions in most contexts. When it comes to stylistic descriptions of what happens (or will happen) in a woman's (or feminine) text, however, there is remarkably little contradiction in the various theorists' claims.[1] Luce Irigaray's positing of feminine multiplicity from the basis of the plurality of female genitalia (lips of the labia) and erogenous zones; Julia Kristeva's theory that an *écriture féminine* is essentially negative (the construct *woman* or *feminine* has meaning only as Other or different from the masculine, which alone is positively asserted to exist); and Sandra Gilbert and Susan Gubar's, or Alicia Ostriker's, argument that women's writing has long existed but that it has been subversive (due to historically determined cultural and psychological constraints on the individual woman)—all lead to basically complementary descriptions of writing. Multiplicity, a negative stance, indirection, and subversion may easily be integrated within a single conception of style, and all aptly characterize Dickinson's poetry.[2]

Again, to clarify: I am arguing that Dickinson's reasons for choosing the language strategies she does and several of the primary characteristics of her language themselves can best be explained by feminist analysis of the stimulus for, and qualities of, women's writing. Furthermore, and as Dickinson herself suggests in several poems, the psychology or aesthetic that prizes the various strategies of disjunction, multiplicity of meaning, and indirection examined in Chapter 2 may itself be gender-linked and feminine. Dickinson does not write as she does because she is a woman; this is not an argument for biological determinism. Nor is she a feminist poet in the political or social sense of that word, as I explain later in this chapter. She is, however, conscious of gender as a defining feature of her life and conscious that gender affects ways of speaking, thus also the construction of her poems.

In 1924 Martha Dickinson Bianchi remembers her aunt as having been "feminist" in "latent tendency." From an early age, the poet appeared indignant "at being counted as *non compos* in a man's world of reality."[3] Certainly her letters and life provide considerable evidence that this is true. Dickinson was quick to assert herself if a correspondent slighted her—whether or not intentionally, and whether or not the form of her rejoinder was direct. She identified strongly with the major women writers of her day, particularly those Englishwomen of the generation preceding her own: pictures of George Eliot and Elizabeth Barrett Browning (along with Thomas Carlyle) hung on her bedroom wall. Dickinson read all she could find on the Brontës, including Mrs. Gaskell's *Life of Charlotte Brontë* and A. Mary F. Robinson's *Emily Brontë*. In a letter, she referred to Eliot as Mrs. Lewes—a name revealing her knowledge and implicit approval of the novelist's long-standing affair with George Henry Lewes, not just familiarity with the works of the public (masculine) author. She offered to give Higginson her copy of Eliot's poems, and read two biographies of Eliot as soon as they appeared (*Life* II, 570, 585). When Samuel Bowles left for Italy, Dickinson asked him to "put one hand on the Head" of Barrett Browning's grave for her; another friend brought her a picture of the grave on his return—a gift he knew she would prize. Dickinson's admiration for Barrett Browning was known widely enough for three separate friends to send her copies of the English poet's portrait (one of which she offered to Higginson, L 271).

In letters, Dickinson frequently refers to or quotes women writers, especially the Brontës, Eliot, and Barrett Browning. Of Barrett Browning and George Sand, who were discouraged by unsympathetic relatives, she writes: "That Mrs. Browning fainted, we need not read *Aurora Leigh* to know, when she lived with her English aunt; and George Sand 'must make no noise in her grandmother's bedroom.' Poor children! Women, now, queens, now!" (L 234). "What do I think of *Middlemarch?*" she responds to her Norcross cousins; "What do I think of glory —" (L 389). At Eliot's death, the poet claims the novelist as her own: "Now, *my* George Eliot" (L 710). Years earlier (in 1854), on reading Barrett Browning's poems for the first time, Dickinson summarizes her response to the poems with the same possessive pronoun: "My crown, indeed! I do not fear the king, attired in this grandeur" (L 171).[4] Walsh claims that Dickinson borrows ideas and phrases in great number from Barrett Browning's *Aurora Leigh,* finding that "at least sixty of Emily's poems can be related to distinct passages in Mrs. Browning's book, with echoes of at least an additional fifty hovering just out of reach."[5]

The strongest specific evidence for a feminine influence on Dickinson's life and art comes in her cumulative responses to Elizabeth Barrett Browning's death. In the year following the English poet's death, Dickinson wrote three tributes to Barrett Browning—her only verse tributes to a contemporary writer. The first follows the posthumous publication of *Last Poems* in 1862: "Her — 'last poems'— / Poets — ended — / Silver — perished — with her Tongue —" (312). This poem is remarkable for the extremity of its claim ("Poets — ended"), but also because Dickinson twice calls attention to the writer's gender, both times as a form of personal identification with the older woman. The poem identifies Barrett Browning metaphorically with music, once by calling her a "Flute" (that is, both an instrument of music and, by metonymy, player of the instrument) and once by comparing her favorably with robins (she has twice their "Tune"). Between these two metaphors, and as an aside in the middle of the sentence, Dickinson becomes curiously literal in her reference to the poet:

Not on Record — bubbled other,
Flute — or Woman —
So divine —

In the context of the metaphors of poet as flute and robin, "Woman" should logically represent a category naturally or essentially poetic: like a flute, woman, or robin, she creates poetry out of herself. Clearly, however, women are neither natural instruments nor musicians, as the skilled pianist Dickinson must have known. The interjection instead seems to be an outbreak of pride, manifest in the speaker's impulsive, and in the immediate context inappropriate, labeling of her subject. The speaker reminds her audience that this great poet is a "Woman" and (unlike Eliot and the Brontës) "on Record" as such. The poem then ends with a question: Dickinson competitively meditates on what it would have been like if she had been the "Bridegroom" to honor the dead poet at her grave: "What, and if, Ourself a Bridegroom – / Put Her down – in Italy?" Preparing the dead, in Dickinson's poetry, is a rite to be guarded jealously and most often a right that the speaker claims of a lover. As husband of the poet, Dickinson would have a special privilege of contact. Significantly, the poem's poet remains a woman: rather than change Barrett Browning's sex and make herself bride to the older poet, Dickinson alters the sex of her speaker.

A second poem commemorates Barrett Browning's death and Dickinson's debt, recalling her request that Bowles touch the Englishwoman's grave for her: "I went to thank Her – / But She Slept –" (363). The third poem recalls the poet's first acquaintance with Barrett Browning:

> I think I was enchanted
> When first a sombre Girl –
> I read that Foreign Lady –

This poem attributes Dickinson's whole poetic calling or "Conversion" to the older woman's poetry. It ends:

> I could not have defined the change –
> Conversion of the Mind
> Like Sanctifying in the Soul –
> Is witnessed – not explained –
>
> 'Twas a Divine Insanity –
> The Danger to be Sane
> Should I again experience –
> 'Tis Antidote to turn –

> To Tomes of solid Witchcraft –
> Magicians be asleep –
> But Magic – hath an Element
> Like Deity – to keep –   (593)

The use of the word "Conversion" and the repeated religious references mark with particular emphasis Barrett Browning's importance in the life of a woman who strenuously and successfully resisted all religious "Conversion," even when under severe pressure from her family, teachers, and peers to believe. According to this poem's language, Dickinson's great religious transformation, her "Sanctifying," is of the "Mind" rather than of the spirit, and it is like "Magic." Although the speaker realizes that choosing enchantment over the expected Christian salvation appears insane to her world, she calls the insanity "Divine" and sees the real "Danger" or sickness in being conventionally "Sane." Should she ever fall into those unhealthy ways again, poetry—particularly the poetry of this divinely insane female predecessor—will save her, will be her "Antidote" against the world's views of her proper activities and role.

Dickinson's description of the "Magic" that saves her as "Witchcraft" underlines the gender identification in the poem. "Sombre Girl" and "Foreign Lady" alike, and unlike their male counterparts, become witches, a specifically female vocation and a subversive one. Witches are feared and punished, not revered, for their craft. Yet they are unmistakably powerful. The contrast between feminine and masculine magic implied by Dickinson's use of "Witchcraft" may be articulated in the following line: "Magicians be asleep" can mean that any poet's "Magic" will last after its maker's death, but it may also contrast the sleepy ignorance of "Magicians" (a word usually masculine in connotation) with the alert "Witchcraft" of this woman.

Barrett Browning provided no major stylistic model for Dickinson, but she did provide proof that a woman could become a poet of international reputation. The Brontës and Barrett Browning were widely known before Dickinson began her serious writing. George Eliot (eleven years the poet's senior) published her fiction from 1858 to 1876, throughout Dickinson's most productive years. With these extraordinary models and with the several American women novelists and poets whose work she enjoyed, Dickinson could imagine herself to be both a serious and a woman writer.

Although Dickinson identified with these writers and cared about their lives, she did not actively support the political campaign for women's rights or, apparently, sympathize with women generally. In her letters, the poet never articulates an interest in the nineteenth-century women's movement; she mentions neither the widely publicized "Woman's Rights" conventions held in Massachusetts between the years 1850 and 1860 (when the poet was between 20 and 30 years old), nor Fuller's 1845 publication of *Woman in the Nineteenth Century,* nor the writings of any other contemporary feminist. And yet she must have been aware of the women's movement through her daily newspaper reading and her father's political career. The Seneca Falls, New York, Convention of 1848 received widespread coverage in the press—albeit mostly negative. Massachusetts hosted the First National Convention of Woman's Rights in Worcester, October 23–24, 1850, and other national or local women's rights conventions in 1851, 1854, 1855, and 1859.[6] In March of 1857, the "petition of Lucy Stone and others for equal rights for 'females' in the administration of government, for the right of suffrage, etc." was brought before the Massachusetts legislature, an event that again received considerable publicity.[7] All these conventions were crowded, and prominent people whom Dickinson respected, in particular Ralph Waldo Emerson (occasionally) and Thomas Wentworth Higginson (consistently), supported their demands—although her father at one point attacked "the women's Suffrage people."[8]

Dickinson's poetry suggests that she is ambivalent about identifying with women. She allies herself with archetypal or mythical women—Eve in several poems and letters, the "Strong Madonnas" of "Sweet Mountains – Ye tell Me no lie" (722), "Madonna" of "Only a Shrine, but Mine" (918)—but she also identifies with archetypal men (Moses, Jacob) and describes the conventional lady as "A Horror" (in "What Soft – Cherubic Creatures," 401).[9] Dickinson repeatedly notes the restrictions of a woman's life ("Born – Bridalled – Shrouded – / In a Day – ", 1072), yet she considers herself to be singular, not a member of an oppressed class.[10] The poet makes abundant use of vocabulary and analogies drawn from a woman's daily life and chores, but she does not use the rhetoric of the women's movement (or of any reform movement) in her poems.[11] Social reform is not Dickinson's concern. The breadth of circumstances in her life in which she sees an unfair differential of power and her association of conventional power and powerlessness with gender reveal the clarity of her vision, not a desire to revolutionize the world. One might speculate that Dickinson shows no interest in class and racial distinctions because these are categories in which she enjoys social privilege. Like most of us, she recognizes power by noting the ways in which it is kept from her. Because she was protected by her father's financial stability and her parents' eagerness to support her at home, several of the political concerns of the women's movement may have seemed irrelevant to her immediate life. Her privilege in the areas of race, class, and social standing, however, may have sharpened her response to the irrational restrictions on behavior that she did see in her life and at home. Dickinson's relative security may have allowed her to note the discriminations of gender hierarchy without the confusion of simultaneous discrimination based on other stigmatized differences.

Without being interested in political feminism, then, Dickinson was extremely interested in the power relations between the sexes. The frequent lack of distinction in her poems between woman and child, and her occasional expression of envy of the child's lot over the woman's, contribute significantly to the evidence that Dickinson associated femininity with powerlessness and therefore with her need to create independent, disguised sources of power for herself.[12] Because power does not inhere in womanhood, its discovery, expression, and survival for a woman must be subversive and oblique. One of Dickinson's primary disguises in the bid for power is the exaggeratedly feminine mask of perpetual childhood. The *Ur*-plot of Dickinson's poems presents its speaker as apparently small, weak, uncertain or apologetic, irrational (to the extent that she relies on contradiction and conundrums), and naively wise—all traditional characteristics of childhood as well as stereotypes of femininity. Mossberg argues that Dickinson's pose of smallness and obedience will protect her from being punished for her cultural "heresies."[13] Nina Baym writes that "the child persona in Dickinson can be read both as the child within human beings generally or more specifically as the child within the *woman,* the child that woman is alleged to be and, crucially in Dickinson's case, the child that the woman is felt to be." Baym notes that Dickinson uses this persona almost exclusively for "the relation of the speaker to masculine figures"; the pose provides room for the needed tension between open resistance and complete acquiescence to the opposed male.[14]

Whether or not they are specifically gendered in the narrative of the poem, Dickinson's speakers assume the culturally feminine role of weakness and self-doubt while in fact powerfully undermining or rebelling against the figure of opposition in the poem's plot. The strategies of the poems, then—their obliquity, oppositional contrast, disruptiveness—are implicitly gender-linked. The speaker may play supplicant to God, child to father, abandoned or neglected love to absent lover, human being to (masculine) death, and so on, but she is always "small" relative to the power she objects to or rebels against, or seeks a closer exchange with.

The pervasiveness of this strategy for disruption can be seen in a number of poems that focus on dramas between a child supplicant and God or a poet and her audience. In an early poem, "I shall know why – when Time is over," the speaker's exaggeration gives indirect expression to her accusation that God or Christ is unjust:

> I shall know why – when Time is over –
> And I have ceased to wonder why –
> Christ will explain each separate anguish
> In the fair schoolroom of the sky –
>
> He will tell me what "Peter" promised –
> And I – for wonder at his woe –
> I shall forget the drop of Anguish
> That scalds me now – that scalds me now!   (193)

Like a student excusing an inadequate teacher or child excusing a parent, the speaker here apparently forgives Christ for failing to answer the ceaseless question of "why" (repeated twice) He allows the "drop of Anguish" she presently suffers. Yet the repetition of "That scalds me now" and the concluding exclamation mark call more attention to her overtly minimized anguish—"drop"—than to her indirect apology for his inadequacy. Moreover, the very posture of apologizing for the divinity's failure to answer essential questions until the answer has become either meaningless or irrelevant amounts to an extraordinary indictment of His justice. The speaker proves herself more generous than Christ both in her willingness to accept His refusal to care for her and in her anticipated empathy at His "woe," despite His apparent indifference to hers.

A simpler and more playful example of God's injustice occurs in a poem where the speaker protests against His claiming "the pretty acre" of garden "that I called mine." The poem concludes:

The station of the parties
Forbids publicity,
But Justice is sublimer
Than arms, or pedigree.

I'll institute an "Action" –
I'll vindicate the law –
Jove! Choose your counsel –
I retain "Shaw"!   (116)

As her "counsel" in a suit against God, the speaker chooses Shaw, the Dickinson's handyman and gardener.[15] Rivalry with God takes more specific form in another early poem (c. 1861):

Over the fence –
Strawberries – grow –
Over the fence –
I could climb – if I tried, I know –
Berries are nice!

But – if I stained my Apron –
God would certainly scold!
Oh, dear, – I guess if He were a Boy –
He'd – climb – if He could!   (251)

Here the speaker is prevented from climbing a fence to get strawberries only by the worry that she may stain her apron and receive a scolding. That God, rather than a nearer father, would scold suggests that these berries represent forbidden fruit of any variety. The poem specifies, however, that it is not the fruit but her climbing "Over the fence" (repeated twice) that is forbidden. A boy would not hesitate to climb because he wears no confining "Apron," nothing that reveals stains. If she were a boy, she too would climb that fence. In her anger at the rule maker who decrees that girls wear aprons and that aprons remain unstained, however, the speaker caustically doubts whether God, as a boy, "could" manage the climb. In a fair contest, she taunts, she would be the better "Boy." But a petty, scolding God has prevented her from even entering the competition in fence climbing, thus cutting off all possibility of reward.

The conditional "could" operates with similar irony in another poem comparing the child/speaker's role with God's, although this time the speaker is again more humane than God rather than more athletic. In "Why – do they shut Me out of Heaven? / Did I sing – too loud?" (c. 1861), the poet concludes:

> Oh, if I – were the Gentleman
> In the "White Robe" –
> And they – were the little Hand – that knocked –
> Could – I – forbid?   (248)

The adjectives describing the speaker or her voice—"little" (twice), "Minor" with its triple pun (as harmonic key, unimportant, and underage), and "Timid"—suggest that the speaker is a girl and that any song of hers would be "too loud." The God who does not like girls to climb does not like them to sing either. This heavenly father, like the unnamed parents of "They shut me up in Prose," evidently prefers that girls be "still" (613).

Although Dickinson does write a number of conventionally religious poems in the tradition of dramatic meditation familiar to her from much contemporary writing and from Herbert's poems, more often she rebels at or acerbically criticizes God's law. He is a "Swindler" in "I meant to have but modest needs" (476), and a sneering "Mighty Merchant" who refuses his customer the one thing she is willing to offer all "Being" for in "I asked no other thing" (621); he is generally indifferent to human trouble or even life—for example, in "It's easy to invent a Life," God's "Perturbless Plan / Proceed – inserting Here – a Sun – / There – leaving out a Man –" (724). The poet calls him "Burglar! Banker – Father!" (49) when he steals a friend from her in death, and the "Approving God" for "Frost," a "blonde Assassin" beheading flowers with repeated "accidental" exercise of his power (1624). God is "jealous" of human happiness, like a child who "cannot bear to see / That we had rather not with Him / But with each other play." (1719). Dickinson frequently uses economic and legal terminology to describe God, usually—as in the examples above—to demonstrate his niggardliness and his untrustworthiness as a judge. One of the most striking examples of legal comparison occurs in "Alone and in a Circumstance" (1167), where the poet indirectly accuses God of an injustice far worse than any human kind:

> If any strike me on the street
> I can return the Blow –
> If any take my property

According to the Law
The Statute is my Learned friend
But what redress can be
For an offense nor here nor there
So not in Equity –
That Larceny of time and mind
The marrow of the Day
By spider, or forbid it Lord
That I should specify.

As in the poem quoted earlier in which the poet trusts her gardener or lawyer Shaw as counsel over God, here human "Statute" is greater protection than His inexplicable, or perhaps nonexistent, law. Dickinson always trusts herself first and all things human second before heavenly salvation or understanding or reward.

Even human language is more useful than God's Word and therefore to be preferred, despite the clear advantages that the absolute creativity and power of the latter would bring. Dickinson begins the following poem with a celebration of language's power generally and with reverberating religious connotation ("A Word made Flesh is seldom / And tremblingly partook"), but ends by contrasting God's Word, Christ, with human "Philology":

A Word that breathes distinctly
Has not the power to die
Cohesive as the Spirit
It may expire if He –
"Made Flesh and dwelt among us"
Could condescension be
Like this consent of Language
This loved Philology.   (1651)

Here again the conditional "Could" calls into question whether divine language is capable of the service human language routinely performs. In "condescension" Dickinson plays on the words "descend," as the Spirit did in the form of a dove at Christ's baptism, and "condescend," with its glance at what may be either God's benign courtesy or His hierarchical system that keeps humanity low. Contrasting God's "condescension" with philology's "consent," the poet appears to say that the ability to expire—breathe as well as die—is crucial in language and perhaps inseparable from its relation to human need and use. God's Word cannot die, but neither, apparently, can it live with us.

The human word, in contrast, is represented by "Philology," by human response (love and study) to language's power rather than by authoritative creation or Adamic naming. Philology represents an exchange between speakers and the categorizable aspects of language, which is valued for its complexity and for its dependence on those to whom it "consents." In this poem human language is twice "loved" (in the adjective and, etymologically, in *philo-logos*) because it communicates *with* us; it consents to our manipulation, which in turn replenishes its meaning. As Dickinson says in another poem, a word "just / Begins to live" when it is spoken (1212). As letter writer, as daughter, sister, and friend as well as in the personae of her poems, Dickinson is a poet of "consent," of the shifting transformation rather than the authoritative establishment of meaning.

The cooperation of language is clearly necessary for such a poet, and perhaps for any poet. Curiously, however, most of Dickinson's poems on poetry are more about the conditions the poet must suffer or overcome than about language or the poet's aesthetic choices; the speaker is only metaphorically a poet. Through their repeated emphasis on the need for escape, or opposition, or defensive contrast of the poet's work with that of some greater or more public figure, these poems define poetry as an aggressive act of expression rather than as an icon or publicly valued art. The speaker's attitude toward her audience often resembles that of the speaker toward God in the poems just quoted, and her metaphorical creation is the method of her rebellion or escape. In some poems, the two types of authority are combined and the poet/speaker stands in opposition to God, as in "Why – do they shut Me out of Heaven?" (248), or "A Word made Flesh is seldom" (1651), or in the ugly-duckling tale "God made a little Gentian," where the poet suddenly makes herself analogous to the ravishing late bloomer and ambiguously threatens: "Creator – Shall I – bloom?" (442). In "I reckon – when I count at all" (569), the speaker claims to value poets, the sun, summer, and "the Heaven of God –", then decides that poets "Comprehend the Whole –" and chooses their rewards over any others, especially over God's:

> . . . if the Further Heaven –
>
> Be Beautiful as they [Poets] prepare
> For Those who worship Them –

It is too difficult a Grace —
To justify the Dream —

As in "A Word made Flesh," God's heaven may be more wonderful, but it is too uncertain and attaining it requires too much loss. She chooses "Poets" over "Heaven," "Philology" over God's "Word."

In "I reckon — when I count at all," poets surpass God in what they offer a reader. Often, Dickinson's poet offers nothing at all except to the poet herself. In "They shut me up in Prose" (613), the speaker compares her adult state as poet to being a "little Girl" shut up in a "Closet — / Because they liked me 'still' —", that is, motionless and silent. The poet, like the girl, however, escapes confinement "easy as a Star" by retreating to movement and sound within her "Brain." When she dances in her own head, "They" cannot know how far she moves, or—as in "Why — do they Shut me out of Heaven?"—how "loud" she sings, or—as Dickinson says in another poem—how often "among my mind, / A Glee possesseth me." In that poem ("I cannot dance upon my Toes — / No Man instructed me —" 326), the speaker's art is great enough to "blanch a Troupe — / Or lay a Prima, mad"; though none "know I know the Art / I mention — easy — Here — / Nor any Placard boast me — / It's full as Opera — ." In this pose, the poet dances and sings for herself alone but knows that her private spectacle is as "full" as the grandest public one. Despite the limitations of her allotted space or formal education ("No Man instructed me"), she produces great art.

In still another poem, the poet is creative only in "moments of Escape," when she eludes the "Goblin" that confines and sexually "Accost[s]" her. Here the poet is first like a bee released to "his Rose" (a reversal of gender that occurs in others of Dickinson's poems, usually marking the speaker's independent mobility). Next she is like a bird in flight and song, then "like a Bomb, abroad" in "bursting all the doors" and dancing until, finally, the "Fright" retakes her and she is "shackled" once again (512). Similarly, in "It would never be Common — more — I said" (430), the speaker seems to be a poet. She "publish[es]" joy in her "Eye," walks "as wings — my body bore —", and deals "a word of Gold / To every Creature — that I met —" until "A Goblin — drank my Dew —" and she finds herself silent, impoverished, infertile again. Unlike the "drop of Anguish" that will last until "Time is over," poetic inspiration (her "moment of Brocade" or "drop — of India") is always threatened and transitory in Dickinson's art.

As the poems just quoted show, and whether the barriers are external or psychological, the poet perceives herself to be beleaguered or shut out, both conditions that demand an aggressive response. Perhaps it is this implicit need for strong action as well as the building pressure of previous repression that occasionally make Dickinson's speakers ruthlessly destructive. In one example, the speaker "dealt her pretty words like Blades," without regard to whether "she hurt" her audience; "That – is not Steel's Affair –" (479). In other poems the poet speaks murderously from what appears to be harmless silence: "A still – Volcano – Life – / . . . Too subtle to suspect / By natures this side Naples –" may be silent for ages and then abruptly open its "lips that never lie –", with the result that "Cities – ooze away –" (601). An apparently "meditative spot" may "disclose" fire beneath its "sod" (1677). "The reticent volcano keeps / His never slumbering plan," Dickinson writes in one poem (1748), but an earlier poem indicates that "the smouldering anguish" will at length "overcome" its reticence or any restriction of "sod"; then "those old – phlegmatic mountains / Usually so still –" release "appalling Ordnance, / Fire, and smoke, and gun, / Taking Villages for breakfast, / And appalling Men –" (175).[16] Volcanoes make their own "Ordnance" or laws, with an indifference to the human population somewhat like God's, and like the dead-shot speaker's with her "Vesuvian smile" in "My Life had stood – a Loaded Gun." The speaker of another poem acknowledges that such an explosion may occur in any soul, not just "in Sicily / And South America." With more than typical inversion, the speaker (threateningly?) brags (1705, lines 5–8):

> A Lava step at any time
> Am I inclined to climb
> A Crater I may contemplate
> Vesuvius at Home

The speakers of these poems do not rebel against a specifically masculine authority; they rebel against any confinement or hardship, or against any accumulation of these experiences. Still, in the nineteenth century, the public world "appalled" by their explosions is one of "Men."

Although disdain is not the primary emotion one would attribute to the rebellious, it often characterizes Dickinson's speakers in their responses to the confining world. The "little Girl" kept in the "Closet" of "Prose" mocks her captors for supposing they can keep her "still" by physically restraining her; the sharp speaker of "She dealt her pretty words like Blades" casually disregards the embarrassment she may cause her audience: "To Ache is human – not polite –" (479); the speaker of "on my volcano grows the Grass" scorns the ignorance of those who view her as harmless: "An acre for a Bird to choose / Would be the General thought –" (1677); speakers frequently eschew "Publication" or recognition of their skill, by contrast or explicitly presenting themselves as above such "Auction" (709). Better than anger because it does not have the same potential for uncontrolled explosion and thus possible self-destruction, disdain nonetheless allows the speaker the same rejection of belittling confinement. In an experimental poem Dickinson even links this enabling scorn with immortality:

> With Pinions of Disdain
> The soul can farther fly
> Than any feather specified
> in Ornithology –
> It wafts this sordid Flesh
> Beyond it's dull – control
> And during it's electric gale –
> The body is a soul –
> instructing by the same –
> How little work it be –
> To put off filaments like this
> for immortality –　　　(1431)

During Disdain's "electric gale" or "might," or "act" (two of Dickinson's five alternatives for "gale"), the soul is released from its confining body, perhaps as the speaker is released from her confining community or from any "filaments" that tie her down.

Anger is the tool of the weak, disdain or condescension that of the strong. To disdain punishment or retaliation, then, becomes one of the poet's strongest tools—both because it allows her the stance of complete control and because it does not make her test the control. Consequently, it offers no risk of defeat. In an early poem, the speaker compares herself to Jesus as a way of marking both her perfect humility at receiving a slight and her potential power:

He forgot – and I – remembered –
'Twas an everyday affair –
Long ago as Christ and Peter –
"Warmed them" at the "Temple fire"

"Thou wert with him" – quoth "the Damsel"?
"*No*" – said Peter, 'twas'nt me –
Jesus merely "looked" at Peter –
Could I do aught else – to Thee?   (203)

Although the analogy makes the question rhetorical (the speaker, like Jesus, will only "look" her reproach), the conditional "Could" suggests that there are other possibilities. If she only reproaches "him," it is because she does not choose to do more (although the fact of the poem itself reveals that the speaker cannot be content just with looking; she must tell "him" that this is all she will do).

As these poems of disdain show, the rejection of authority and the assertion of personal ability or power take any number of forms in Dickinson's poems. Opposition is more often against an unnamed deed or individual than it is specific, and gender remains for the most part implicit in the speaker's address to a masculine other, in her relatively powerless initial or present stance, and in the overall assumption that Dickinson's speakers are female. The pattern of need to achieve independence, however, is unambiguously clear. The poet is not always isolated, and may even speak from a plural community as a kind of protective reassurance of her own right, but she is almost invariably involved in some kind of opposition and equally often aware of the transitory nature of both her poetic and the external authority's power.

Margaret Homans argues that women's writing differs from men's because although women, like the speakers of Dickinson's poems, know and feel they are at home in their (Western) culture, their voices have been typically suppressed and repressed. Drawing from the work of both American and French literary critics and theorists of language, Homans posits that "there is a specifically gender-based alienation from language that is characterized by the special ambiguity of women's simultaneous participation in and exclusion from a hegemonic group (with the qualification that while 'hegemonic' usually refers to white, ruling-class men, it can also refer in context to men of any woman's own race or nationality, who are hegemonic relative to her)."[17] Homans recognizes that there are several kinds of silencing, as well as different kinds of alienation or exclusion from language use. She argues, however, that "while victimization takes relatively overt forms with respect to race or nationality, the silencing and oppression experienced by women as women are masked as their choice."[18] Homans's hypothesis that women simultaneously participate in and feel alienated from language may help explain Dickinson's gifted manipulation of language in contorted and cryptic forms, and her alternatively pleading and antagonistic stance toward the powers of her world. The thematic key points in Dickinson's world are the speaker's opposition to, yet desire for, some other figure or thing, and the lack of a just and reliable law. These are the very points that feminist theories help to explain, especially in the context of stylistic disjunction and instability.

Theorists from Virginia Woolf on have been concluding that for cultural and historical reasons a woman's writing is different from a man's, or that—put in the terms of more recent criticism—to inscribe the feminine requires language resources and techniques different from those used in "masculine" writing (which is to say almost all Western writing).[19] In their stylistic aspects nearly all the theories are speculative rather than descriptive, but the descriptive details that one does find correspond to techniques of Dickinson's language manipulation with a consistency far beyond what mere coincidence would generate.

The most common claim is that women's writing is nonlinear. For American and British theorists, this claim typically follows a sociological or historical reference to women's domestic work. For example, Virginia Woolf writes: "The book has somehow to be adapted to the body, and at a venture one would say that women's books should be shorter, more concentrated, than those of men, and framed so that they do not need long hours of steady and uninterrupted work. For interruptions there will always be."[20] Josephine Donovan argues similarly that the circumstances of daily life appear to shape women's artistic products. Moreover, women's typical inhabitation of the domestic sphere, with its repetitive and interruptible tasks and cycles, "contributes to a consciousness that is aware of contingency, that perceives itself bound to chance, not in total control."[21] From a historical perspective, Judith Fetterley identifies short form with a relaxed or loosened control. Using Dickinson as a primary example of

the "tiny tale" writer, Fetterley argues that nineteenth-century American women prose writers did their best work in short form, perhaps because it provided greater freedom of expression:
"Writers who wished to avoid . . . conceptual dependency or who wished to experiment with artistic form might well have chosen to work in genres less formalized, less pretentious, and less predetermined [than the novel] and therefore more open, fluid, and malleable to their uses . . . in territory less clearly marked, the woman's story . . . could perhaps be better told."[22]

Women's writing may be like quilt making; both stem from the "organization of material in fragments," a process that encourages rearrangement, new form.[23] Rachel Blau Du Plessis, with reference to Woolf and to Anais Nin, sees women's writing in the form of a journal: "I knew more, said more than I knew. The writing is in the interstices, the meaning is between. It is created in the relationship between, between the elements, they are put down at random, and they flare up they are not said by chance; they know better. I allow this to enter, the blankness which I don't control."[24] In similar terms, Dickinson speaks of a word coming "unsummoned" to the searching poet: "Not unto nomination / The Cherubim reveal —" (1126). In another poem she writes: "Your thoughts dont have words every day / They come a single time / Like signal esoteric sips / Of the communion Wine" (1452). A poet may be her own surprised audience, stunning herself "With Bolts of Melody!" (505). Like the quilt maker, Dickinson's poet and philologist must work *with* pieces of meaning and form; they require the "consent" of language. As Woolf, Donovan, Fetterley, and Du Plessis would expect, Dickinson's poems are short, often nonlinear and fluid in form, and they reveal a consciousness that without anxiety knows itself to be incapable of complete control.

As the comparisons of women's writing with quilts and journals suggest, several critics see the lack of iconographic product as characteristic of feminine art. Gayatri C. Spivak claims that women, as they have been "socially defined" in the West, "understand a kind of work which does not in fact lead to . . . a totemized object, like a book."[25] The "feminist program," she argues, involves a "deconstruction of the opposition between private and public."[26] Anais Nin reasons that "writers know their text as a form of intimacy, of personal contact, whether conversations with the reader or with the self. Letters, journals, voices are sources for this element . . . expressing the porousness and nonhierarchic stances of intimate conversation in both structure and function."[27] Dickinson's poems are "Letter[s] to the World," literally in her use of the poems in—and as—letters and figuratively in the open address of the poems to an ambiguous "you." They are both conventionally formal (stanzas in meter and rhyme) and formless (unsyntactic, irregular in stanza, meter, rhyme). They are specific messages to friends and at the same time complex metaphorical statements written to an audience beyond her time and community.

Luce Irigaray perhaps imagines a form like Dickinson's when she theorizes that all writing that inscribes the feminine is "unidentifiable" and "multiple." A text written in the feminine is always changing, she claims. More specifically, the syntax of such a text would "involve nearness, proximity, but in such an extreme form that it would preclude any distinction of identities, any establishment of ownership, thus any form of appropriation."[28] Thus a feminine text will differ from a masculine in the multiplicity of its linguistic particulars as well as in its overall form. Woolf anticipates this syntactic argument in her historically based observation that the sentence of great male writers is "unsuited for a woman's use." It is too rigid, contains too much of "I."[29] Combining historical and theoretical perspectives— and playing on the homonym of the linguistic and legal "sentence"— Paula Treichler similarly speculates that the tyranny of the (linguistic) sentence has carried over into literature in ways that emphasize the syntactic over the semantic, or law over meaning, and thereby curtail those aspects of language with which women are most concerned: "One can generalize and say that signs alone are of less interest to women than are the processes of signification which link signs to semantic and pragmatic aspects of speaking. To 'escape the sentence' is to move beyond the boundaries of formal syntax."[30] Julia Kristeva claims that non-sense multiplies sense; fragmentation (which high-lights semantics rather than syntax) challenges the ("phallic") posture of mastery or control in language and thereby allows for the creation of new and unprivileged meanings.[31]

One could hardly be more multiple than Dickinson is in her practice of leaving variant word choices marked in the margins of bound copies of her poems, or in her different choices of words or line arrangements for the mailings of a single poem to more than one friend. Similarly, her multiple and overlapping uses of "it" in a poem and her mid-poem changes of a speaker's gender or gender association mark a disinclination to "appropriate" meaning. The multiplicity of meaning in Dickinson's poems also stems from their characteristic fragmentation. As I discuss in the grammar, commas and dashes break up a poem's syntax; the omission of words and phrases or of appropriate end punctuation calls the completeness of sentences into question; lack of standard reference for pronouns makes poems sound like fragments from an ongoing conversation or monologue where the reference has already been made clear. Individual poems are even in a sense fragments of Dickinson's complete poetic production—with the qualification that the cumulative fragments never make a single whole: there are too many for any single arrangement or pattern to account for. However one solves the puzzle of her work, pieces will remain.

From historical, cultural, and psychological perspectives, feminist theorists tend to describe women's writing as *non*linear, *in*formal, fragmented, loosening control—that is, in terms of what it is not or what it reacts against. Kristeva goes so far as to say that a "feminist practice" can only be negative, in opposition to what already exists. As a social construct, *woman* itself is "something that cannot be represented, something that is not said, something above and beyond nomenclatures and ideologies."[32] Margaret Homans makes this argument with specific reference to Dickinson. Working from a Derridian model of centrist (phallic) and marginal (Other) discourse, Homans sees Dickinson's experimentation with language as a reaction against phallogocentrism or centrist law, not a positive construction in itself. Dickinson seeks a language different from that of the tradition that has preceded her, Homans contends, in and through which she may constitute a different kind of self. In both these uses, "different" is primarily oppositional: the poet knows more about the inadequacy of her present state than about a world that would be adequate. As a consequence, language itself is "double" for the poet: it acts to break down what is known and then to establish the boundaries for new meaning. It is not based on absolute truth or a romantic unity but is primarily fictitious.[33] Hagenbüchle similarly posits the nondialectical quality of Dickinson's poetry and implies that its essential character is negative. As he demonstrates, her poems are metonymic, not metaphorical. Where metaphors, "due to their relationship of equivalence, presuppose a stable world," metonymy encourages negation, indeterminacy, the disruption of expected patterns.[34]

As these same critics realize, however, it is problematic and ultimately misleading to characterize either women's writing or Dickinson's poetry primarily in terms of negation or opposition or difference. Kristeva responds to this implicit problem of feminist theory by arguing that the negation of an *écriture féminine* establishes a "process of differentiation" rather than "a fixed opposition ('man'/'woman')."[35] Kristeva (as well as other theorists) identifies an assertive, positing stance with the masculine and a multiple, antagonistic or destructive stance with the feminine, yet she finds that "all speaking subjects have within themselves a certain bisexuality which is precisely the possibility to explore all the sources of signification, that which posits a meaning as well as that which multiplies, pulverizes, and finally revives it."[36] Using this terminology, one would say that Dickinson's poetry stylistically emphasizes the multiplying, rupturing aspect of creation over the positing, controlling one, or the feminine over the masculine form, and yet it ultimately achieves that "bisexuality" Kristeva claims as the foundation for exploring meaning.

Again using Kristeva's language, one might even say that Dickinson reveals her poetic genius in her creation of a spiraling movement from "feminine" disruption to "bisexuality." While working within and through the restricting and negative conditions of being a nineteenth-century woman poet, Dickinson constructs a poetry that speaks from those conditions yet in its creativity is enormously affirming. Woolf concluded from her reading that women writers had to be creatively experimental because there was no syntax or language that expressed a woman's experience: "Whole flights of words would need to wing their way illegitimately into existence," she writes, "before a woman could say what happens when she goes into a room."[37] Dickinson creates "whole flights of words," transforming the world's inadequate language into an adequate language of her own.

Difference stimulates Dickinson. As Homans writes, the "rhetoric of sameness," found especially in poems where the speaker addresses another woman and thus metonymically another self, "points ultimately towards a lack of language . . . The sense of silent closure in the poems about two women suggests that it is the overcoming of hierarchy, not the absence of it, that is conducive to poetry."[38] Without antagonism, Dickinson loses important stimulus to her full speech or voice, but the antagonism does not culminate in bitterness or a desire to conquer, only a desire to get rid of the limiting barrier. This may explain why Dickinson apparently felt her poetic audience to be primarily male (despite the fact that she sent by far the greatest number of her poems to Sue). As Karl Keller writes, "Imagining her audience to be male gave Emily Dickinson opportunity to play the deviant. Perhaps she could have played that among women, too, but she would not have had to be as brisk, as nasty, as coy, as teasing, as sure. These postures were created by the men in her mind."[39] Dickinson was at her best talking at a distance and against authority, not within a community.

Dickinson negates or subverts established meanings in order to create new ones. Rather than attempting to "fix" an opponent or an opposing meaning, she works through oppositions to the point where she can question them—as she does, for example, in "In lands I never saw—they say," where the speaker sets "Alps" against "A Myriad Daisy" and then asks "Which, Sir, are you and which am I / Upon an August day?" (124). The poet concludes similarly in "I make His Crescent fill or lack" (909), which contains a double inversion of expectation. First the speaker announces her surprising complete "control" of his "Nature" and "Tides" (stanzas 1 and 2); then she undercuts this hierarchy by revealing the larger truth of their relation:

> But since We hold a Mutual Disc –
> And front a Mutual Day –
> Which is the Despot, neither knows –
> Nor Whose – the Tyranny –   (909)

Typically in Dickinson's poems, the speaker creates an oppositional base for her own sense of self or power (like the fantastic singular/plural "A Myriad Daisy" or her control of the moon/man's shape and conditions) before revealing that the two powers or roles are equal, and perhaps indistinguishable. Dickinson's language negates exclusivity in meaning. The poet establishes a whole new grammar for the articulation of new meanings through the constructive disruption of set form.

Several of the language features mentioned in this chapter have long been seen as "feminine" in ways not at all feminist. Multiplicity of meaning, irrational or metaphorical progressions, disruptive or marginal discourse characterize much of the poetry of every age and, despite the preponderance of male poets, have often been culturally labeled as feminine; but whereas before these features were attributed to women's language because of supposed defects in women's nature, they are now claimed by feminists as a part of a conscious aesthetic.[40] Other elements of language are not seen as feminine at all and have been claimed particularly by the Modernist period—for example, the distrust of any defining order or fixed truth, the need to create new forms of language. Even if it is primarily women today who use the techniques themselves that have come to be grouped under "women's style," the techniques themselves and the choices to use them are not inherently feminine. As Du Plessis reminds the reader at the end of her discussion, "female aesthetic" is just a name for those practices available to any group [or, I would add, individual] that wants to overturn or criticize "the dominant forms of knowing and understanding."[41]

Women's "style" or "aesthetic" is neither exclusive nor prescriptive. Feminist critics write repeatedly that "it is impossible to *define* a feminine practice of writing"; it cannot be "theorized, enclosed, coded."[42] Yet, they assert, it does exist and can be recognized by its relation to standard language, to the present order of meaning. Helene Cixous writes, "A feminine text cannot fail to be more than subversive":

> It is volcanic; as it is written it brings about an upheaval of the old property crust, carrier of masculine investments; there's no other way. There's no room for her if she's not a he. If she's a her-she, it's in order to smash everything, to shatter the framework of institutions, to blow up the law, to break up the "truth" with laughter.[43]

Women's historical simultaneous exclusion from and participation in the use of language may affect their use of disruptive qualities in writing. Du Plessis states that "women of achievement . . . undergo 'male' socialization while they have been marginalized; that would explain the prevalence of both/and vision in Richardson, Woolf, Lessing." A woman may be an "insider" by virtue of her wealth, race, and family connection, but she remains an "outsider" by virtue of her sex, her relation to power. Thus her position is "double"; "How then could she neglect to invent a form which produces this incessant, critical, splitting movement?"[44] According to Cixous, women are capable of writing "(in) the inbetween, inspecting the process of the same and the other without which nothing can live" because they have had to live in the male world, to renounce their own knowledge (their bodies) to learn his. This gives women both a double perspective and potentially greater verbal adroitness: "Those who have turned their tongues 10,000 times seven times before not speaking are either dead from it or more familiar with their tongues and their mouths than anyone else."[45] Dickinson, one feels, is familiar with her tongue.

The relation of Dickinson's language to her gender is complex, like the relation of her language to biblical or Puritan plain style or to Emerson's exuberant fluidity; yet recognizing Dickinson's gender as a powerful influence on her style clarifies one's understanding of the depth of her antagonistic stance and the corresponding depth of her need to keep that antagonism indirect, in the hope that she will gain by approval the power and status she loses by birthright as a woman. Like her need to maintain distance between herself and those she loves, Dickinson's disruptiveness stems from her desire: if she valued the world and her place in it less, she would no doubt rebel less against its injustice and restrictions.

In this study I propose various explanations for why Dickinson writes as she does. She writes antagonistically, that is, in opposition to an existing order that attempts to repress her voice or undermine her seriousness. The disruptions of her style, from this perspective, mark her rejection of the conditions of thought and action in which she has been raised; her language is a nineteenth-century anticipation of possibilities for an *écriture féminine*. Or, in an indirect acknowledgment that she indeed possesses some force and control, Dickinson writes protectively, "slanting" language to shield her audience from the too-bright lightning of Truth, from the volcanic power of her speech and understanding. Or she writes defensively, to protect herself from a world that she desires too much and is too much affected by; she can continue her writing, that is, her life as she has chosen it, only by keeping it at a physical and metaphorical distance, both represented and maintained in the ellipses of her language. Or Dickinson uses ungrammatical, compressed, densely metaphorical language because there is no other way for her to express her meaning; she cannot say what she sees or experiences using legitimate or conventional means because they could not express it. This last—that Dickinson writes as she does because it is the only way for her to speak adequately—is the explanation I would choose if I could take only one. But it stems, I believe, from the dynamics of the others.

To speak her mind, Dickinson feels that she must keep audible both her love of the world and of language and her rejection of its attempts to keep her "still." To lapse on the side of love or uninhibited intimacy would be to risk consummation, being subsumed in an order so much more powerful than she is that she would have no voice or words but those of its law: the dialectically differentiated spheres of masculine authority or feminine sentimentality. But to give up the possibility of fulfilled love or communication altogether would, she fears, leave her with no comprehensible language at all. To choose, as she does, language that attempts to communicate as clearly and as much as possible while remaining faithful to an unorthodox perception and while protecting its speaker allows the poet both the sweetness of the "Rose" and a sharp consciousness of the conditions for "Essential" expression. Poetry is both Dickinson's means of rebelling against the world and her way of communicating her love to it. Gender is the cohering factor of influence in the development of her poems' compressed, disruptive, doubling style.

As the poet's identification with the "Queens" Elizabeth Barrett Browning and George Sand and with "*my* George Eliot" indicates, gender also underlies her confidence in the new poetic language she creates, a connection she reveals in the whole spectrum of her speaker's roles. In her rebellious mode, explosion is one of Dickinson's favorite metaphors for expression; she is a volcano or a dancing bomb. When reflective and philosophical, she stresses the "Screws" of expression, her need for philology's "consent." In her more contented modes, poetry is analogous to flight. Furthermore, her speaker's metaphorical flight in these poems occasionally attains a stability that could rest only on the author's innate certainty of her poetic power—whatever the world might think of it. In a poem that it is nearly impossible to read without thinking of the poet herself, Dickinson writes:

> She staked her Feathers — Gained an Arc —
> Debated — Rose again —
> This time — beyond the estimate
> Of Envy, or of Men —
>
> And now, among Circumference —
> Her steady Boat be seen —
> At home — among the Billows — As
> The Bough where she was born —   (798)

Through apposition, the poet identifies "Men" (exclusively male or generic, as the public world) with "Envy" or any prohibiting emotion she must rise above. The debate over whether to fly, however, is entirely her own, and once she has taken the preliminary daring steps into flight, she finds herself "At home." Like the protagonist of this poem, Dickinson feels most secure when at a distance from her audience, and she creates the desired distance both physically in her life and metaphorically through the lack of direct self-reference and the general level of difficulty in her poems. The extraordinary, peculiar language of Dickinson's poetry leaves the reader grounded, like the "Men" of the poem, but entices the reader close enough to wonder at her flight.

Notes

Index

Notes

1. Letters to the World

1. For other critics combining analysis of Dickinson's language with attention to her life, see Charles R. Anderson, *Emily Dickinson's Poetry: Stairway of Surprise* (New York: Holt, Rinehart and Winston, 1960); Albert Gelpi, *Emily Dickinson: The Mind of the Poet* (Cambridge, Mass.: Harvard University Press, 1965) and *The Tenth Muse: The Psyche of the American Poet* (Cambridge, Mass.: Harvard University Press, 1975); David Porter, *The Art of Emily Dickinson's Early Poetry* (Cambridge, Mass.: Harvard University Press, 1966) and *The Modern Idiom* (Cambridge, Mass.: Harvard University Press, 1981); Robert Weisbuch, *Emily Dickinson's Poetry* (Chicago: University of Chicago Press, 1972); and Suzanne Juhasz, *The Undiscovered Continent: Emily Dickinson and the Space of the Mind* (Bloomington, Ind.: Indiana University Press, 1983).

2. Sharon Cameron takes this association further, reading "Screws" as a metonymy for death: only through death does the symbol come into being; *Lyric Time: Dickinson and the Limits of Genre* (Baltimore and London: The Johns Hopkins University Press, 1979), 195–196.

3. The Dickinson family owned a copy of the 1844 printing of the 1841 edition of Noah Webster's *American Dictionary of the English Language.* Although it is not included in Dickinson's Webster, the poet no doubt also knew that *screw* carried much the same colloquial meanings in the nineteenth century that it does today; Harold Wentworth and Stuart Berg Flexner, *Dictionary of American English* (New York: Thomas R. Crowell Co., 1960; 1967).

4. *Dickinson and the Romantic Imagination* (Princeton: Princeton University Press, 1981), 125. Feit Diehl is speaking of the poet's move away from Romantic dependence on nature, and the corresponding lack of referentiality in her use of language. Although I believe Dickinson uses both the world of referential objects (nature) and her own imagination as the source of meaning while Feit Diehl seems to argue more exclusively for the imagination, I find her characterization of Dickinson's language apt.

5. Barbara Mossberg writes at length about Dickinson's role as letter writer in her family and the differences between mother's and daughter's relations to the written word. Mrs. Dickinson had the reputation in her family of being "too busy" to write. Her unwillingness to set pen to paper was even a family joke; as Emily writes Austin once: "Mother was much amused at the feebleness of your hopes of hearing from her – She got so far last week once, as to take a pen and paper and carry them into the kitchen"; *Emily Dickinson: When a Writer Is a Daughter* (Bloomington, Ind.: Indiana University Press, 1983), 40, 42.

6. "Pen-portrait" of Emily Dickinson, in Joseph Lyman's *The Lyman Letters: New Light on Emily Dickinson and Her Family* (Amherst, Mass.: University of Massachusetts Press, 1965), 78.

7. Karl Keller characterizes Dickinson as a "tease" in "Notes on Sleeping with Emily Dickinson" in *Feminist Critics Read Emily Dickinson,* ed. Suzanne Juhasz (Bloomington, Ind.: Indiana University Press, 1983), 69–72. Juhasz claims outright that Dickinson's letters "are always love letters." In the letters, she argues, Dickinson practices a "seduction carried out by flattery, so that the compliment serves as the essential rhetorical act"; "Reading Emily Dickinson's Letters," *ESQ,* 30, no. 3 (1984), 171.

8. Richardson to Sophia Westcomb, c. 1746. From *The Selected Letters of Samuel Richardson,* ed. John Carroll (Oxford: Clarendon Press, 1964), 65.

9. Mabel first visited the Dickinson "Homestead" on September 10, 1882, to play the piano and sing for Austin's sisters and mother. In what has often been described as a scene typifying her reclusiveness, the poet listened from the hallway (unseen) and then sent in a glass of sherry and a poem to thank their guest ("Elysium is as far as to / The very nearest Room," 1760). Mabel commented in her diary that Emily had not seen anyone but the family in years. One week later, she sent the poet a painting of Indian Pipes and received another poem in return. Mabel frequently played and sang for the Dickinson sisters. Polly Longsworth, *Austin and Mabel: The Amherst Affair and Love Letters of Austin Dickinson and Mabel Loomis Todd* (New York: Farrar, Straus, Giroux, 1984), 3–5.

10. Juhasz, "Reading Emily Dickinson's Letters," 179.

11. I have no hesitation in reading this phrase as a reference to the poet's difficulty in expressing herself in conventional English, or what she might regard as "English" altogether, despite Barton Levi St. Armand's recent recovery of the old assertion that "'Saxon' was a code-word for her lover," whose loss she here mourns; *Emily Dickinson and Her Culture: The Soul's Society* (Cambridge: Cambridge University Press, 1985), 328, n.4.

12. Quoted in Millicent Todd Bingham, *Ancestor's Brocades: The Literary Debut of Emily Dickinson* (New York: Harper and Brothers, 1955), 314–315.

13. As a rule, Dickinson copied the poems out before mailing them to friends. As far as her editors can tell, usually her fair copy and the epistolary one were written within a short time of each other and contain relatively minor variations.

14. For other variations in the second version, see Johnson's *Poems of Emily Dickinson.* The copy to "Her" is if anything more coquettish than the one to "Him," although most of the changes are minor (for example, "Until tomorrow" becomes "until the evening"—evidently because the letter would be delivered then).

15. That Dickinson loved Susan seems beyond debate. The character of that love included strong romantic and erotic components; however, understanding the relationship of the two women—both before and after Sue's marriage to Austin—requires a recognition of the nineteenth century's acceptance and even encouragement of passionate friendships between women. On this subject, see Carroll Smith-Rosenberg's "The Female World of Love and Ritual: Relations between Women in Nineteenth-Century America," *Signs,* 1 (Autumn 1975), 1–29; and both Lillian Faderman's essay "Emily Dickinson's Letters to Sue Gilbert," *Massachusetts Review,* 28 (Summer 1977), 197–225, and her more extensive study *Beyond the Love of Men: Romantic Friendship and Love between Women from the*

Renaissance to the Present (New York: William Morrow, 1981).

16. This idea could be stated differently: the reader imposes his or her biases of interpretation on the poem, and Dickinson's language is so flexible and rich that it supports a broad range of readings and emphases.

2. A Grammar

1. For example, Brita Lindberg-Seyersted's meticulous description of features of Dickinson's language and William Howard's pioneering descriptive essay on her vocabulary provide invaluable information to a critic of language. Lindberg-Seyersted, *The Voice of the Poet: Aspects of Style in the Poetry of Emily Dickinson* (Cambridge: Harvard University Press, 1968); and Howard, "Emily Dickinson's Poetic Vocabulary," *PMLA*, 72 (March 1957), 225–248.

2. See, for example, Robert Weisbuch, *Emily Dickinson's Poetry* (Chicago: University of Chicago Press, 1972); Jean McClure Mudge, *Emily Dickinson and the Image of Home* (Amherst, Mass.: University of Massachusetts Press, 1975); Rebecca Patterson, *Emily Dickinson's Imagery* (Amherst, Mass.: University of Massachusetts Press, 1979); and Suzanne Juhasz, *The Undiscovered Continent: Emily Dickinson and the Space of the Mind* (Bloomington, Ind.: Indiana University Press, 1983).

3. Samuel Levin, "The Analysis of Compression in Poetry," *Foundations of Language,* 7 (1971), 39. See also the discussion between Levin and Eugene R. Kintgen in *Foundations of Language,* 9 (1972), 98–102: "Nonrecoverable Deletion and Compression in Poetry," and "Reply to Kintgen."

4. Jack L. Capps, *Emily Dickinson's Reading, 1836–1886* (Cambridge, Mass.: Harvard University Press, 1966), 24.

5. Capps, *Emily Dickinson's Reading,* 120.

6. Jane Donahue Eberwein, in *Dickinson: The Strategies of Limitation* (Amherst, Mass.: University of Massachusetts Press, 1985), sees Dickinson's use of compression as an aspect of her general pose of smallness. The poet often poses as a child, identifies herself with small animals, and speaks of herself as physically slight (while she in fact seems to have been of average or moderately tall height). Although at first glance the short lines and texts do make Dickinson's poems look comparatively small, or slight, the poet's pose of littleness and the compression of her language seem to me to work fundamentally at cross-purposes: Dickinson's disguise makes her inconspicuous, whereas her language is conspicuous, striking. See especially Eberwein's chapter "'My Little Force Explodes': The Poetics of Distillation."

7. Eric Auerbach, *Mimesis: The Representation of Reality in Western Literature,* trans. Willard R. Trask (Princeton, N.J.: Princeton University Press, 1953), 110.

8. For example, George Herbert, one of Dickinson's favorite poets, wrote highly elliptical, dense, and archetypally personal (in contrast to personally confessional) poetry.

9. Richard Ohmann, "Generative Grammar and the Concept of Literary Style," *Word,* 20 (1964), 438.

10. The second percentage figure comes from an earlier study of conjunctions by Francis Christensen in *Notes toward a New Rhetoric: Six Essays for Teachers*

(New York: Harper and Row, 1967), 46. Card's essay "Frequencies of Some Sentence Connectors" appears in *Studies in Linguistics in Honor of Raven I. Mc-David, Jr.,* ed. Lawrence M. Davis (University, Ala.: University of Alabama Press, 1972), 251–261.

11. The sample poems are 90, 190, 290, 390, 490, 590, 690, 790, 890, 990, 1090, 1190, 1290, 1390, 1490, and 1590. I do not count pronoun connectors because Dickinson frequently omits pronouns in her sentences (especially when consecutive sentences of parallel structure begin with a pronoun and copular verb—the sentences where pronoun connectors are most prominent) and because Dickinson also uses pronouns that imply a previous statement where there is none. It is clear, however, that pronoun connectors are still her most frequently used connectors, as they are in Card's sample.

12. Adverbs of time, order, and place—which account for only about 4.7 percent of connectors in Card's sample—account for another 16 connectors, or 22 percent, in these 16 poems. Other connectors are "not" (used three times); "more," "such," "as," and "that" (used twice); and "equally," "neither," "whose," and "only" (used once).

13. Janel Mueller, *The Native Tongue and the Word: Developments in English Prose Style 1380–1580* (Chicago: University of Chicago Press, 1984), 17.

14. Auerbach, *Mimesis,* 71. The use of symmetrical or simply additive *and* is typically associated with children's speech, although Mueller points out that the association is not altogether appropriate. Recent studies show that both adults and children connect sentences with *and.* Children do use paratactic connection more often and more exclusively than adults, but they use it to join fewer phrases together (Mueller, *The Native Tongue,* 102).

15. Auerbach, *Mimesis,* 110.

16. Robin Lakoff's "If's, And's, and But's about Conjunction" differentiates between symmetric and asymmetric uses of *and:* with asymmetric *and,* the order of events connected is fixed (A, B + C is not the same as B, C + A), while with symmetric *and* there is no fixed order of relation (A + B = B + A). *Studies in Linguistic Semantics,* ed. Charles J. Fillmore and Terence Langendoen (New York: Holt, Rinehart, and Winston, 1971), 115–149.

17. Stanley B. Greenfield sees Blake's syntactic ambiguity in "Tyger, Tyger" as performing the same function. The ambiguous reference of the lines "What dread hand? / And what dread feet?" identifies the creator with the thing created by ceasing to differentiate between them. "Grammar and Meaning in Poetry," *PMLA,* 82 (1967), 377–387.

18. Vivian Pollack notes an example of self-revelation in syntactic doubling in the poem "Her sweet Weight on my Heart a Night" (518), where the ambiguous syntax of the line "When, stirring, for Belief's delight" "fuses the identities of the speaker and her lover" and thereby allows "an image of physical intimacy rarely found in Dickinson's poetry of womanly love." *Dickinson: The Anxiety of Gender* (Ithaca, N. Y.: Cornell University Press, 1984), 149.

19. Although "oil" has been a part of the English language long enough to be considered native (from Old French and Latin) and although Dickinson generally would use such a word in contrast to the more learned and more recently foreign "Essential," here the common acceptance of the phrase, her

mediating dash, the abstraction, and the two capital letters in contrast to the characteristics of the following phrase make "Essential Oils" a unit, and one of distinctly higher class and greater exoticism than "are wrung." In general, I use "latinate" interchangeably with "foreign-derived" to signify those words of recent enough borrowing that they retain some elevated, exotic, or foreign flavor (most of these words are in fact latinate). This practice sounds more subjective than it is; as Lindberg-Seyersted notes, linguists follow the same general rule of thumb.

20. Allen Tate, "New England Culture and Emily Dickinson," in *The Recognition of Emily Dickinson,* ed. Caesar R. Blake and Carlton F. Wells (Ann Arbor, Mich.: University of Michigan Press, 1964), 165. Howard remarks on this tension in "Emily Dickinson's Poetic Vocabulary," 235, and Lindberg-Seyersted spends several pages detailing Dickinson's uses of contrast as a structuring, semantic, and figurative device in her poems (*Voice of the Poet,* 89–103).

21. Juhasz, *The Undiscovered Continent,* 29.

22. Howard, "Emily Dickinson's Poetic Vocabulary," 235.

23. To the extent that Dickinson was familiar with American poetry from the Colonial period and certainly in her knowledge of hymns, she would have been familiar with the mingling of latinate and native words as a way of placing God's power and wisdom on the earth and in the mundane.

24. Jan Mukařovský, "Standard Language and Poetic Language," in *Linguistics and Literary Style,* ed. Donald C. Freeman (New York: Holt, Rinehart and Winston, 1970), 43, 56. Mukařovský defines the function of poetic language as consisting "in the maximum of foregrounding of the utterance. Foregrounding is the opposite of automatization, that is, the deautomatization of an act; the more an act is automatized, the less it is consciously executed; the more it is foregrounded, the more completely conscious does it become" (43).

25. Roland Hagenbüchle ("Precision and Indeterminacy in Emily Dickinson's Poetry," *ESQ,* 20, no. 2, 1974, 33–56) also notes that generally in Dickinson's poems "some established feature (hymn, rhyme, level of style; intellectual, social and religious structures) functions as background or expectation horizon in the reader whom Dickinson strategically disappoints" (p. 40). Hagenbüchle's review essay "New Developments in Dickinson Criticism" in *Anglia,* 97 (1979), 452–474, provides an excellent summary of language-oriented analysis of Dickinson's poetry up to 1979.

26. Carol Brown Pasternack argues that disjunction is an essential aspect of Anglo-Saxon poetry; parts of Anglo-Saxon texts that were thought to have different authors or to belong to different poems are in fact disjunctive parts of a single whole. "Disjunction: A Structural Convention in Old English Poetry," Ph.D. diss., University of California, Los Angeles, 1983). The disjunction of Dickinson's poems has at least once led to similar confusion. R. W. Franklin argues that "I tie my Hat – I crease my Shawl" (which Johnson numbers as poem 443, written c. 1862) is really two poems: "I tie my Hat – I crease my Shawl" and the final two stanzas of another poem, "A Pit – but Heaven over it" (which Johnson numbers as poem 1712, no date). Both poems, Franklin claims, were written ca. 1862.

27. For a history of the editing of Dickinson's poems and a description of the present state of her manuscripts, see Johnson's introduction to *The Poems of Emily*

Dickinson, especially xxxii–xlviii; see also R. W. Franklin's introduction and appendixes to *The Manuscript Books of Emily Dickinson* (Cambridge, Mass.: Harvard University Press, 1981).

28. Brita Lindberg-Seyersted, *Emily Dickinson's Punctuation* (American Institute, University of Oslo, 1976), 23–24. In her introduction Lindberg-Seyersted also uses E. L. Thorndike's article "The Psychology of Punctuation" (*The American Journal of Psychology,* 61, April 1948, 222–228) to support her argument that punctuation individualizes a writer, and to suggest that punctuation points toward personality as well as to style. Lindberg-Seyersted's monograph first appeared in *Studia Neophilologia,* 37, no. 2 (1965).

29. Johnson's variorum edition of the *Poems* does not correct any aspect of the poet's spelling, grammar, or punctuation; however, his later edition (*The Complete Poems of Emily Dickinson,* Boston: Little, Brown, 1957) does.

30. See Lindberg-Seyersted's summary of this literature in *Punctuation,* passim, and 28–29. She, too, considers the poet's slanting marks best reproduced typographically as dashes, although she notes that typographical dashes are more obtrusive on the page than the poet's handwritten marks. Sewall provides further summary of this material and reference to the advice young Emily may have remembered from her grammar and composition books in his *Life* (II, 349–350 n). As he notes, dashes were used frequently as marks of emphasis in the nineteenth century. Austin and Lavinia, like Emily, used the dash profusely in their letters.

31. In her fascicle copy of this poem Dickinson places the numbers 1, 3, 2, and 4 at the beginnings of these lines, suggesting that the stanza might instead read: "The Feet, mechanical, go round – / A Wooden Way / Of Ground, or Air, or Ought – / Regardless Grown, / A Quartz contentment, like a stone –". I give the lines as she first wrote them. Either way, the punctuation breaks the lines phrase by phrase.

32. Lindberg-Seyersted claims that dashes clarify phrase boundaries as well as interrupting them. She gives as an example the line "For Frigid – hour of Mind –" from "A Shady friend – for Torrid days –" (278). The linking of "hour" and "Mind" seems to me, however, to have more semantic than syntactic significance.

33. Sirkka Heiskanen-Mäkelä, *In Quest of Truth: Observations on the Development of Emily Dickinson's Poetic Dialectic* (Jyvaskyla, 1970), 183. Joanne Feit Diehl also makes the interesting argument that Dickinson's dislocation from the Romantic tradition allows her greater leeway than her male contemporaries and predecessors to question that tradition. The questions that for Keats would have seemed overweening pride and would have undermined his attempt to find a peace and order in the world are for Dickinson a necessity if she is not to feel swallowed by that world. *Dickinson and the Romantic Imagination* (Princeton, N.J.: Princeton University Press, 1981), 101–103.

34. I am indebted to Bonnie Costello's intuitive discussion of Elizabeth Bishop's use of questions for this insight. "The Impersonal and the Interrogative in the Poetry of Elizabeth Bishop," in *Elizabeth Bishop and Her Art,* ed. Lloyd Schwartz and Sybil P. Estes (Ann Arbor, Mich.: University of Michigan Press, 1983), 109.

35. For a fuller discussion of the implied threat in this poem, see pp. 543–544 of Lynn Keller and Cristanne Miller, "Emily Dickinson, Elizabeth Bishop, and the Rewards of Indirection," *The New England Quarterly*, 57, no. 4 (1984), 533–553.

36. In the sample poems I have chosen, for example, possible capital letters that Johnson does not reproduce as capitals in his texts include "Ourselves" in "This was a Poet" and "Every," "Cordial," and "An" in "My Life had stood – a Loaded Gun." For the sake of simplicity, I follow Johnson's standardizations in reprinting the poems here.

37. Counting the first word of each line, the numbers run as follows: 132 nouns, 22 adjectives, 13 verbs, and 64 function words, mostly conjunctions. I have counted pronouns and verbals according to their grammatical usage as nouns or adjectives. Dickinson occasionally capitalizes a function word or an adverb in the middle of a line, but, as this sample shows, the occurrence is relatively rare.

38. Howard, "Emily Dickinson's Poetic Vocabulary," 230, 240–243, 248.

39. These adjectives occur in poems 290, 298, 390, 409, 510, 627, 721, 724, 1382, and 1400.

40. For a description of the apparent irrationality of English determinations that some nouns may be counted (shoes, chairs, coins) and others may not (footwear, furniture, money), see James D. McCawley's "Lexicographer and the Count-Mass Distinction" in *Adverbs, Vowels, and Other Objects of Wonder* (Chicago: University of Chicago Press, 1979), 165–173.

41. Both Howard and Lindberg-Seyersted comment on this fact as one of the primary characteristics of Dickinson's poetry. Josephine Miles, in *Eras and Modes in English Poetry*, rev. ed. (Berkeley: University of California Press, 1964) provides statistical evidence that the ratio of Dickinson's verbs to her nouns and adjectives is very high in comparison with that of most poets.

42. Lindberg-Seyersted, *Voice of the Poet*, 116.

43. Grace Sherrer, "A Study of Unusual Verb Construction in the Poems of Emily Dickinson," *American Literature*, 7 (1935), 37–46. Sherrer sees most of Dickinson's uninflected verb constructions as archaic forms of the subjunctive. According to Lindberg-Seyersted, altering a verb to create the subjunctive mood was already out of style in the nineteenth century. There was some inclination to revive that form from 1855 to 1880, but even then the use of any verb but "be" in the subjunctive mood was considered archaic. She takes her information from Thyra Jane Bevier's "American Use of the Subjunctive" in *American Speech*, 6 (February 1931), 211.

44. George Whicher, *This Was a Poet: A Critical Biography of Emily Dickinson* (New York: Scribner's Sons, 1938), 93; Lindberg-Seyersted, *Voice of the Poet*, 248.

45. Thomas H. Johnson, *Emily Dickinson: An Interpretive Biography* (New York: Atheneum Press, 1967), 93; David Porter, *The Art of Emily Dickinson's Early Poetry* (Cambridge, Mass.: Harvard University Press, 1966), 139. Charles R. Anderson reads the verb forms of "Essential Oils" as signs of the permanence of art and the "absolute truth" of her claim in *Emily Dickinson's Poetry: The Stairway of Surprise* (New York: Holt, Rinehart and Winston, 1960), 67.

46. The variant for "Maintain," "Do reign," supports this argument by making the trees sovereign but over nothing in particular.

47. Dickinson may be using an archaic form of the subjunctive here: "It is as [if] a Vesuvian face were to let [or were to have let] its pleasure through." The archaism is uncommon, however. Furthermore, even if the poet intended the subjunctive here, it remains unclear whether it is past or present subjunctive, and thus the suggestive contrast of present smile with accomplished explosion holds.

48. George Wright, "The Lyric Present: Simple Present Verbs in English Poems," *PMLA*, 89 (1974), 563–579.

49. Hagenbüchle describes Dickinson's poetry as characteristically indeterminate; it is typified by "pure *deixis*—Rilke's *reiner Bezug*—without any corresponding referent whatever," as in "Dickinson's 'absolute' use of the pronoun: 'Him you chasten that is He'" ("Precision and Indeterminacy," 42, 43). One could say that Dickinson's pronouns without definite reference are "absolute"; they may refer to infinity as easily as to some biographical context. Although I agree with Hagenbüchle's description of the poet's language generally, I would not say that it typically has no corresponding referent.

50. I use "he" here and everywhere for Dickinson's lover or antagonist when she does not specify gender because where gender is specified those figures are most often male.

51. I include "like" in this list even though it is not strictly speaking a function word because its use resembles that of prepositions more than that of adjectives or adverbs in modern (including nineteenth-century) spoken English. In this sentence, "like" is an adjective functioning as a subjective complement after the implied "is" (no diligence is like that), and "that" is the object of an understood preposition such as "to."

52. See Mary Daly in *Gyn/Ecology* on the implicit authority and assertiveness of passive voice constructions; "Spooking by the Passive Voice: Grammar," *Gyn/Ecology* (Boston: Beacon Press, 1978), 324–329.

53. From "Tyrian Businesses," II, 3, *The Maximus Poems* (New York: Jargon/Corinth Books, 1960).

54. Miles, *Eras and Modes*, 2. In contrast, phrasal syntax emphasizes substantival elements, "the phrasal and coordinative modifications of the whole statement," and is "cumulative." It tends to look toward blank verse or the ode and a vocabulary of "lofty ceremony and enthusiasm"; it corresponds to high or sublime style, cosmic and "receptive" philosophies. Actions are subordinate to the substance presented. Of American poets, Miles finds that Longfellow, Emerson, Lanier, Pound, Williams, Stevens, and Eliot, to name a few, write without predominantly either phrasal or clausal structures, or in a balanced mode of poetic statement; Whitman, H. Crane, and Moore write verse that is predominantly phrasal; and Cummings writes in a predominantly clausal mode.

55. Elizabeth Perlmutter, "Hide and Seek: Emily Dickinson's Use of the Existential Sentence," *Language and Style*, 10 (1977), 109–119.

56. In *The Chinese Written Character as a Medium for Poetry*, ed. Ezra Pound (New York: Arrow Editions, 1936), 35. See Christine Brooke-Rose, *A Grammar of Metaphor* (London: Secker and Warburg, 1958), on the potential metaphorical

richness of the copula. Few poets in English, she notes, have taken advantage of this potential.

57. Juhasz talks about this function of the copula in *The Undiscovered Continent,* 32.

58. "Negation," Hagenbüchle writes, "is of such importance in Emily Dickinson's poetic oeuvre that one is tempted to speak of a *poesis negativa*" ("Precision and Indeterminacy," 40). Margaret Homans in *Women Writers and Poetic Identity: Dorothy Wordsworth, Emily Brontë, and Emily Dickinson* (Princeton, N.J.: Princeton University Press, 1980) and Joanne Feit Diehl in *Dickinson and the Romantic Imagination* (Princeton, N.J.: Princeton University Press, 1981) claim that Dickinson's characteristic use of negation stems from her more general opposition to, or desire to negate, nature; in *Emily Dickinson: When a Writer Is a Daughter* (Bloomington, Ind.: Indiana University Press, 1983), Barbara Mossberg traces negation to the poet's need to negate her presumed identification with her mother—that is, with standard expectations for women.

59. According to S. P. Rosenbaum's *A Concordance to the Poems of Emily Dickinson* (Ithaca, N.Y.: Cornell University Press, 1964) she uses *not* 828 times. The only words she uses more often are, in order of decreasing use, *the, a, to, and, of, that, it, in, is,* and *for.*

60. See, for example, Derrida's "Structure, Sign, and Play in Discourse of the Human Sciences," in *The Structuralist Controversy: The Languages of Criticism and Sciences of Man,* ed. Richard Macksey and Eugenio Donato (Baltimore: Johns Hopkins University Press, 1970), 247–272.

61. Jane Eberwein, "Doing Without: Dickinson as Yankee Woman Poet," in Paul J. Ferlazzo's *Critical Essays on Emily Dickinson* (Boston: G. K. Hall, 1984), 216.

62. According to Janel Mueller (*The Native Tongue,* 97–99), and using the rhetorical figures "ellipsis," "prolepsis," and "anacoluthon," contemporary linguists and literary and language historians agree that speech prominently exhibits these elements.

63. See *The Voice of the Poet.* Lindberg-Seyersted is extremely thorough in her documentation of speechlike elements in Dickinson's poetry. I give a brief overview of the poet's use of colloquialism here.

64. Bonnie Costello, "The 'Feminine' Language of Marianne Moore," in *Women and Language in Literature and Society,* ed. Sally McConnell-Ginet, Ruth Borker, and Nelly Furman (New York: Praeger, 1980), 221–238. Costello argues that Moore's themes or "morality" and style are one, and that "the central morality of her style (and the chief source of its vitality) is a resistance to the complacencies of thought and language" (224). In reviewing critical notions of the "feminine," she refers to criticism on Moore and Edna St. Vincent Millay by T. S. Eliot, Randall Jarrell, R. P. Blackmur, John Crowe Ransom, Roy Harvey Pierce, and Suzanne Juhasz (222–223).

65. Mudge makes this claim in the context of acknowledging the skill of men like Henry James and Nathaniel Hawthorne in depicting the nuances of a house and its objects. *Emily Dickinson and the Image of Home* (Amherst, Mass.: University of Massachusetts Press, 1975), 143.

66. Sandra Gilbert, "The Wayward Nun beneath the Hill: Emily Dickinson and the Mysteries of Womanhood," in *Feminist Critics Read Emily Dickinson* (Bloomington, Ind.: Indiana University Press, 1983), 23.

67. Francine Frank and Frank Ashen summarize literature on stereotyped perception of gender difference in language use in their chapter "Talking Like a Lady: How Women Talk" in *Language and Sex* (Albany: State University of New York Press, 1983), 25–51. A study by Carole Edelsky, for example, shows that sixth-grade children have already adopted stereotypes of language behavior identical to those of adults (29–30). The effect of stereotypes on perception of language is also a major and repeated theme of Cheris Kramarae's *Women and Men Speaking* (New York: Newbury House, 1981), 92–99, 151.

68. For example, in "'Women's Language' or 'Powerless Language'?" William M. O'Barr and Bowman K. Atkins conclude from the evidence of their courtroom study that features of "women's language" correlate more closely to social status than to gender. Reprinted in *Women and Language in Literature and Society,* 93–110.

69. Kramarae reviews research showing that in all-female groups narrative is a communal activity rather than a sequence of autonomous speeches, as it tends to be in all-male groups. Women orient much of their speech to serving the linguistic or discursive needs of their conversational partners. *Women and Men Speaking,* 13–17, 20–21, 75–76, 105, 133, 144.

70. Pamela Fishman, "Interaction: The Work Women Do," in *Language, Gender, and Society,* ed. Barrie Thorne, Cheris Kramarae, and Nancy Henley (Rowley, Mass.: Newbury House, 1983), 89–102. This collection of essays also contains the best annotated bibliography of recent work on language and gender.

71. *Recollections of a Southern Matron* (New York, 1838), 256. Quoted in Barbara Welter's *Dimity Convictions: The American Woman in the Nineteenth-Century* (Athens, Ohio: Ohio University Press, 1976), 29.

72. Cited in Welter, *Dimity Convictions,* 30.

73. Cited in Welter, *Dimity Convictions,* 38.

74. Cristanne Miller, "Language and Gender in Popular Magazines," paper presented at the MLA, Washington, D.C., December 1984.

75. An editor of *Self* magazine reported that articles written by men for their magazine require as much but not more editing than articles written by women (personal communication, November 1984).

76. Writers discussing the indirection of women's forms include Adrienne Rich, "Vesuvius at Home: The Power of Emily Dickinson" in *Lies, Secrets, and Silences, Selected Prose 1966–1978* (New York: W. W. Norton, 1979; originally published in 1976), 157–183; Suzanne Juhasz in *Naked and Fiery Forms, Modern American Poetry by Women: A New Tradition* (New York: Octagon Books, 1976) and *The Undiscovered Continent*; Elaine Showalter, *A Literature of Their Own* (Princeton, N.J.: Princeton University Press, 1977); Sandra Gilbert and Susan Gubar, *The Madwoman in the Attic: The Woman Writer and the Nineteenth-Century Literary Imagination* (New Haven, Conn.: Yale University Press, 1979); Terrence Diggory, "Armored Women, Naked Men: Dickinson, Whitman and Their Successors," in *Shakespeare's Sisters: Feminist Essays on Women Poets,* ed. Sandra Gilbert and Susan Gubar (Bloomington, Ind.: Indiana University Press, 1979),

135–150; Margaret Homans, *Women Writers and Poetic Identity: Dorothy Words-worth, Emily Brontë, and Emily Dickinson* (Princeton, N.J.: Princeton University Press, 1980); Cheryl Walker, *The Nightingale's Burden: Women Poets in America, 1630–1900* (Bloomington, Ind.: Indiana University Press, 1982); and Alicia Ostriker, "The Thieves of Language: Women Poets and Revisionist Mythmak-ing," *Signs,* 8 (August 1982), 69. Kramarae reviews empirical support for these literary claims (*Women and Men Speaking,* 143–144, 129–130). See also Marjorie Harness Goodwin's "Directive-Response Speech Sequences in Girls' and Boys' Task Activities" (*Women and Language in Literature and Society,* 157–174).

77. For a fuller discussion of Dickinson's indirect presentation of herself in the poems, particularly as it may relate to her gender, see Lynn Keller and Christanne Miller's "Emily Dickinson, Elizabeth Bishop, and the Rewards of Indirection." Lindberg-Seyersted estimates that two-fifths of Dickinson's poems "revolve around an explicit 'I'" (*Voice of the Poet,* 33).

78. *Women and Men Speaking,* 70.

79. Hagenbüchle, "Precision and Indeterminacy," 35, 40–45.

3. Reading the Poems

1. "Essential Oils – are wrung" is not included here because I have discussed it extensively in Chapter 1.

2. All variants listed here are from a semifinal draft of the poem in packet 19. In a fair copy addressed to Sue, Dickinson adopted all the changes suggested in the packet copy; Johnson uses the copy addressed to Sue as the final version, as I do here (Johnson, *Poems* I, 238–239).

3. Rebecca Patterson, *The Riddle of Emily Dickinson* (Boston: Houghton Mifflin, 1951), 129. Joseph Duchac (*The Poems of Emily Dickinson: An Annotated Guide,* Boston: G. K. Hall, 1979) cites two readings of this poem in which "He" is Wadsworth: Richard Bridgman's "Emily Dickinson: A Winter Poet in a Spring Land," *Moderna Sprak,* 56, no. 1 (1962), 1–8; and John B. Pickard's *Emily Dickinson: An Introduction and Interpretation* (New York: Barnes and Noble, 1967). In one of the most recent books of Dickinson criticism, Wadsworth reappears as the poet's lover (or secret "husband") and the primary influence on her art: William H. Shurr, *The Marriage of Emily Dickinson: A Study of the Fascicles* (Lexington, Ky.: University Press of Kentucky, 1983).

4. Clark W. Griffith reads the poem as an expression of the poet's fear of the masculine (*The Long Shadow: Emily Dickinson's Tragic Poetry,* Princeton, N.J.: Princeton University Press, 1964, 171–173, 180). Charles Anderson ("From a Window in Amherst: Emily Dickinson Looks at the American Scene," *New England Quarterly,* 31, June 1958, 157) sees "Him" as a preacher; William R. Sherwood (*Circumference and Circumstance: Stages in the Mind and Art of Emily Dickinson,* New York: Columbia University Press, 1968, 108–109) and Sewall (*Life* II, 451n, 703) argue that "He" is a preacher but not necessarily Wadsworth, though evidently considering Wadsworth the strongest candidate for "His" identity. Cleanth Brooks, R. W. B. Lewis, and Robert Penn Warren see "Him" as God (*American Literature: The Makers and the Making,* New York: St. Martin's Press, 1973, 1238).

5. Robert Weisbuch, *Emily Dickinson's Poetry* (Chicago: University of Chicago Press, 1972), 98–99. As I do, Weisbuch notes the combined creative and destructive images of the poem.

6. Inder Nath Kher, *The Landscape of Absence: Emily Dickinson's Poetry* (New Haven, Conn.: Yale University Press, 1974), 18, 107, 132.

7. Adrienne Rich, "Vesuvius at Home: The Power of Emily Dickinson," in *Lies, Secrets, and Silences, Selected Prose 1966–1978* (New York: W. W. Norton, 1979), 105.

8. David Porter, *Dickinson: The Modern Idiom* (Cambridge, Mass.: Harvard University Press, 1981), 285.

9. Although Dickinson provides no pronoun referent for "you," we may assume that "you" and the speaker are female. In the most frequently recurring drama of her poems, Dickinson matches a female victim or speaker with a larger, threatening or authoritarian male figure (sometimes a non-gendered "They"). Often, as in this poem, the speaker or "I" has no explicit gender, but the patterns of Dickinson's metaphorical representations of women and the smaller size or lesser power of the speaker suggest femininity: the speaker is often a flower or bird. When Dickinson's poems involving a potentially romantic couple are homoerotic, both figures are always female. This is logical; since Dickinson writes from her own experience and knowledge in her poems, most of her speakers will be female. On Dickinson's use of male speakers, see the first chapter of Rebecca Patterson's *Emily Dickinson's Imagery* (Amherst, Mass.: University of Massachusetts Press, 1979), 1–29.

10. In Ralph Waldo Emerson's "Fate," in *Complete Works,* 12 vols. (Cambridge, Mass.: Riverside Press, 1883), VI, 25.

11. Questioning the extent of Dickinson's sexual experience is of less importance and interest than acknowledging the fact of her passionate nature. This reclusive poet is remarkably frank in letters and poems about her own passion.

12. In *Emily Dickinson: When a Writer Is a Daughter* (Bloomington, Ind.: Indiana University Press, 1983), Mossberg argues that the poet feels she is in handicapped competition with Austin to be the best "son."

13. Johnson dates the poems by year according to Dickinson's handwriting, which varies quite markedly during her life. There is no way to tell, however, if a poem was written near the time to which we can date the first extant copy. The poems that Dickinson collected in fascicles seem nearly all to be copies of poems written initially on other sheets of paper and probably at other times.

14. I have been aided in my reading of this poem particularly by the lengthy analyses of Robert Weisbuch, *Emily Dickinson's Poetry,* 25–39; Albert Gelpi, "Emily Dickinson and the Deerslayer: The Dilemma of the Woman Poet in America" in *Shakespeare's Sisters: Feminist Essays on Women Poets,* ed. Sandra M. Gilbert and Susan Gubar (Bloomington, Ind.: Indiana University Press, 1979), 122–134; and Sandra Gilbert and Susan Gubar, *Madwoman in the Attic: The Woman Writer and the Nineteenth-Century Literary Imagination* (New Haven, Conn.: Yale University Press, 1979), 608–613.

15. Annette Kolodny better than anyone else has compiled and discussed the evidence of our culture's masculine identification of the landscape as feminine, specifically as mother and sweetheart: *The Lay of the Land: Metaphor as Experience*

and History in American Life and Letters (Chapel Hill, N.C.: University of North Carolina Press, 1975) and *The Land before Her: Fantasy and Experience of the American Frontiers, 1630–1860* (Chapel Hill, N.C.: University of North Carolina Press, 1984).

4. Influences on the Poet's Language

1. Herman Melville, *Billy Budd, Sailor (An Inside Narrative),* ed. Harrison Hayford and Merton M. Sealts, Jr. (Chicago: University of Chicago Press, 1962), 75.

2. Frederick Tuckerman, *Amherst Academy: A New England School of the Past* (Amherst, Mass., 1926), 97.

3. Sewall refutes the myth that Dickinson was isolated socially and spiritually at Mount Holyoke because she did not convert (*Life* II, 362–364). It is also important to note in this age of greater religious variety that one could be a regular churchgoer and generally adhere to the principles of Christianity without being "a Christian." The poet's letters contain several references to sermons and ministers that she heard until she became completely reclusive in her early thirties.

4. Thomas H. Johnson, *Emily Dickinson: An Interpretive Biography* (Cambridge, Mass.: Harvard University Press, 1955), 151.

5. James R. Kugel, *The Idea of Biblical Poetry: Parallelism and Its History* (New Haven, Conn.: Yale University Press, 1981), 300.

6. Dickinson alludes to the gospel of Matthew seventy-four times in her poems and letters, more than twice as often as to any other book of the Bible. Jack L. Capps, *Emily Dickinson's Reading, 1836–1886* (Cambridge, Mass.: Harvard University Press, 1966), 40–41, 192.

7. One of the primary initial arguments of Mueller's *The Native Tongue and the Word: Developments in English Prose Style 1380–1580* (Chicago: University of Chicago Press, 1984) has to do with the complexity and effectiveness of a conjunctive and paratactic style. Mueller notes that the shift of subject (here from third to first person) occurs frequently in scripturalism and in spoken language; it also occurs frequently in Dickinson's poetry.

8. Kugel, *The Idea of Biblical Poetry,* 10.

9. There are more extreme examples of Dickinson's repetition, but they follow the same pattern of functional repetition and semantic variation. For example, in "Mine – by the Right of the White Election!" (528), six of the poem's nine lines begin "Mine –" and four begin "Mine – by the . . ." Like "It was not Death," this poem never identifies its subject, what the speaker insists is "Mine."

10. Morris Croll, "The Baroque Style in Prose," ed. John M. Wallace, in *Style, Rhetoric, and Rhythm: Essays by Morris Croll* (Princeton, N.J.: Princeton University Press, 1966), 207–237 (originally published in 1929). Subsequent citations of Croll in the text will be indicated by giving page numbers in parentheses. Croll speaks only of biblical prose, but Kugel argues at length that the lack of meter in Hebrew makes the Romance language distinction between poetry and prose meaningless. At its most "poetic," biblical language employs

the greatest number of "heightening features" to create the greatest intensity (*The Idea of Biblical Poetry,* 85–86).

Dickinson wrote to Higginson: "For Prose [I have] – Mr Ruskin – Sir Thomas Browne – and the Revelations." "For Poets," she names only Keats and the Brownings (L 261). Millicent Todd Bingham and Mabel Loomis Todd published Herbert's stanzas as Dickinson's in the first edition of *Bolts of Melody: New Poems of Emily Dickinson* (New York: Harper and Brothers, 1945).

11. James Davidson ("Emily Dickinson and Isaac Watts," *Boston Public Library Quarterly,* 6, 1954, 141–149) mentions the former two books. Capps mentions only the latter, stating that it belonged to the poet's father (*Emily Dickinson's Reading,* 187). All three were enormously popular in the nineteenth century.

12. Watts concludes his hymn "There is a land of pure delight" (626) with the stanza: "Could we but climb where Moses stood, / And view the landscape o'er; / Not Jordan's stream, nor death's cold flood / Should fright us from the shore." Dickinson parodies this vision of heaven in "Where bells no more affright the morn" with her wish for a "town" (or "Heaven") where "very nimble Gentlemen" can no longer wake sleeping children. Her poem concludes: "'Oh could we climb where Moses stood, / And view the Landscape o'er' / Not Father's bells – nor Factories, / Could scare us any more!" (112). Watts's hymn is in his *Psalms, Hymns, and Spiritual Songs* (Boston: Crocker and Brewster, 1834).

13. According to Davidson, Watts's psalms and hymns were frequently smoothed out by editors because of this irregularity and harshness. *Church Psalmody,* however, one of the Watts books belonging to the Dickinsons, was virtually unchanged by editors ("Emily Dickinson and Isaac Watts," 143).

14. Mueller argues that modern English as a whole has been deeply influenced by scripturalism, primarily through translations of the Bible preceding the King James version (*The Native Tongue and the Word*). American adoption of some characteristics of biblical style seems to be more specific and more closely tied to biblical authority than were the earlier British borrowings from scripturalism.

15. Perry Miller, "An American Language," in *Nature's Nation* (Cambridge, Mass.: Harvard University Press, 1967), 208–240. Subsequent page references to this essay will appear in parentheses in the text.

16. Think of the inevitable opening apologia in Puritan writing, from Bunyan's *Pilgrim's Progress* to the "foolish, broken, blemished Muse" that Anne Bradstreet claims for herself in her "Prologue."

17. William Ames was the most articulate proponent of the plain style. The passages quoted in the text are from his "Conscience with the Power and Cases Thereof" (1643) and *The Marrow of Sacred Divinity* (1643) as cited respectively in Larzer Ziff's *Puritanism in America* (New York: Viking Press, 1973), 14, and Perry Miller's *The New England Mind: The Seventeenth Century* (Boston: Beacon Press, 1939), 301.

18. From Ames's *Marrow of Sacred Divinity,* quoted in Miller, "An American Language," 219.

19. In *The American Democrat* (New York: Alfred A. Knopf, 1931; a reprint of the 1838 edition), 108–116.

20. Given the context of the poem, it must be the old Sea that says "Go" to the new or "Brook"-Sea. The Brook-Sea speaks last, addressing the older "Waters."

21. Capps, *Emily Dickinson's Reading*, 173–174.

22. Ralph Waldo Emerson, *Complete Works*, 12 vols. (Cambridge, Mass.: Riverside Press, 1883). This quote is taken from vol. I, 31. Subsequent quotations from Emerson will be cited in the text as *Works*, with volume and page number.

23. Ernest Fenollosa, *The Chinese Written Character as a Medium for Poetry*, ed. Ezra Pound (San Francisco: City Light Books, 1969), 20–21, 23; originally published in 1936.

24. "An Introductory Dissertation on the Origin, History and Connection of the Languages of Western Asia and Europe, with an Explanation of the Principles on which Language are Formed," ix–lxxi. It is possible that Webster's interest in etymological derivations in this essay and throughout his dictionary influenced Dickinson's similar interest, but there is no special reason to assume this connection. More likely, Webster's derivations provided empirical support for an interest and habit the poet had already developed on her own.

25. Webster, "State of English Philology," in *A Collection of Papers on Political, Literary and Moral Subjects* (New York, 1843), 365.

26. Sandra Gilbert and Susan Gubar, *The Madwoman in the Attic: The Woman Writer and the Nineteenth-Century Literary Imagination* (New Haven, Conn.: Yale University Press, 1979), 584.

27. See, for example, poems 75, 184, 274, 281, 311, 413, 670, 817, 1181, and 1400 for ghosts and 167, 195, 253, 472, 788, 841, 938, and 1004 for haunting.

28. Gilbert and Gubar, *Madwoman in the Attic*, 585–586.

29. Cheryl Walker, *The Nightingale's Burden: Women Poets in America, 1630–1900* (Bloomington, Ind.: Indiana University Press, 1982), 88, 116, 87.

30. Mary Abigail Dodge, from "My Garden," *Atlantic Monthly*, 1862. Reprinted in *Provisions: A Reader of Nineteenth-Century American Women*, ed. Judith Fetterley (Bloomington, Ind.: Indiana University Press, 1985), 421–445.

5. The Consent of Language and the Woman Poet

1. To simplify my text, from here on in the chapter when speaking of feminist theory or theories in general, I will use the phrase "women's writing" to cover the various territories delineated by the terms "feminine writing," or "feminist writing," or "women's writing," or *écriture féminine*. When referring to work of individual theorists, I will use their terminology without further explanation.

2. For primary statements of these positions, see Luce Irigaray's *This Sex Which Is Not One* (Ithaca, N.Y.: Cornell University Press, 1985), originally published in 1977; Julia Kristeva's *Desire in Language: A Semiotic Approach to Literature and Art*, trans. Leon S. Roudiez, Alice Jardine, and Thomas Gora (New York: Columbia University Press, 1982) or excerpts from her work in *New French Feminisms: An Anthology*, ed. Elaine Marks and Isabelle de Courtivron

(Amherst, Mass.: University of Massachusetts Press, 1980), 137–144; Sandra Gilbert and Susan Gubar's *Madwoman in the Attic: The Woman Writer and the Nineteenth-Century Literary Imagination* (New Haven, Conn.: Yale University Press, 1979); and Alicia Ostriker's "The Thieves of Language: Women Poets and Revisionist Mythmaking," *Signs,* 8 (1982), 69.

3. Martha Dickinson Bianchi, *The Life and Letters of Emily Dickinson* (Boston and New York: Houghton Mifflin, 1924), 26, 27.

4. Vivian R. Pollak identifies the volume of poems that Henry Emmons gave the poet as Barrett Browning's (they were previously thought to be Poe's) in "Dickinson, Poe, and Barrett Browning: A Clarification," *New England Quarterly,* 54 (March 1981), 121–124.

5. John Evangelist Walsh, *The Hidden Life of Emily Dickinson* (New York: Simon and Schuster, 1971), 108. I am skeptical of Walsh's claim that Dickinson borrowed so heavily but have no doubt that *Aurora Leigh* was an important poem to her. It is also clear that the two women shared a vocabulary and, to some extent, a common sensibility, as reflected in the passages Walsh designates.

6. There was a second National Convention on October 15–16, 1851 (again in Worcester), The New England Woman's Rights Convention in Boston on June 2, 1854, and other women's rights conventions in Boston on September 19–20, 1855, and on May 27, 1859.

7. The quotation marks around "females" evidently demarcate the language of the legislature. This quotation and the information on women's rights conventions are taken from *History of Woman Suffrage* by Elizabeth Cady Stanton, Susan B. Anthony, and Matilda Joslyn Gage (New York: Charles Mann, 1887), I, 215–262; and Angela Y. Davis, *Women, Race, and Class* (New York: Random House, 1981), 52.

8. Jay Leyda, *The Years and Hours of Emily Dickinson* (New Haven, Conn.: Yale University Press, 1960), II, 218. The period from 1850 to 1860 coincides with Edward Dickinson's most active political involvement in state affairs, making it almost inevitable that his daughter would have heard of or participated in discussion of the "woman question" at home. Furthermore, there was sufficient coming and going between Worcester, Boston, and Amherst in the Dickinson family for the poet to have received personal word about the women's rights campaign.

9. In *Women Writers and Poetic Identity: Dorothy Wordsworth, Emily Brontë, and Emily Dickinson* (Princeton, N.J.: Princeton University Press, 1980), Margaret Homans discusses Dickinson's use of Eve in poems and letters (169–176, 194), as do Gilbert and Gubar in *Madwoman in the Attic* (648–650) and Barbara Mossberg in *Emily Dickinson: When a Writer Is a Daughter* (Bloomington, Ind.: Indiana University Press, 1983), 150–156. Sandra Gilbert uses the metaphor of poem 722 for the title and as the central metaphor of her essay "The Wayward Nun Beneath the Hill," in *Feminist Critics Read Emily Dickinson,* ed. Suzanne Juhasz (Bloomington, Ind.: Indiana University Press, 1983), 22–44.

10. Dickinson is no exception to her times in taking this position. Judith Fetterley writes that "on the subject of women's oppression, the collective voice of mid nineteenth-century American women writers is essentially muted and indirect." Josephine Donovan's history of feminist thought characterizes most

early nineteenth-century feminism as "liberal Enlightenment" thought, more interested in the natural doctrine of equal rights than in the radical notion of gender as class. In *Provisions: A Reader from Nineteenth-Century American Women* (Bloomington, Ind.: Indiana University Press, 1985), 12; and *Feminist Theory: The Intellectual Traditions of American Feminism* (New York: Frederick Ungar, 1985), especially chap. 1.

11. "Slavery," for example, was the favorite nineteenth-century metaphor for social ills. The temperance people used it to describe drunkards (slaves to the bottle), evangelists used it for sinners, and labor reformers used it for the proletariat or lower class as well as the women's movement using it for women and, of course, abolitionists' talking about actual slaves before the war. Dickinson uses the word "slave" in only one poem ("The Lamp burns sure – within," 233), and "slavery" not at all.

12. Gilbert and Gubar (*The Madwoman in the Attic,* 587–594) and Mossberg (*When a Writer Is a Daughter*) note that the child pose bears direct relation to Dickinson's ambivalence about adult femininity and female sexuality. As a child, the poet/speaker does not have to take on the responsibilities and demureness of a woman; at least part of her wildness and unorthodoxy is excused (although Gilbert and Gubar and Mossberg also argue that the child pose becomes a crippling habit for the poet). As boy, Dickinson is freest of all: there she finds the double advantages of childhood and maleness.

13. Mossberg, "Emily Dickinson's Nursery Rhymes," in *Feminist Critics Read Emily Dickinson,* 45; and *When a Writer Is a Daughter,* 90–91.

14. Nina Baym, "God, Father, and Lover in Dickinson's Poetry," in *Puritan Influences in American Literature,* ed. Emory Elliott (Urbana, Ill.: University of Illinois Press, 1977), 207, 208. Like Gilbert and Gubar, Baym sees the child pose as more of a dilemma for Dickinson that a strategy for successful coping.

15. Dickinson may also be referring to the well-known Massachusetts judge and lawyer Lemuel Shaw.

16. Dickinson often uses "Man" or "Men" in contrast to herself or to a community. In these poems, the poet seems to play on the ambiguity between the word's generic use and its specifically masculine reference. Among others, examples of this ambiguously generic reference occur in: "Publication – is the Auction / Of the Mind of Man –", where "We – would rather / From Our Garret go / White – Unto the White Creator / Than invest – Our snow –" (709); "Myself was formed – a Carpenter," where the speaker's tools and bench join her to argue "Against the Man": "We – Temples build – I said –" (488); "I cannot dance upon my Toes," where "No Man instructed me –" (326); and "She staked her Feathers – Gained an Arc," where the poet rises above "the estimate / Of Envy, or of Men –" (798). See my article "How 'Low Feet' Stagger" in *Feminist Critics Read Emily Dickinson,* 144–145.

17. Margaret Homans, "'Her Very Own Howl': The Ambiguities of Representation in Recent Women's Fiction," *Signs: Journal of Women in Culture and Society,* 9, no. 2 (1983), 205.

18. Ibid., 198.

19. Simone de Beauvoir articulates what has become one of the primary assumptions of much current feminist criticism: that woman is not a biological

creature but a construct of patriarchy. Thus a woman may be masculine in her writing.

20. Virginia Woolf, *A Room of One's Own* (New York: Harcourt, Brace, 1929), 135.

21. Josephine Donovan, "Towards a Woman's Poetics," *Tulsa Studies in Women's Literature*, 3, no. 1/2 (1984), 102.

22. *Provisions*, ed. Judith Fetterley (Bloomington, Ind.: Indiana University Press, 1985), 15.

23. The quotation is from Sheila de Bretteville, cited in "For the Etruscans: Sexual Difference and Artistic Production—The Debate over a Female Aesthetic" by Rachel Blau Du Plessis and Members of Workshop 9, in *The Future of Difference*, ed. Hester Eisenstein and Alice Jardine (Boston: G. K. Hall, 1980), 135.

24. *The Future of Difference*, 137.

25. Gayatri Spivak, from "A Dialogue on the Production of Literary Journals, The Division of the Disciplines and Ideology: Critique with Professors Gayatri Spivak, Bill Galfton, and Michael Ryan," in *Analecta*, vol. 6 (1980), 84.

26. Spivak, from "Explanation and Culture: Marginalia," in *Humanities in Society*, 2, no. 3 (1979), 204.

27. From *The Diary of Anais Nin*, vol. 1 (1931–1934), ed. Gunther Stuhlmann (New York: The Swallow Press and Harcourt, Brace and World, 1966), 34; quoted by Du Plessis in *The Future of Difference*, 131.

28. Irigaray, *This Sex Which Is Not One*, 134. In describing Dickinson's work, I would modify Irigaray's implicit claim of infinite multiplicity to one of controlled or limited multiplicity. Dickinson does attempt to establish meaning; she simply does not attempt to fix it. Puns, syntactic doubling, and other forms of word play that create simultaneous and varying possibilities of meaning are a central element of her style. Her language is "multiple," just not infinitely so.

29. Woolf, *A Room of One's Own*, 151, 133.

30. Treichler elaborates on this claim in her discussion (it would be ridiculous to say that men are more interested in signs than in meaning, as the comparison in the quotation might imply), arguing that men find the signs of our language more adequate to their sense of reality and are therefore more comfortable relying on them than women are. From "Escaping the Sentence: Diagnosis and Discourse in 'The Yellow Wallpaper,'" in *Tulsa Studies in Women's Literature*, 3, no. 1/2 (1984), 70.

31. Kristeva, *New French Feminisms*, 137. Du Plessis quotes or interprets Adrienne Rich, Frances Jaffer, Lessing, and Woolf to be making similar claims about their own art, or about women's experience, speaking of meaning "always in motion" (*The Future of Difference*, 132–134).

32. Kristeva, *New French Feminisms*, 137.

33. Homans, *Woman Writers and Poetic Identity*, 34–36, 165, 211.

34. Roland Hagenbüchle, "Precision and Indeterminacy in Emily Dickinson's Poetry," *ESQ*, 20, no. 2 (1974), 40. Feit Diehl suggests that Dickinson avoids direct reference as being a kind of consummation; "Desire alone insures permanence," and so the possessiveness of naming or fixed reference would entail

loss; in *Dickinson and the Romantic Imagination* (Princeton, N.J.: Princeton University Press, 1981), 94.

35. Kristeva, *New French Feminisms*, 165.

36. Ibid.

37. Woolf, *A Room of One's Own*, 156.

38. This is the subject of Margaret Homans' essay in *Feminist Critics Read Emily Dickinson:* "'Oh, Vision of Language!' Dickinson's Poems of Love and Death," especially pp. 120–130. The quotation is from p. 124. Feit Diehl similarly argues that Dickinson depends on the existence of an outside Other, a "Composite Precursor" toward which she is both antagonistic and dependent for her ability to write poetry. *Dickinson and the Romantic Imagination*, passim and pp. 15, 18–19.

39. Karl Keller, "Sleeping with Emily Dickinson," in *Feminist Critics Read Emily Dickinson*, 69, 70.

40. Makward calls attention to this change in "To Be or Not to Be . . . A Feminist Speaker"; *The Future of Difference*, 100.

41. *The Future of Difference*, 149.

42. Helene Cixous, "The Laugh of the Medusa," trans. Keith Cohen and Paula Cohen, reprinted in *The Signs Reader: Women, Gender and Scholarship*, ed. Elizabeth Abel and Emily K. Abel (Chicago: University of Chicago Press, 1983), 283, 287. Cixous's essay originally appeared in 1976.

43. Ibid., 292.

44. *The Future of Difference*, 135. Homans makes this argument in "'Her Very Own Howl.'" Du Plessis writes about this aspect of women's art and psychology at greater length in her *Writing beyond the Ending: Narrative Strategies of Twentieth-Century Women Writers* (Bloomington, Ind.: Indiana University Press, 1985).

45. Cixous, "The Laugh of the Medusa," 291.

Index of First Lines

Index